Seven Hundred Kisses

D0343253

Seven Hundred Kisses

A *Yellow Silk*

BOOK OF EROTIC WRITING

EDITED AND WITH AN INTRODUCTION

BY Lily Pond

HarperSanFrancisco
An Imprint of HarperCollins*Publishers*

Permissions begin on p. 271 and are considered a
continuation of the copyright page.

HarperSanFrancisco and the author, in association with
The Basic Foundation, a not-for-profit organization
whose primary mission is reforestation, will facilitate
the planting of two trees for every one tree used in the
manufacture of this book.

A TREE CLAUSE BOOK

SEVEN HUNDRED KISSES: *A Yellow Silk Book of Erotic Writing.*
Copyright © 1997 by Lily Pond. All rights reserved.
Printed in the United States of America. No part of this
book may be used or reproduced in any manner
whatsoever without written permission except in the
case of brief quotations embodied in critical articles and
reviews. For information address HarperCollins
Publishers, 10 East 53rd Street, New York, NY 10022.

HarperCollins Web Site: http://www.harpercollins.com
HarperCollins®, ☰ ®, and HarperSanFrancisco™ are
trademarks of HarperCollins Publishers Inc.

Library of Congress Cataloging-in-Publication Data
Seven hundred kisses : a yellow silk book of erotic
writing / edited and with an introduction by Lily Pond.
ISBN 0–06–251484–9 (pbk.)
1. Erotic literature. I. Pond, Lily. II. Yellow silk.
PN6071.E7S47   1997   96–38100
810.8'03538—dc21

97 98 99 00 01 ❖ RRDH 10 9 8 7 6 5 4 3 2 1

Contents

Introduction

There is one person you'll meet in this book who's not to be found in any of the pornographic anthologies crowding yesterday's bookstore shelves. Is it the dark-haired smoldering beauty, heavy-lidded, whose black negligee strap has begun to stray down her shapely white shoulder? Nahhh. She'd be elsewhere.

What about the tow-haired workman, tanned muscles rippling beneath his faded and soft blue workshirt, open to the waist revealing his golden chest hairs? No. Sorry. But I can tell you where to look.

Maybe the black-leather-clad couple, sporting implements, wearing frightening shoes and supercilious scowls on their faces? Nope. Not here either.

Well, I'll let up on the suspense, though you've probably guessed already. The person you'll find here is you, you, a regular person, a person who stubs his toe, and his heart, who swells with love, in her soul, in her private parts, you, at the moment private is made public, when frustration turns to passion: in a barnyard, in an unkempt room. These are people who do have feelings—which help, which get in the way, which are contradictory. These are people with no answers. These are people who will go to the ends of the earth. These are people who are scared, loving, baking bread, unrolling a nylon stocking.

And you the reader are also here: not as a voyeur but as a participant. Part of the thrill of porn, an essential medium (just not this one), is distance on the part of the reader. No messy identification with the humans interacting—they aren't humans, they're disembodied skin with movable parts, they sweat, they come, they make loud noises. Then they go back into a box until the next time you rewind and again they sweat, they come, they make loud noises.

The people in this book will spend the day with you; like the characters in all great literature, they will become part of your vocabulary. They will inform your lovemaking, they will enrich your moments of sweat, come, and loud noises rather than intruding with their own.

This is their gift to you; enjoy them. Let them help you own that which is most yours already, and in so doing let them give you eros, or at least remind you how erotic you already are.

Yellow Silk, in its fifteen years as a quarterly magazine, has always sought to broaden this culture's concept of eros, not only to bring it home off the high-priced glossy shelves of the local well-lit convenience stores, but also to strip it of its elastic accoutrements. It's such an erotic world out there, that to narrow the definition of eros, as this culture often has, is to rob us of the richest experience of living possible. We hope we have succeeded in bringing that erotic ethos to this book as well.

Find the exquisite erotic nugget buried all but forgotten in the mind of Tobias Wolff's protagonist, the one sweet moment of true love in one man's whole life. Find Mary Mackey's surreal vision of an altered universe where, in love, all differences fall away, and Carlos Fuentes's wildly bawdy shipboard one, where wordplay serves to whet the appetite and wet the whistle, so to speak. Jane Hirshfield explores the subtle, mystical place of all connection, Walter Mosley, the downright rub of need between man and woman.

Whether it's Timothy Liu's dark AIDs-world vision of grasping at love, or Dorianne Laux's simple grasping, Alison Fell's delightful interspecies parable or Jane Smiley's tale of irresistible, obsessional love, you will find here the whole range of human love and loving. And with it you will find your own abilities for both expanded.

Turning the magazine into a book has been a wonderful transition, and in addition to the longtime readers and the writers who have gracefully helped make this change possible, I'd like to thank two men: David Eisenmann, my friend and lawyer, for his wisdom, patience, intelligence, and silliness, and my editor, Kevin Bentley, for his foresight, his smarts, his great taste, and his wicked sense of humor. Nice touch, don't you think, to have two men for midwives?

And if you are new to *Yellow Silk*, I open-armed welcome you. I hope it's good for you too. I hope after reading this book that the eros of the world blows around you like the wind, that you can hear its siren call on the wings of morning and on the covers of the last thing at night. And that you can answer.

LILY POND

MARCH 11, 1997

A Sun To Shine on Them

JOHN GOLDFINE

He thought: Angus Aaroam Cameron, man of many slippery vowels and knocking consonants, the Scottish tongue-twister, the Celtic kiltie, yon glorious laddie of the thistle-oh, muckle bonny Highland prickle and prick, goddamn him.

—Aren't you on Angus time? Isn't your meter running for him?

—I don't know what you mean.

—You'll be with him, fucking him in you-can-count-the-fucking-hours. So why me, now?

Closer she came, closer, closer, sarong towel wrapped around the steaming pink of her. And she smiled at him, shyly, ignoring the meter talk . . .

—I love you too, you know that.

True, and he loved her when he wasn't too furious to remember it.

She came so close there was no distance left. But he wanted something from her, not intercourse, not a soft cuddle afterwards, something else, and now he stepped back, declining.

—I can't do this.

Then she is in Italy with Angus Aaroam Cameron, the Scottish etcetera, and he is two weeks alone at home with her chores and her animals and a job, his job, and in truth feeling sorry enough for himself when it all pushes in.

And it snows and snows and then there is a thaw and rain, coating the snow with a skim of ice, and then the cold slides in again, hard, and when the full moon arrives on January 27 and rises to its peak, the night is so bright with the moon and the ice that the three dogs wake up thinking it's morning and they pace and scratch and whine and caper on the bedspread until they wake him up to start their day.

He is fooled not just by the silver light everywhere but also by his daily reliance on these dogs welcoming dawn. He sweeps the covers into a triangle, sheets creamy in the moonlight, the smallest dog tossed onto its back by the vigor of his sweeping motion.

The dogs jump down from the bed, race ahead, watch him over their shoulders, plunge in a heap by the door until he opens it, runs with them across the porch, opens the storm door, and turns them out into the cold cold night air. He doesn't lean into the night to see the thermometer screwed to the door jamb because his naked skin is already shrinking from the surround, telling him more than he wants to know. He also suspects by the diffuse quality of the light and the lack of distinction in the east that he and the dogs are all astray. He turns the fluorescent on in the kitchen, it blinks once, twice, and he squints at the clock: twenty of two.

—Jesus Christ, goddam dummies, internal clock bullshit, my fucking word, twenty of two.

He has been asleep such a short time he doesn't even need to urinate or sip a swallow of orange juice straight from the Rubbermaid for dry mouth. Back to the kitchen door, which he opens but doesn't close completely behind him for fear of it locking, although a key hangs hidden on a nail, then the porch which he skips across barely touching the jute mat, the storm door.

—Come on little guys, come on come on, what the hell are you up to, you idiots.

The dogs gallop past, race into the kitchen, and dance for their breakfast snack—vainly—realizing after a moment that, no, it isn't morning, that he has gone back to the bedroom, no snack—while he lies under the cold covers, no heat left in last night's soapstone, cursing the mutts for fools, laughing at their dejected careers as they troop back to the bedroom, nails click-click-clicking on the uncarpeted floors, tags jingling. The collie lies with a sigh on a rucked floor pillow, the two small ones jump up and settle in, one by his head, one in the small of his back. Three hours until chores, nearly five until dawn.

He wakes to dimness, not the false silver light, but dimness genuinely promising daylight.

—What time is it? As he turns, the alarm sounds and he is out and up. Two of the dogs foray and return, but the littlest dog, again tossed onto his back, now is reluctant to leave his spot on the blanket. No time here for prima donnas. He claps his hands and the chilled room crackles with his will. The dog eyes him sideways, decides he is serious, heaves up stiffly and again all four race for the kitchen door, the storm door, and then the dogs for the snowbanks outside. He peeks at the thermometer: twenty-three below. Two roosters crow, the sound sharp in the thin air, also fuzzled by the wrapped-up barn, but the sharp and soft of it are contradictory data to comb through another time—how long can he live naked on the porch in an atmosphere raking his senses?

He leaves the dogs to it, trots to the bathroom. It will be two minutes to shave, another minute to wash his face and armpits, and the dogs will be okay, okay for two minutes.

But he rushes and is using Ivory, not shaving cream, so gashes his throat under his jaw, dabs on toilet paper. He hasn't time to bleed because before the blood can clot he will need to put on his shirt, flip the collar, tie the tie—and if the blood stains the collar, forcing a change of shirt, his whole day will begin to dissolve.

The shirt carried down last night from the unheated upstairs goes on without stain, the rest of the clothes too, and back to the dogs, pressing for their breakfast snack. Over four hours since their moonlight rehearsal, now the collie gets a scoop, the middle one a handful, the littlest one another handful but of special old-dog old-heart kibble.

Over his sweater and tie combo goes his barn coat, its shoulders streaked with epaulets of brown, black, and white chicken shit. On his head, a black watch cap. The green plastic pail filled with water the night before. The rubber boots. The leather mittens. Is he ready?

Through the window in the kitchen door, he looks west where it is still night. Over his shoulder, the east—a red sliver in the east precursor of the goading hours until bed, the soapstone, the dogs at his head and back. Ready but unwilling, he is ready.

The path to the barn is iced, the snowbanks high enough to knock the water pail, confusing his balance. The red barn door he rolls back a foot or two, and the old gelding releases a roar and another, another.

No word exists for the sound and it continues, continues, the worst thing in his morning many mornings, until he has found the metal grain scoop, dug out a scoop of old-horse high-protein gray-green pellets, fought open the stall door the old gelding has spent the night wedging shut with half-chewed hay and his angrily kicked and endlessly fruitlessly nuzzled and licked rubber pail, and poured the grain into the freshly-righted pail.

Then the sound stops. Most mornings.

This morning the gelding lunges a second too soon, hits his elbow, knocks the grain out of the scoop and onto the stall mat before it can reach the bucket. Half-blind, the head goes into the empty bucket, then comes out in full throat, betrayed so profoundly that in all history or philosophy never has any human bitterness expressed itself with half as much force.

—Shit, goddammit you fucking asshole. Goddam goddam fucking bitch bullshit asshole cocksuckers, stupid fuckhead asshole. He returns to the galvanized barrel of pellets and gets a second scoop.

—Bitch, bitch, to leave me with this the bitch, her and Angus MacFuckhead. The old gelding is plunging in place, expanding in the ten-by-ten stall until it is nearly filled with impatience and despair. The gelding caroms off the two-by-eights, his hair whistling against the rough boards, moving faster and faster. The stall could collapse around him.

—Jesus! Jesus Jesus Jesus! Alright it's here, it's here! Again he enters the stall. The grain goes in. The old gelding shuts up. Now the other two begin.

—Shut up you stupid fucks, shut the fuck up!

In a rage he hurls the empty scoop in the direction of the fat horse. It clangs against the corrugated metal siding above him and drops into the stall. The fat horse spins as if to escape, sees the barn wall blocking his way, and races in a tight circle around his stall, avoiding the rocking scoop, searching for some way out.

He finds a plastic scoop without a handle and noses it into the semi-frozen corn oats molasses mixture until he has enough to distract the fat horse—a cup or two. He goes in the stall, dumps the grain in the bucket, retrieves the scoop and when he leaves, the fat horse is snuffling his food, the flying scoop forgotten.

The third horse, the mare, is arch-necked and blowing, her eyes rolling.

—Oh fucking relax. He gives her her grain.

The bantams scuffle in the hay, looking under their wings, stretching necks and shaking heads. With the plastic scoop he flings cracked corn, in an arc as dusty and geometric as a galactic loop of stars. The alpha birds move after the corn in a desultory way, the rest are too demoralized by the cold to fight for it. They grumble and look under their wings some more.

He puts a scoop of old-horse pellets in the paddock bucket outside, a tiny scoop of mixed grains in the other horses' paddock buckets, sets the water pail on a level spot on the icy ramp, opens a haybale.

He turns out the old gelding who races, high-trots down the aisle and onto the ramp, head swivelling to locate the old-horse pellets.

Special treatment for the fat horse: he picks up the aluminum stall shovel and half leans on it. He drops his right mitten despite the cold so that he can release the stall door hook-and-eye, pry up the wire loop over a nail which backs up the hook-and-eye, and slide rightwards the two-by-four failsafe bar, which backs up the other two closures—three goddamn closures for the fat horse who once was discovered out of his stall and droopy-headed colicky hanging over the galvanized barrel with its hypnotic grain mixture.

He finds his mitten and lifts the shovel to port arms.

—Come on you fucker. I dare you, just try it. He'd like nothing better than for the fat horse to just try it, but the fat horse eyes the shovel sideways and hand-gallops off, snaking his head teeth-first toward the stacked haybales as though, if he could only stop a second, he might snap one and pull it down in passing, which indeed he did one time, pulling not only the one but forty or fifty others stacked above. So the next time the fat horse was turned out, he was there pitiless behind the fat horse's tucked and rolled rump beating with passion its astonished amplitude with the flat of the aluminum shovel screaming

—Get out of here you fucker! Git!

And for a moment the surprised and muscular squat of the rump as it leaped forward might have come off the Parthenon frieze. Now the shovel is only a reminder and the snaked head vestigial but also a reminder of the horse's barely banked nature.

And finally the mare, frantic at being herd-last, so the likeliest prey of any wolf or tiger.

—Git git git, all of you. Git!

He watches them for a moment in their paddock: the gelding bores into his bucket, oblivious; the fat horse eats, eyes the mare sidling over to her bucket, flips his head angrily to warn her off her own feed, realizes he should be eating instead of flipping, eats. . . .

Before the fat horse is done with his own grain, he rushes over to claim hers. She circles around behind the old gelding to the fat horse's bucket and finishes what he has left behind.

They settle down, the man and the three horses.

He starts to slide the door shut, preliminary to latching it, barring it, turning on the electric fence, charging back to the house and pulling together his work gear. But. Stops. Notes: the steam from the horses' nostrils. And across the pasture the backlit woods, black but with chinks, the light there promising in five minutes when the sun is higher to be unbearable. Snow pinkening in the space between the long tree shadows.

—Ahh. Ah shit. Ah shit.

The colors, the cold air steaming, the three quiet horses—defeat him.

A cat winds by his ankle, out into the paddock. He doesn't feed the cats until he returns from work tonight.

—Shit. Hey Kitty, c'mum c'mum.

He can't remember cat names, whimsical cat names she has summoned.

—Here Kitty. The cat turns, comes back in. He slides the door fast, bars it, turns on the electric fence. Too much time wasted on pastel colors and rural scenes and goddam cats, too much—he frowns. He stomps back the path to the house, empty pails banging in his hands, counting cadence

—And fuck and shit and fuck and . . .

But he laughs at himself as he counts, shakes his head, smiles, then laughs aloud.

—Shit.

He pictures her, bent under two pails of water ten days ago on this same path—shit, the bend in her back stabs him now. Shit, poor Angus Aaroam with his awful shrew wife. The wife might as well have a name of consonants alone, gritting and choking, for all the peace she gives poor Angus—who wouldn't want some comfort? And how could his own wife resist giving it and getting in return at least a Scot's peck, solace for twenty years of his scowls?

—Ah shit. Shit shit shit.

He shakes his head, shit, but without his willing it, his chest opens, sternum warming and uncreaking as though all the ribs had found a sun to shine on them. By the time he reaches the porch door, each rib has burst into leaf, southern birds sing there. He gives himself up to that, forgets all the rest.

He laughs again, shrugs, deciding that the time until she returns from Italy is a patchwork of small and simple things to do and then be done with.

—Next round of chores I'll be my fucking old self again. No doubt, no fucking doubt.

But he isn't, doesn't come on that fucking old self again that afternoon or night or next day or next.

One morning he snaps the paper open and checks the Rome weather, hoping she and Angus are getting some small warmth, a sun to shine on them.

At the airport he hugs her.

Is everything okay? Her voice diminishes so as not to provoke. Chores?

—Chores! Jesus Fucking Christ deliver me from chores. But he's smiling. Yes, everything's fine, no problem.

—Really?

—Yeah, the little guys, the mutts, they woke me up one morning at twenty of two for their goddamn breakfast.

She smiles, he hoists her carry-on to his shoulder.

—What happened?

And, as he opens his mouth to tell her, oh how the leaves rustle, the birds in his chest sing.

Animal Skins

THAISA FRANK

A few weeks before she left for the mountains, she said to him: Do you know that if I touch you in a certain way, you'll feel like a vole? They were in bed, reading. She put out her cigarette, touched him softly, and he felt he had silky fur. He'd never seen a vole, but had an instant understanding of different gradients of earth, just the way she understood layers of snow—depth-hoar, crystal-snow— he'd heard her talk about them. Then she stroked him with the back of her hand and he was racing along the ground. What was I then? he asked. You were a fox, she answered.

She was going to the mountains alone—that was the understanding. She was a professional skier, so the separation made sense. Still, there was tension surrounding her trip because she was going to ski in country that had avalanches. One night he read a book about mountain rescue, and realized that all the techniques required another person. He mentioned this and she said she wasn't afraid.

That evening he watched her pack and had an insatiable desire to follow her. What animals will you see? he said. I have no way of knowing, she answered. He persisted, saying that he wanted her to touch him so he could become each animal on her journey. She said she didn't want to be bothered, and soon they had a fight in which she said his reading the book about mountain rescue was a form of meddling and he said he could read any damn book he pleased. She got into bed and began to smoke. The smoke reminded him of powder snow—the kind that can cause avalanches.

All that month he thought about her in the mountains, especially when he was in bed, trying to re-create the feeling of her hands. He thought about being an animal in snow, imagined her finding him, a moment of locked eyes.

As soon as she came back, he made her tell him every animal she'd seen. Foxes mostly, she said. And maybe a few deer. The usual. She was standing by the closet unpacking clothes, looking relaxed, a little smug. The animals I expected to see, she added.

He came over and gripped her by the shoulders—at a distance, so he could see her eyes. They were bright, as though they had seen acres of snow, great impossible bolts of it, traversing an entire country. He hesitated, then stroked her lightly, turning her into an animal he'd never seen. Who am I? she said. I have no idea, he answered. He carried her to the bed and put her under piles of blankets, an avalanche of sorts, far away from the mountains. Don't think about anything, he whispered, everything is known inside the skin.

Apollo and The Seven Whores

CARLOS FUENTES, TRANSLATION BY ALFRED MAC ADAM

6:47

I told them I wanted nothing from them, that I was just offering them a little pleasure sail. Get a little sun, Snow White told them, let a little light into the place where the sun doesn't shine, assholes. No one said anything about money. I only asked that there be seven, including Snow White. But she wasn't going for it. I'm the Wicked Stepmother, she said with an ineffable smile, I'm the one who offers the poisoned apple. But I, generous to a fault, insist on assigning her the role of heroine. The day began gloriously, and the seven I picked (Snow White insisted on being the Wicked Step-mother and not giving up her own role; I insisted on calling her Snow White) were delighted to go out for a sail, with no demands, just to get a little tan, to kick back a little, practice napping, be somewhere else. . . . That's what Snow White told them to bring them around. I only asked for a minute to pick up my things at the hotel. I didn't give up my room. I threw the few things I brought with me in my bag, making sure I had my shaving kit, my tooth-paste and toothbrush, deodorant. The girls would look divine in the sunlight, despite a sleepless night and the dancing. I could tell I looked gray, unshaven, bloodshot, dry skin. The different drinks I'd had gathered into a fist inside my head, hammering at it. The girls saw me and probably said to themselves, We won't have any prob-lems with this wreck. I barely had time to look at myself in the mirror. With revulsion, I thought about the coffee-colored recep-tionist in his *guayabera*. He wasn't there. How right they were to let him out only at night; sunlight would destroy him.

8:00

They may have begun to see me differently when I showed them how much I knew about handling a beautiful ketch with fixed sta-bilizer, twin masts, boom, and two jibs. Thirty-six feet long, a beam of nine feet, and a thirty-foot displacement, it cut a fine figure leav-ing the docking area on its way to the bay, running on the auxiliary motor, with my firm hand on the tiller to take it out of Acapulco. Then, leaving control of the helm, I passed it to Snow White, who al-most fainted with shock, amid the giggles of her ladies-in-waiting, so I could raise the mainsail and then the mizzen, all with precise movements, tying cables, setting bitts to wind other cables around them, tying down the boom with a clove hitch and the jibs with a couple of half hitches.

I clamped down a cable that looked loose.

I made everything fast and shipshape.

The ketch was ready for any adventure. A sensitive craft, faith-ful, that followed every movement of the person who loved her and sailed her well, it was the most beautiful ornament of a splen-did day, the kind only the Mexican Pacific knows how to give. Like a poem I learned as a child, anyone who's seen a sea like this and still wants to get married can only do it with someone like the sea itself.

Ireland boils in my veins. Even more the black Ireland of a descendant of Spain, a castaway it seems, Vincente Valera is my name, but my ambitions are much more modest than those in that poem of my childhood. Vincente Valera is my name, and the name of my ketch, to the boorish satisfaction of the hotel receptionist, is *The Two Americas*.

Snow White and her seven girl-dwarfs stare at me in admiration and if I don't marry the sea, I'll have to settle for going to bed with them. All seven? Two Americas, one Apollo, and seven whores? What a salad!

9:16

I took the helm again. I think the girls had never seen one of their customers carry out maneuvers they'd only seen done by the boatmen in the port. The morning was cool and blazing hot at the same time: the brilliant, dry heat redeems everything in Acapulco—the ugliness of the buildings, the filth on the streets, the misery of the people amid the tourist boom, the blind pretense of the rich that there are no poor here, all inexplicable, all unjust, all probably, after all is said and done, irredeemable.

In the eyes of the seven dwarfs, I saw something like an immediate admiration, which did not demand from the guy cast as the macho more than a series of strong, well-defined acts to take control of their feminine veneration. Of course, I tried much too hard. My head was splitting, I felt I needed a bath, an aspirin, and a bed more than I needed all this work; but when we were out to sea, far from the corrupt fingernail of the bay, the Sun and the Pacific, that glorious husband and wife team that overcomes all unfaithful storms and even the most hurricane-plagued divorces, embraced all of us, the eight women and me, in an irresistible way. I think we all had the same idea: if we don't give ourselves over to the sea and the sun this morning, we don't deserve to be alive.

The minibar on *The Two Americas* was well stocked, and there were also some platters of Manchego cheese and Spanish ham along with sliced jicamas covered with powdered chile. No sooner did the girls discover them than they devoured them, all feeding each other, while Snow White shrugged her shoulders and poured some drinks. She came over to me, holding out a glass. I should have said no, but she insisted on drawing a face in the air, on top of my own, as if she'd guessed what my dream was, as if she were trying to hypnotize me. So I left her with the tiller again, whereupon she again became nervous. "Just keep going straight ahead. There are no trees on the road," I said laughing, both of us laughing, creating a strange link between the two of us.

I had an idea. I wanted to teach the girls something. I thanked my lucky stars that the hotel people had put a rod and reel on the ketch. I announced to them that I was going to teach them to fish. They all laughed out loud and began to make jokes. One after the other, they played word games, the custom in both Mexico City and Los Angeles, sister cities where language is used more for self-defense than for communication, more to conceal than to reveal. The wordplay digresses, camouflages, hides: from an innocent word you try to squeeze a filthy word, so that everything comes to have a double meaning or, if you're lucky, a triple meaning.

I say they laughed a lot and that their collective voice was like the sound of birds. But their jokes were crude, physiological, more suitable for vultures than for nightingales. The fishing rod was the object of myriad phallic metaphors; the hook became a dick, the bait a pussy, flying fish became flying fucks, and soon every squid, ray, oyster, or snapper in the vast sea metamorphosed into every imaginable sexual object and word. After a night of giving themselves over to the energy of their bodies, it was as if the girls had sweated out all their corporeal juices. Now their heads were lubricated, and they could dedicate themselves to the art of language. But it was foul language which produced a chain reaction of hilarity among them and, at the same time, seemed to affirm the fact that they were in some way superior beings, owners of language as opposed to the owners of money, castrators of the "decent" language of the master, the boss, the millionaire, the tourist, the customer.

I should probably confess that my poor Anglo-Saxon similes, extremely brutal, were no competition for the metaphoric pyrotechnics of the gang of seven girls, loosened up in their collective giggle. Their camaraderie and their instant commitment to joking were contagious, but I stopped listening to them, oh my sad condition, your sad cuntdition? cunt, runt, grunt, cuntinue please, yes give me a hand here, a handjob here? a handkerchief? you need a fingerbowl, no, a fingerfuck, Dallas, Texas, not Dullass but good ass, good as gold, no Gold Finger, oooh! not a Cold Finger, oh oh seven, you mean up up six, six is a lot for a teeny little twat, well I give tit for twat. Not one pun unturned.

While they fooled around, I copped a few feels. The pretext, as I said, was to teach them how to fish, to use the rod and hook, and to do it, I stood behind each one and taught her to cast, carefully, so no one would get hurt. I hugged each one, sitting each of them on my lap, teaching them to fish, my hands around each waist, on each thigh, and on each and every sex, feeling in short order the excitement of my own when I dared to rub their nipples and then to slide my hand under their bikini top, or into the bikini bottom and put my finger full of their juices into the mouth of . . .

I began to sort them out, my seven dwarfs, as they began to get hot and asked me to teach them to fish: Now it's my turn; No it's mine, you cut in, bitch.

No. This one must be Grumpy because she resisted my advances saying No, I'm not like them, now you've got me pissed off; get your hands off me. Another had to be Dopey because she only laughed nervously when I felt her up and pretended not to notice, without being able to control the comic movement of her ears. The third must be Sleepy because she pretended I wasn't touching her and acted the part of the tourist while I stuck my finger up her wet, excited vagina, as if that could tell me the temperature of the other six and announce the tidal wave of sex that was rolling in.

I had identified Doc, who simply looked very serious, while Bashful wouldn't come close, as if she was afraid of me, as if she'd met me before.

Sneezy was the one who drove me crazy, the first one to sink her nose into my pubic hair and begin to sneeze as if she were coming down with hay fever. And the seventh, who would be the most hardworking and careful, unbuttoned my shirt and stretched

me out naked on the deck of the ketch that Snow White was steering in complete ignorance, without daring to ask: What do I do,
now what do I do?

Without even daring to admonish her wards: You can look, you
can listen, you can even sniff, but around here you can't touch anything.

They touched everything I had, the seven demonic dwarfs of
Acapulco. The seven whores of the marvelous Apollo who had out-
done himself, who had completely realized his capabilities in that
moment when I lost the notion, which I'd just attained, of the indi-
viduality of each one of them. They were only what I had said they
were: dopey, dreamy, sneezy, diligent, and wise, enterprise and sensuality. They were obscure angers and palpitating desires, all together. They lacked faces, and I imagined my own under the sun,
under the shadows that covered me, naked on a ketch that was
heading straight for the middle of the ocean, farther and farther
(Snow White never changes course, doesn't protest, doesn't say a
word, an argonaut, a whoronaut, an argoinvalid paralyzed by the
sea, the breeze, the sun, the adventure, the danger, our increasing
distance from terra firma), and I only know that seven eighteen-
year-olds (on the average) are making love to me.

I see seven asses that sit on my face and offer themselves to my
touch and my mouth. I want to be honored and to notice differences, to individualize. I want to glorify them in that culminating
moment. I don't want them to feel bought. I don't want them to
think they're part of a pack. I want them to feel the way I felt when
I got the Oscar, king of the world, and they, my seven dwarfs, my
queens. Asses as hard as medlars and smooth as peaches. Asses as vi-
brant as eels and as patient as squid. Asses that protect the dark
essence, the smooth, slight hair of the Indian woman. The impossible protection of the wide hips, the impossibly slim waists, the
thighs of water and oil that surround, defend, and protect the sacred place, the sanctuary of the vagina, my seven asses this morning
which I smell, touch, desire, and individualize.

Seven cunts seven. Cunt the flesh of a freshly peeled papaya,
rose-colored, untouched, like a carnivorous, perfumed pearl. Palpitating cunt of a wounded pup, just separated from its mother,

pierced by the damned arrow of an intrusive hunter. Cunt of a pure spring, water that flows, without obstacles, without remorse, without concern for its destiny in the sea that will drown it like a salt gallows. Night cunt poised to spring in full daylight, kept in reserve for the weakness of the day, vaginal night in reserve for the day when the sun no longer shines and the woman's sex should occupy the center of the universe. Fourth cunt of the Acapulco girls, fourth, fortress, cunt like a furnished fortress, warm, inviting, expecting its perfect guest. Fifth cunt, the fifth the best, a metallic cunt with veins that refuse to be mined and give up their gold, asking the miner that he first die of suffocation in the heart of the tunnel. Glorious cunt of eucharistic libations, sixth, sexth, religious cunt, Irish, black, what would my waspish WASP wife Cindy say, whiteanglosaxonprotestant who tries to hand me her boring genealogical charts: You don't know how to enjoy yourself, Vince, unless you think you're sinning, miserable celluloid Apollo, inflammable, perishable, take me as a woman, as a human being, as your equal, not as a symbol of your spiritual odyssey, son of a bitch, I'm not your communion or your confession, I'm your woman, I'm another human being, why the hell did I ever marry an Irish Catholic who believes in the freedom of sin and not in the predestination of the flesh!

I flee from that: I want to enjoy the final cunt, the seventh seal, the cunt without qualities, the sexual purgatory without heaven or hell, but with my name tattooed on the entrance to the vagina, Vince Valera, conquered Apollo: the seven on my dick, the seven sucking me, one after another, one sucks, the next sticks her finger up my ass, the third kisses my balls, the fourth shoves her cunt in my mouth, the fifth sucks my tits, the sixth licks my toes; the seventh, the seventh rubs her huge tits all over my body, tells the others what to do, bounces her breasts in my eyes, drips them on my balls, glides a nipple over the head of my dick, and then each one sucks me. But not only them: the sun, the sea, the motor of *The Two Americas*—they all suck me.

The impassive stare of Snow White sucks me as she continues in her useless pose with her hands on the tiller. Uselessly, because all the rules of her kingdom are being broken and she can do nothing but stare at us with an indifferent absence which must be that of God Himself when He sees us revert to the condemned but indispensable condition of beasts.

Uselessly, because *The Two Americas* has already attained its inertia and only goes farther into the sea, just as my sex goes further into just one, just one of the seven holes offered this morning to my absolute surrender, the demand that I be given everything, that nothing be held back, that I not find a single pretext to be here or flee, marry or divorce, sign a contract or aspire to a prize, impress a boss, smile to a banker, seduce a columnist as we have dinner at Spago's, nothing, nothing more than this: the simultaneous ascent to hell and heaven, the unleashed palpitation of my chest, the awareness that I drank too much, that I idiotically did not sleep, my heart gallops and my stomach twists, I haven't shaved, my cheeks scrape the divine ass of Dopey as the thorns scrape Christ's face, the sun falls on us like lead rain, the breeze stops, my pain becomes ubiquitous, the sound of the motor disappears, the sun goes out, my body runs out like water, the laughter of the seven dissipates, there are no longer seven holes, there is only one hole into which I weightlessly fall, there are not seven nights, there is only one night, I softly enter it without vacillation, predestined as my wife, Cindy, wanted, without a heart or a head now, pure erect penis, pure phallus of Apollo in the mouth of a bordello muse who caresses my face and whispers in my ear: "This is your ideal face. You'll never have a better one. This is the face for your death, Daddy-o."

12:01

I just died, when the sun passed its zenith. I just died screwing. I was just killed, aboard *The Two Americas*, by the biggest blow job in the history of sex.

12:05

"What are we going to do?" asks Snow White, her hands wrapped tightly around the tiller, as if our not capsizing really depended on it, not daring to sweat, her hands more rigid than my sex, which refuses to die with me.

My dick is still stiff, expecting the second coming, but in reality, I realize, it only predicts, with its excessive hardness, the total stiffness, the rigor mortis that will soon take control of my body, which is still limp, tanned, and unshaven. Is every man's secret dream to have a permanent erection, the thing doctors call priapism? Well, God's just given me one, as much an act of grace as giving military genius to a conquistador, a poetic star to a writer, a good ear to a musician, language to a translator . . .

The dream into which I sink tells me many things, and one of them is this: Vince Valera, you no longer have to prove your masculinity on screen. You've proven it in life. And now, in death, you are going to be the hardest, most unbendable slice of cold cuts that ever descended from an Irish mother. Only the worms from County Tyrone will be able to deal with you!

Shit, I tell myself, I'm talking about my body from the outside. The voice of the Lord is right. Inside, what's going to happen to me inside? Everything that happens to me is passive, a final consequence, a last sigh. My nails and hair keep on growing. This is the first thing I know for a fact.

Bells

STEFANIE MARLIS

What if we saw our hearts as if for the first time;
one sitting like a buddha,
another, shuffling like a man without a home.
Compassion means the heart's desire, bright or bitter,
    counts twice—
like a king in checkers. Like a lover's words
when he touches certain scars:
all these years later the wound's doubly fierce, doubly

healed, and the morning is a rosy glove
pulled onto your whole body.
You hear the bells from the seminary
and for as long as they ring your heart is without a wish.

Blue

MARY MACKEY

One day
suddenly
without warning
everyone in the world
turned blue
not the pale
washed-out blue
of a summer sky
or the gray-blue
of old silk
but full turquoise
bright and hard as
a Navajo stone
set in silver

at first
there was mass panic
governments fell
commerce collapsed
immigration officials went
into shock
and were found wandering along
fortified borders

singing snatches of old
Lawrence Welk tunes

on battlefields all across
the planet
blue soldiers
ran screaming from each other
no one knew who to shoot
no one knew who to hate
the enemy was suddenly
beatified
gorgeous and familiar
as the palm of one's own
hand

in Brazil
three abandoned children
from a cardboard favela
walked unrecognized
through the biggest shopping
mall in Rio
and were accidentally
presented with promotional balloons

in Berlin
five Turkish families
sat on benches in the Zoo
for most of the afternoon
unnoticed and undisturbed

in Miami
a Haitian cab driver
was inadvertently hired
to teach advanced French
at an exclusive
girls' school

as time passed,
the confusion deepened

landlords had to be sedated
real estate agents were found
curled in the fetal position
around For Sale signs

in Chicago alone
over 200 loan officers
attending a convention
at the Airport Hilton
suddenly took Jesus as
their Savior

but for lovers
blueness was a gift
the world around them
opened up
blossoming and blossoming
like a great, blue cornflower
innocent and strange
they lay in each other's arms
blue lips to blue lips
blue breasts to blue breasts
making long, blue love

and when the blue nights
came down at last
and the blue sunsets
hovered over their beds
their blue laughter could be heard
as soft as silver bells
as they whispered to each other
those magic words:
azure
cobalt
indigo
lobelia
gentian
aqua.

Bullet in the Brain

TOBIAS WOLFF

The line was endless. Anders couldn't get to the bank until just before it closed and now he was stuck behind two women whose
loud, stupid conversation put him in a murderous temper. He was
never in the best of tempers anyway, Anders—a book critic known
for the weary, elegant savagery with which he dispatched almost
everything he reviewed.

With the line still doubled around the rope, one of the tellers
stuck a Position Closed sign in her window and walked to the back
of the bank, where she leaned against a desk and began to pass the
time with a man shuffling papers. The women in front of Anders
broke off their conversation and watched the teller with hatred.
"Oh, that's nice," one of them said. She turned to Anders and
added, confident of his accord, "One of those little human touches
that keep us coming back."

Anders had conceived his own towering hatred of the teller,
but he immediately turned it on the presumptuous crybaby in
front of him. "Damned unfair," he said. "Tragic, really. If they're not
chopping off the wrong leg, or bombing your ancestral village,
they're closing their positions."

She stood her ground. "I didn't say it was tragic," she said. "I
just think it's a pretty lousy way to treat your customers."

"Unforgivable," Anders said. "Heaven will take note."

She sucked in her cheeks but stared past him and said nothing.
Anders saw that the other woman, her friend, was looking in the
same direction. And then the tellers stopped what they were doing,
and the customers slowly turned, and silence came over the bank.
Two men wearing black ski masks and blue business suits were
standing to the side of the door. One of them had a pistol pressed
against the guard's neck. The guard's eyes were closed, and his lips
were moving. The other man had a sawed-off shotgun. "Keep your
big mouth shut!" the man with the pistol said, though no one had

spoken a word. "One of you tellers hits the alarm, you're all dead meat. Got it?"

The tellers nodded.

"Oh, bravo," Anders said. "Dead meat." He turned to the woman in front of him. "Great script, eh? The stern, brass-knuckled poetry of the dangerous classes."

She looked at him with drowning eyes.

The man with the shotgun pushed the guard to his knees. He handed the shotgun to his partner and yanked the guard's wrists up behind his back and locked them together with a pair of handcuffs. He then toppled him onto the floor with a kick between the shoulder blades. He took his shotgun back and went over to the security gate at the end of the counter. He was short and heavy and moved with peculiar slowness, even torpor. "Buzz him in," his partner said. The man with the shotgun sauntered along the line of tellers, handing each of them a Hefty bag. When he came to the empty position he looked over at the man with the pistol, who said, "Whose slot is that?"

Anders watched the teller. She put her hand to her throat and turned to the man she'd been talking to. He nodded. "Mine," she said.

"Then get your ugly ass in gear and fill that bag."

"There you go," Anders said to the woman in front of him. "Justice is done."

"Hey! Bright boy! Did I tell you to talk?"

"No," Anders said.

"Then shut your trap."

"Did you hear that?" Anders said. " 'Bright boy.' Right out of 'The Killers.' "

"Please be quiet," the woman said.

"Hey, you deaf or what?" The man with the pistol walked over to Anders. He poked the weapon into Anders' gut. "You think I'm playing games?"

"No," Anders said, but the barrel tickled like a stiff finger and he had to fight back the titters. He did this by making himself stare into the man's eyes, which were clearly visible behind the holes in the mask pale-blue and rawly red-rimmed. The man's left eyelid kept twitching. He breathed out a piercing, ammoniac smell that shocked Anders more than anything that had happened, and he was beginning to develop a sense of unease when the man prodded him again with the pistol.

"You like me, bright boy?" he said. "You want to suck my dick?"

"No," Anders said.

"Then stop looking at me."

Anders fixed his gaze on the man's shiny wing-tip shoes.

"Not down there. Up there." He stuck the pistol under Anders' chin and pushed it upward until Anders was looking at the ceiling.

Anders had never paid much attention to that part of the bank, a pompous old building with marble floors and counters and pillars and gilt scrollwork over the tellers' cages. The domed ceiling had been decorated with mythological figures whose fleshy, toga-draped ugliness Anders had taken in at a glance many years earlier and afterward declined to notice. Now he had no choice but to scrutinize the painter's work. It was worse than he remembered, and all of it executed with the utmost rarity. The artist had a few tricks up his sleeve and used them again and again—a certain rosy blush on the underside of the clouds, a coy backward glance on the faces of the cupids and fauns. The ceiling was crowded with various dramas, but the one that caught Anders' eye was Zeus and Europa —portrayed, in this rendition, as a bull ogling a cow from behind a haystack. To make the cow sexy, the painter had canted her hips suggestively and given her long, droopy eyelashes, through which she gazed back at the bull with sultry welcome. The bull wore a smirk and his eyebrows were arched. If there'd been a bubble coming out of his mouth, it would have said, "Hubba hubba."

"What's so funny, bright boy?"

"Nothing."

"You think I'm comical? You think I'm some kind of clown?"

"No."

"You think you can fuck with me?"

"No."

"Fuck with me again, you're history. *Capeesh?*"

Anders burst out laughing. He covered his mouth with both hands and said, "I'm sorry, I'm sorry," then snorted helplessly through his fingers and said, "*Capeesh*, oh, God, *capeesh*," and at that the man with the pistol raised the pistol and shot Anders right in the head.

The bullet smashed Anders' skull and plowed through his brain and exited behind his right ear, scattering shards of bone into the cerebral cortex, the corpus callosum, back toward the basal ganglia, and down into the thalamus. But before all this occurred, the first appearance of the bullet in the cerebrum set off a crackling chain of ion transports and neurotransmissions. Because of their peculiar origin, these traced a peculiar pattern, flukishly calling to life a summer afternoon some forty years past, and long since lost to memory. After striking the cranium, the bullet was moving at nine hundred feet per second, a pathetically sluggish, glacial pace compared with the synaptic lightning that flashed around it. Once in the brain, that is, the bullet came under the mediation of brain time, which gave Anders plenty of leisure to contemplate the scene that, in a phrase he would have abhorred, "passed before his eyes."

It is worth noting what Anders did not remember, given what he did remember. He did not remember his first lover, Sherry, or what he had most madly loved about her, before it came to irritate him—her unembarrassed carnality, and especially the cordial way she had with his unit, which she called Mr. Mole, as in "Uh-oh, looks like Mr. Mole wants to play," and "Let's hide Mr. Mole!" Anders did not remember his wife, whom he had also loved, before she exhausted him with her predictability, or his daughter, now a sullen professor of economics at Dartmouth. He did not remember standing just outside his daughter's door as she lectured her bear about his naughtiness and described the truly appalling punishments Paws would receive unless he changed his ways. He did not remember a single line of the hundreds of poems he had committed to memory in his youth so that he could give himself the shivers at will—not "Silent, upon a peak in Darien," or "My God, I heard this day," or "All my pretty ones? Did you say all? O hellkite! All?" None of these did he remember; not one. Anders did not remember his dying mother saying of his father, "I should have stabbed him in his sleep."

He did not remember Professor Josephs telling his class how the Spartans had released Athenian prisoners from their mines if they could recite Aeschylus, and then reciting Aeschylus himself, right there, in the Greek. Anders did not remember how his eyes had burned at those sounds. He did not remember the surprise of seeing a college classmate's name on the jacket of a novel not long after they graduated, or the respect he had felt after reading the book. He did not remember the pleasure of giving respect.

Nor did Anders remember seeing a woman leap to her death from the building opposite his own, just days after his daughter was born. He did not remember shouting, "Lord have mercy!" He did not remember deliberately crashing his father's car into a tree, or having his ribs kicked in by three policemen at an antiwar rally, or waking himself up with laughter. He did not remember when he began to regard the heap of books on his desk with boredom and dread, or when he grew angry at writers for writing them. He did not remember when everything began to remind him of something else.

This is what he remembered. Heat. A baseball field. Yellow grass, the whirr of insects, himself leaning against a tree as the boys of the neighborhood gather for a pickup game. The captains, precociously large boys named Burns and Darsch, argue the relative genius of Mantle and Mays. They have been worrying this subject all summer, and it has become tedious to Anders; an oppression, like the heat.

Then the last two boys arrive, Coyle and a cousin of his from Mississippi. Anders has never met Coyle's cousin before and will never see him again. He says hi with the rest but takes no further notice of him until they've chosen sides and Darsch asks the cousin what position he wants to play. "Shortstop," the boy says. "Short's the best position they is." Anders turns and looks at him. He wants to hear Coyle's cousin repeat what he's just said, but he knows better than to ask. The others will think he's being a jerk, ragging the kid for his grammar. But that isn't it, not at all—it's that Anders is

strangely roused, elated, by those final two words, their pure unex-
pectedness and their music. He takes the field in a trance, repeating
them to himself.

The bullet is already in the brain; it won't be outrun forever, or
charmed to a halt. In the end, it will do its work and leave the trou-
bled skull behind, dragging its comet's tail of memory and hope
and talent and love into the marble hall of commerce. That can't be
helped. But for now Anders can still make time. Time for the shadows to lengthen on the grass, time for the tethered dog to bark at
the flying ball, time for the boy in right field to smack his sweat-
blackened mitt and softly chant, *They is, they is, they is.*

Coyote and the Shadow People

E. BETH THOMAS

My wife of many years suddenly
died, left me knocking around
the empty dwelling, lone seed
in a brown shell.

The death spirit took pity.
To once again taste of my wife
I vowed constancy to him,
and he made me a guest

in his spirit world, guiding me
through gates I couldn't see.
At my side amorphous, he led me
over a plain, observing a herd

of horses that to me were
grass flats and blue sky—

nothing more. We neared the dead,
where we picked and ate berries

that to me were air and miming motions
of my mouth and hands. I mimicked
his every ghostly move, as if
watching myself in a hazed pool of water.

As I followed him, her edges in my mind
softened—my hands wanted
to seize real twigs, snap them
to hear the noise.

I waited. Breathed deep from the chest.
The spirit led me to a lodge
I couldn't see, a wife I couldn't see,
food she prepared and we ate

which I couldn't see. I scooped
prairie dust in my palm to feel
its solid trickle through my fingers,
to still their trembling. My skin

prickled with her.
Your sunset will be our dawn
the spirit told me. As darkness dropped
its cloak on the day,

people emerged, fingers of color
slowly painted on the dark canvas.
My wife sat beside me, her lips
curved in a smile, and I accepted

the magic as real. I ate. I drank.
I tended fires with friends who passed
long ago. Around me always hung
my wife's smile, amulet.

I parched in the desert days,
my skin growing tight on my bones,

drank in the night's coolness.
The spirit returned and bid me farewell.

Go, he said, and bring your wife.
Cross five mountains in five days.
Do not touch your wife
until the fifth day has passed

and she will be yours again.
Four days passed. I watched her shape
grow solid, smelled her sweat,
knotted my joy round an ache

in my gut. We reached our final
campsite and her face glowed
with heat, owning its sweat,
snapping my knots—my hands

broke towards her even as her mouth
formed in horror
STOP—
one touch. My fingers burned
from her skin and she vanished.

The spirit appeared, fleshed
in his fury. You did not obey.
You had begun humanity's return
from the dead. You erred

and make death final for all.

Dulled, I retraced our steps,
fumbled through the spirit's rites
of passage. My feet bled

from trudging, small moans fell
from my lips, darkness leveled the day.
I sat cross-legged, watching stars
poke pin-holes of light

in the sky. The horizon flushed rose
and my skin grew hot. My throat dried.
I sat a week's rotation of sky,
alone.

I was too filled with love.

I left its bones in the prairie dust.

Each Touch the Future

DAVID BIESPIEL

To say *yes*, a whisper, *yes*, a nerve.
Mornings, mornings: the foghorns' song.
The stiffbacked surf-fishermen cluster,
Undiluted, around the blueing bass. Steam
Rises from its gills that still open.
Gulls hang on in the sky when I enter
You again, as in a dream of flying —
The beginnings of air seen or felt

Or fallen into. As into water.
You are not water but a body
I know, each dune in your wrist.
Mornings, mornings: the foghorns unbroken.
Like words, you keep rising under
So that we are, when we are, one air.

Fall Courting Rituals

LISA LEITZ

what I do in the car
when the kids aren't with me
very much concerns Bill (I can tell
by his yellow hat), half of the cropduster brother
team, he's racing me down twenty-four
as he sprays sweet corn
And I listen to the radio too loudly
and drive with my skirt up
and the window unrolled
even as the peppery stink of insecticide
slaps into my throat and hair.
He does a showoff tight hop over a poplar windbreak
and finishes the narrow strip just before
the Jelmberg's, tilting his wings zigzag,
I see you. And here I am roaring to Moses Lake,
a little off course because I'm not smiling
or digging for graham crackers,
like a bird off the migratory pattern
I could do anything.

Only-Child Agriculture

LISA LEITZ

Bags of sweet corn line the floor, and Walt is still naked,
palms yellow from drawing chalk eggs
        on the chickenhouse

hell yes, I have to get it shucked and blanched
before more earwigs plip happily to the floor,
    quite a move up
from Harvey Herigh's cornfield—but now the kid
needs a popsicle, or he's climbed up on a table—
There's cherries in June, nectarines in July.
Then apples, and potatoes sifting onto the floor
I can't keep up. Now he's walking up
with two white buckets of Concord grapes and spiders
his cap still in the truck, probably upside
down and filled with spilled wheat or a couple Braeburns,
he only wishes there were more yellow fingerprints
    on his pants,
he's ready to feed me into fertility, stockpiling food
    for the big family
he drenches me with every night,
millions of children looking for a warm safe place
well we have enough to feed the world.

Geography

EDWARD SMALLFIELD

Purple flowers. Wide as trumpets, so delicate they wither in my fingers. Where are you? On the balcony, I suppose, watching as the
crowd from the ferry disappears in the streets above the harbor.
Sun works on your face, a careful pencil, perfecting your skin.
Later, when I touch your cheek, I feel sun concealed inside you. I
close my eyes, see those flowers again. When I touch one, I find a
membrane, sensitive as the inside of your mouth. While we make
love, a little light trickles around the curtain. A wind knocks our
shirts from the balcony. Afterwards, when we walk downstairs to

pick them up, it's so late that we don't bother to dress. Your red shirt and my white one shine under the streetlight. When a car stops, and the driver asks us why we're naked, we tell him we're dead people who've returned to gather lost garments. He believes us because he doesn't speak our language. Then we slip into his cab and you promise him a coin he's never seen before. Where, he asks, is your asphodel? so we try to pick some in the field beside the road. We can't find asphodel, so we choose fennel, flagrant at this time of year. We drive all night, in circles, around the island. When we stop in small stores for beer, or in restaurants to eat lamb, the driver explains that we're naked because we're dead. No one questions this story. Maybe they're convinced by our fennel, or by our nakedness. Maybe they know that lovers, like the dead, inhabit a country of their own, closed to everybody else. Because we didn't have time to wash after making love, our bodies smell of seawater. As we drive around the island, the driver stops at every beach, and we wash each other. We add more salt to our salt, wetness to our wetness. Near dawn, when we return to the street outside our hotel, the driver asks if we want to go back to our country. No, we tell him, we've decided to stay a while, and he looks at us strangely. When we leave the cab, he waits. We find a small cafe in the basement of a house across from the hotel. The bartender dozes with her head on the bar. A few couples sway on the dance floor. The piano player laces a little Bach into his blues. Yellow blossoms blaze on the fennel you hold over your head.

Grayton Beach Cottage

TARA BRAY

She slides both hands into her pants,
not with her usual groggy-sweet sensuality,

but with her eyes wide open, taking
in the light that bends down from concrete

walls. She wonders if others have come
to this, before her, unable to contain the vastness

of the dark sea, the ragged storm clouds,
haunting brown pelicans, the white-capped teeth

that bite into themselves. A woman hungry
enough to feed from her own emerald salt.

Harry Pickering

KARL HARSHBARGER

I

Harry Pickering, associate professor of English, but actually a specialist in nineteenth-century American literature, made the first of what was to be a series of important discoveries on this cold and forbidding February morning: he had actually bounded up the stairs towards his office after his nine o'clock class. He only realized this afterwards when he found himself stopping at the top to catch his breath. And even then he didn't remember quite how it had happened, just something about his grabbing hold of the railing and swinging around the first landing and then grabbing hold again and launching himself up more stairs. Having caught his breath and now walking down the hallway he made a second discovery, that he was almost whistling, right in the middle of the hallway with students passing by all wrapped up for winter, some tune out of his boyhood, as if he were whipping along on his bike with the wind singing past.

So, thought Harry Pickering, my goodness, what was all this? Because as he inserted the key in his office door he realized he simply felt—how else to put it?—unusually good. No. More. A lifting feeling. A surge of well-being. But why? And where did it come from? On a day like this?

"Good morning, Dr. Pickering."

Two students passing him in the hall, the girl wrapped in a gigantic muffler.

"Good morning, good morning."

He lingered watching the two students. The last time he'd felt like this, who knows, maybe he'd even bounded up the stairs then, Clifford Leach had caught him in the hallway (directly under where he now stood, by the way) and told him that although it wasn't official yet his tenure decision had been affirmative. Then two days later President Bynoski calling him in and shaking his hand. That had been all unreal, too, as if everything would only go right the rest of his life and nothing could ever again go wrong.

But now? Still standing in front of his office door Harry Pickering quickly cast himself over the morning's events. Nothing unusual. An ordinary breakfast with his wife, a walk to the College over those bumpy and icy sidewalks, and, yes, the nine o'clock class had had its moments, but then it often went well, not always, but often enough.

So, Harry Pickering told himself, let it go. And trying to make a bit of a joke out of it as he opened his office door, he reminded himself that in all due modesty there were some mysteries of life that would ever remain beyond him, for example his wife's filing system, the origin of the universe, and why not, the way he felt this morning? Accept it as a gift. Leave it at that.

Except that this surging sense of well-being wouldn't leave it at that, because even when he saw his scholarly desk against the wall (as opposed to his teacher's desk where he talked to students) all covered with notes laid out in order, and especially as he sat down and looked at the title of his next article written out in the upper left-hand corner, "The Reactive Image: The Triad in Melville's *Moby Dick*," he thought, wondering all the time as he was thinking it, no, no, no, there was no way he was going to work on *Moby Dick* today, something so, well, yes, be honest, he was thinking it, he shouldn't hide it from himself, so trivial. Trivial? *Moby Dick*? Trivial? Nonsense! Perhaps he, himself, or his own work, trivial. But not *Moby Dick*. And in any case, he always stayed the course. Through up days and down days. Through all those mental tricks and machinations. Those quite predictable assaults. The secret? Not to stop, not to give in.

But as he leaned forward over the previous days' notes to find just the proper entrance slot, that sense of "trivial" hung above him. And, so, just for the moment anyway, Harry Pickering gave up looking for the entrance slot and leaned back in his chair.

It had to be something in the morning's events. He started to go back, trying to remember how he felt when he woke up, but then put it to himself another way. Was it actually necessary to stay the course every blessed morning between ten o'clock and one o'clock? In general, yes, a good idea. He enjoyed it, always had been attracted to it, the clear formulation of the idea, the force of the revealing argument, the clarity in chaos. But then, hadn't he been more diligent than most? Didn't he deserve some time off every once in a while? Wasn't a certain amount of rest a good idea? And, after all, my God, look at the weather. February!

Harry Pickering got up, put his hands in his pockets, went over to his office window and studied the bleak and dark forms of the College buildings against the snow. How depressing it seemed. Really! The beginning of winter was all right, the first blizzard, the insane way the wind raged, flinging skies full of snow around, slowing everything to a stop. But later, well, week after week, the snow everlastingly on the ground. . . .

So, another discovery. Harry Pickering found himself pulling on his coat and hat and gloves, closing and locking his office door, going down the stairs, past Clifford Leach's office and the large lecture room where, God knew, someone held forth, wrapping his scarf up around his neck, pushing against the huge door of Old Main and stepping out into the crushing cold.

Naturally the sidewalks were rock-like with ice. That's what happened after a snow when the students walked to class the next morning. Now it would be weeks and weeks before the ice gave way, unless Buildings and Grounds came with picks and sledge hammers, which, of course, they wouldn't.

Just when he'd reached that point when he thought the front of his face couldn't stand the cold any longer, thank God, the warmth of the Union, coats flung about, never enough hooks, students sprawled all over the place, only the faculty sitting straight and proper. As Harry Pickering moved out of his coat he looked for Sommerfield and Smith up at their little place on the semi-balcony on the right, but it had been so long since he'd been here at this time of the morning that he'd forgotten that they had ten o'clocks this semester. Maybe one of them was holding forth in the main lecture room. So that left the "Young Turks," Irwin, Orrmann, Stone, McCormick, Fisher, and Beckham at the big table in front of the huge window. Hadn't that group disintegrated yet? Did they still meet here? Every morning? Thank God for his own strength of discipline.

Nevertheless, there was nothing for it, so he pulled up a chair and as he did so he noticed he received a few perfunctory waves, nothing very welcoming, but then that's probably because as one of the tenured members of the faculty, established, so to speak, he didn't really belong here with them. Just as well. Or maybe it was because Irwin, with those long arms of his, was in the middle of telling some incredible story about the failings of the Admissions Office, something to do with actually promoting another college by mistake. Pickering studied Irwin as he talked, jabbing those hands up and down. No, he didn't like him, a wound-up comer like that, all talk, all sparkle, all go. But somehow it didn't make any difference what Irwin was saying or whether he was a comer or a goer because as the cold he'd picked up from crossing the iced sidewalks eased out of him Harry Pickering found that strange, even almost unbearable sense of well-being flowing into him again. It was almost as if he now held some wonderful secret inside of himself, some explosion of good news.

But what was this good news? Again, Harry Pickering tried to make a joke to himself about it, something about the origins of the universe, but the joke didn't quite work for him, and so he gave it up and simply reviewed the morning's events again. Nothing his wife had said or done. Nothing on the walk over to the College. No one he'd met in the halls. And, yes, the class had gone well, the way he'd trapped the students into that discussion of the character of Othello. The Novotney boy had gotten it first, and then the dispute between Novotney and the Miller girl, Susan Miller, yes, the way she'd gone after Novotney, her eyes almost blazing. Quite an argument, some of the other students even embarrassed. Ah, Susan Miller! Was that it? Was it that simple? Another crush on a coed? Certainly a beautiful girl, always so well dressed, today the bright blue scarf thrown around her neck matching her long very dark blue skirt (see, he had noticed), and, admit it, he loved her long blond, almost golden, hair which he often studied when the students busied themselves writing. But still, nothing unusual, nothing that hadn't happened to him tens of times (hundreds of times?) before, and happened to other professors, too, he assumed. No. Susan Miller couldn't really account for this new feeling, this surge inside of him. This feeling came from somewhere else, somewhere extraordinary. And sitting there half listening to the talk around him, a kind of fainting feeling came to him, almost a dizziness, as if a void had opened up in front of him.

"Look at Harry!" said Irwin.

Harry Pickering pulled back from the void on Irwin's voice and saw all the others looking at him.

"You're the cat who's swallowed the canary."

What a strange look from all of them! The pain in their faces!

"Come on, tell us!" That was Lothar Fisher. The little copy-cat.

"No, no," said Harry. "That's my secret."

"But that's no fair," said Lothar, with a quick glance at Irwin.

Afterwards as they were all pulling on their coats and scarves and gloves, Irwin made it a point to stand next to Pickering, almost towering over him. And it happened so strangely. Irwin winked down at him. But no ordinary wink. Very slow and deliberate. As if Irwin understood something.

II

On Monday morning walking to class he had almost forgotten Friday's great surge of feeling. The weekend had been rather ordinary. On Saturday morning he and his wife had done their shopping, and on Saturday afternoon he corrected one set of student papers and had gotten through half a set of others. That night he and his wife had driven to a party in Iowa City given by her major professor in her Ph. D. program at the university. The party had depressed him somewhat, all that graduate student talk, rather sophomoric, so brittle, deconstructionism and all that, and then he and his wife had gotten back late to Addison. At least they were able to sleep in Sunday morning—one of the advantages of not having children. In the afternoon a pleasant coffee and cake at the Sommerfield's, although he could have done without Mary Sommerfield going on and on about the new president. That evening, while his wife made notes on her thesis, he finished off the rest of the second set of his student papers. While he was working in one room and his wife in the other, he had a generalized kind of idea of making love to her when they went to bed, but somehow that didn't work out.

In any case, his only concern walking to the College on Monday morning was wrapping himself well enough against the cold and watching his feet on the bumpy frozen snow. Running into Lothar Fisher didn't help his mood because that meant he would have to endure that same kind of graduate school conversation again. But actually, probably because of the cold, Lothar didn't have that much to say and more or less just fell in and walked beside him, only dropping back when the piled-up snow made the sidewalk too narrow.

But Friday's mood returned suddenly and powerfully. He and Lothar had waited at Highway 6 to let a string of farm trucks pass, and then had no more than crossed over and stepped up on the sidewalk (really the ice on top of the sidewalk) when that surge of powerful uplift, that sense that everything was right in his life and nothing could ever possibly go wrong again, exploded through him. My God! What was happening! The feeling was so incredible, so luscious, so wonderful, so, well, spring-like, really, blasting spring-like, so opposite to the cold and the snow and the dark sky and bleak forms of the College buildings, that nothing could be sillier than Lothar walking, slightly hunched, his scarf almost covering his face, beside him. But, come on, what was happening? And, why just as he reached campus? Just as he stepped up on the sidewalk?

"See you at the Union?" said Lothar, getting ready to veer off towards his little office in the Annex behind Old Main.

"I'll be working."

"Well, have a good day."

Harry Pickering let himself be carried along by the wave of students converging on Old Main, even past the main lecture hall where most of them were going, and once he reached the stairs, my God! found himself wanting to bound up them again. But he stopped himself, although, still, he allowed himself a swing and a lunge at the first landing. Then the whistling again, or at least the urge to whistle, the image of himself as a boy whipping along on a bike, his fishing pole sticking out behind.

So, oddly, it was with a sense of relief that he collected his books in his office and actually walked down the stairs, past the big lecture room and down to the end of the hall and turned into room six, for his nine o'clock morning session of "Literary Foundations." An almost full class. Good. But on purpose he didn't look at anyone—Susan Miller in particular—while he set down his material and opened his roll book, went over the names pretending to check on attendance figures, and then purposely avoiding the eyes of the students looked up and out the window to the dark clouds beyond. Aware that the latecomers had arrived and that one of those latecomers had shut the door, he now carried his gaze down away from the window over the students in the classroom, down the front row to Susan Miller, and, yes, she looked as beautiful as ever, this time in designer jeans and a white angora sweater, but, no, he didn't think so, and continued down the row to the end where Novotney sat and back again towards Susan Miller.

It was at this point that Harry Pickering made a much, much larger discovery. It wasn't Susan Miller at all. It was the girl next to her, a Miss Chenery, the somewhat short one with the close-cropped black hair and the rounded face. Her name? Of course, her last name was Chenery, he knew that, but her first name? Did he even know it? He experienced the same sense of dizziness and emptiness in front of him, a void, almost as if he might fall, as he retreated to his roll book to find her first name. Because this girl hardly ever said anything, was just there morning after morning. Her name: Peggy. Peggy Chenery.

Quite aware of his beating heart (and in some corner of his mind thinking, my God, what was this, a cheap novel, beating heart and all that?) and retreating once again to his roll book, he noticed that this Peggy Chenery had been present for every class since the beginning of the semester and that her name appeared between Cane above it and Doggett below it. Having determined that, he decided to sneak one more quick glance before he would be actually obligated to begin the lesson, and again purposely looked out the window and then down the row of students past Susan Miller and almost like an electric shock past this Miss Chenery. Had he been caught? Because without question, beyond any question at all, this energy emanated from her.

Harry Pickering took a deep breath (more out of a cheap novel?) and began the class. First, he reviewed the discussion on Friday concerning *Othello* and posed again the basic question which had concerned them. Othello had every reason to believe Desdemona and no reason to believe Iago, or at least more reasons to believe Desdemona, and yet he chose to believe Iago. Why?

Ralph Novotney's hand shot up.

"Yes," said Pickering.

"I want to add to something I said on Friday."

"By all means," said Pickering.

You never knew about these students. Novotney had made up a little presentation because he now pulled out a piece of paper and began to talk from it. At least this was Addison College, so all the other students turned in his direction to listen. And with the class facing that way, including this Miss Chenery, Harry Pickering now found the opportunity to study her more objectively. No, certainly not a girl he would have picked out. Not bad looking. Good looking in a plain kind of way, a round face, or an oval face, close-cropped hair, and dressed much more conservatively than the other girls. Some of them had a practiced sloppiness which was nevertheless attractive (down to the holes in the jeans), but more and more, a sign of the times? many like Susan Miller went in for fashion, long skirts, matched blouses, brushed and almost glowing hair. But this Peggy Chenery dressed very simply, a straight skirt, possibly a little short, coming just over her knees, and a simple sweater with a pin above her left breast. Wasn't that what girls used to do . . . put their boyfriend's pin on their sweater? So, being careful not to seem too obvious, Harry Pickering studied the pin as well as he could from the desk, but it only seemed ornamental, and, anyway, he pulled himself away because he realized that he had been staring at the curve of her breast, the way it lifted into her sweater, and the dizziness and sense of void came back to him.

To recover, he brought his gaze back to Novotney, where it should have been all the time, nodded, moved his gaze out the window, then back down the front row past the others and Susan Miller to this Miss Chenery, a quick look at her breasts, no, don't do that, he told himself, and then noticed, what was that, some kind of necklace with a ring dangling at the end of it? And wasn't it a man's ring? A man's class ring? And didn't that mean she was engaged, or, if not engaged, pinned? Or did girls still get pinned? Wasn't that rather old-fashioned? But then she looked a little old-fashioned.

The class turned back towards Pickering because Ralph Novotney had stopped talking.

"Yes, I find much of what you say very worth considering," Harry Pickering said. "You've really put some thought into that."

"I find Othello an absolutely fascinating character," said Novotney.

"One of Shakespeare's most intriguing."

"He's both simple and complex."

"I think Ralph's made him too complex." This was Susan Miller cranking up for the attack. "I think he's over-reading."

"But the more important question is," said Pickering, fending off her attack, "was Shakespeare actually aware of what he was doing? We must deal with the question of intention." He had no idea at all why he had jumped to Novotney's rescue, but having done it, now relaxed into the entirely predictable discussion which followed, Don Doggett (what a name!) leading off from the back row. Pickering again stole a glance at Miss Chenery, but this time directly without going to the window first. There she sat, bent over just a bit, a left-hander, cribbing notes into her notebook, a look of almost childish concentration on her face, trying to make sense of Doggett's nonsense. What was it about her? What had hit him so hard? It certainly wasn't her unusual good looks. No one would pick her out. Of course, not bad looking, even if a little short, but not overweight exactly. And she had her youth, the soft, clear complexion of her cheeks. But then they all had that. All the coeds. So why her? Especially since he hadn't noticed her before and didn't even know her first name? And just then she looked up and he barely got his eyes away, and there it was again, the electric shock, his heart setting off like crazy (yes, yes, the cheap novel), because hadn't she felt his eyes on her, wasn't that why she looked up? And hadn't he been caught?

III

At age thirty-seven Harry Pickering felt quite fortunate in his marriage, especially as he surveyed the wreckage around him. Of course, there was the matter that he and his wife had no children and she (as a consequence?) had decided to study for her Ph.D. in Iowa City, and all this would have to be worked out when she actually got her degree. There was little chance that the College would hire her, and he wasn't sure he wanted that. But, that aside, he felt their marriage rested on solid ground and he was absolutely sure she had been true to him. As an undergraduate he had done his share of playing around, who hadn't, but even by graduate school he had started looking for a wife, and when in his Ph.D. program at Hopkins he met Clare he committed himself to her. There had been opportunities from time to time, most recently at the Christmas MLA when the woman Spanish professor from UCLA followed him up to his room and he almost had to close the door in her face. And even, yes, students. Once he was teaching a course in Restoration drama and a coed had come in for a paper conference and told him in a way that left no room for interpretation that her stage name should be "Miss Needit."

Ah, yes, of course, he had had his share of crushes. A whole string of lovelies in his classes. But, then, who hadn't. Maybe not Clifford Leach or maybe not (possibly) Claus Lanchinskcy, but over the years Pickering had come to the conclusion that having crushes on coeds was perfectly normal, it happened to almost all the faculty members, and the thing to do was not hide this from oneself but admit it. Usually he told his wife. Or, more truthfully, at least he didn't try and hide it from her if she sensed it and asked about it. Sometimes when it came out they even laughed about it.

But crushes were one thing and going beyond that pleasant fantasy quite another. Harry Pickering strongly disapproved of those few faculty members who broke the code and actually had affairs with students. For example, two years ago, really, in one of his last official acts, President Bynoski had had to get rid of Peterson because of his affair with the Hawkins girl. And Pickering had refused to join those other faculty members, like Clifford Leach, who tried to defend Peterson.

Therefore as Harry Pickering moved through the rest of his day after his nine o'clock class and allowed the impressions of Miss Chenery to settle, if that was the word, the path before him gradually became clearer. He could not pretend that he understood what was happening to him, the almost violence of his emotions. But one thing was for sure. He was certainly not going to allow anything untoward to happen between him and her. Perhaps she was in love with him. No, no, not perhaps. Obviously. For some reason. You never knew why. Yet, even so, there was something going on he didn't understand. Clearly she had offered her soul up to him. Maybe that was it. Her whole soul. Perhaps that's what he was picking up across the divide between her chair and his desk, so to speak. Her soul. All right, he decided. He would accept her soul. He would accept it as a gift and let it flow inside of him. Let it prop up this February life. A nice gift for a dark and cold February. And the weather in March was questionable, too, so March might need propping up as well. But probably by April the weather would improve, the warmth would return, it most certainly would, and all this would fade away. The main thing with a gift like this was not to mistreat it. Not to harm it. Cherish it.

Harry Pickering gave himself this good advice a number of times during the day, as he was lecturing to his twelve o'clock class, as he was having lunch with Sommerfield at the Steer, as he held student conferences in the afternoon, and once towards five o'clock as he was getting ready to go home and the sky outside his office window had already gone black, allowed himself this good advice again, then having received it, and in a sense thinking he now deserved it, leaned back in his chair and let the wonderful, warm sense of uplift, this Miss Chenery, this strange offer of her soul, infuse through him again. And in that moment, as he felt himself almost lifted out of his office, he remembered the pin on her sweater just above her breast, and then remembered looking at it from his desk in class to see if it signified a tie to some boy, then catching himself looking at the rise in her breast, and now lost himself in a fantasy as his hand traveled downwards from the top of her blouse, his thumb and finger undoing the first button. He pulled himself back from this edgy dizziness.

No, he told himself, no. Not only, no, but he must be sensible and recognize the element of danger here. More than an element of danger. He had tenure. Of course, he had tenure. But what was the word for it? Moral turpitude. A horrible kind of phrase. They could always bring that out against him. The Administration didn't have to use those kind of formal charges against Peterson because Peterson didn't have tenure and that kind of protection, so they just denied him his next contract. Nothing of the dirty business had been brought out into the open. The Hawkins girl even stayed and graduated. But there were ways to get a tenured member of the faculty. Two ways, he now remembered. Financial exigency and moral turpitude. No, no, no. He must be careful. Again, he reminded himself, as he was reminding himself more and more today, he should accept her soul as a gift and like all nice gifts which come unbidden, a holy gift, really, he must not mistreat it.

Then, suddenly, almost horribly, sitting there in his office on this late Friday afternoon with everything dark outside his window, he remembered something else. Last Friday morning. He had been sitting with the Young Turks after his nine o'clock class in the Union and afterwards they had all gotten up and were standing around pulling on their coats getting ready to go back out into the cold and Irwin had rather purposely come right up to him and, there it was, the wink. Had Irwin guessed? Was he only the first to know?

IV

That was on Monday. By Tuesday evening he had found a solution for it all. It went like this. He wasn't attracted to Peggy Chenery at all. His mind had pulled a trick on itself. Certainly it was all understandable, considering the wretchedness of the month of February and the long weeks before spring, but no matter how you looked at it, this Peggy Chenery just didn't make sense. Perhaps she had fallen in love with him. Well, all right. But she wasn't that good a student, probably not all that bright, never distinguished herself in any way in his class—he hadn't even known her first name—and certainly had only average looks. She was simply not his kind of coed. What had happened, he decided, or at least proposed to himself, floated the theory, as it were, was that his real attraction, and perhaps an attraction, well, he should admit it, that had gotten out of hand, aimed at Susan Miller. He could understand that. She was the beautiful one, the one with the blazing eyes, really, a stunning beauty, who always rose to the attack against Ralph Novotney. And it was the middle of February. But, so his theory went, for some reason he was not able to admit this entirely understandable attraction to himself and, in order to handle it better, in order, indeed, to make it less dangerous (another very laudable goal), had transferred his desire towards the less acceptable Peggy Chenery.

Why not?

At least that was his theory. And so on this Tuesday evening he developed a plan to test it. The plan went like this: All of the students in his nine o'clock class needed to come in to see him about their major class paper. Normally he would have seen them during his office hours or other special hours set up in the afternoon. But he could always change that. And so on Wednesday morning he would make what he hoped would be received as the entirely reasonable announcement that class as such was canceled for today and he would hold student consultations in his office, not for all the students, that would be too many, but, oh, let's say for today, the students in the first row. That was a clever trick which no one could see through because such a choice seemed absolutely arbitrary, yet wasn't, since Pickering knew both Susan Miller and Miss

Chenery always sat in the first row. Always. But here was the real genius of the plan. He would also announce that he would see the students in no particular order and they were just to line up however they wanted outside his office door. It seemed clear to Pickering that if Susan Miller were in love with him, an entirely reasonable supposition now, she would surely choose the last position in line in order to have more possible private time with him, and, well, if this Miss Chenery were in love with him, she would do the same.

As it happened, Ralph Novotney presented himself at his office door first.

"Please sit down," said Pickering, indicating the chair right next to his own, beside the desk that he used for interviewing students.

"You must be some kind of athlete," said Novotney.

"I beg your pardon."

"You ran up those stairs."

"Did I?"

"Did you run track in college? You must be in great shape."

"You see, I didn't go to a college. I went to Harvard."

"Sorry," said Novotney, not laughing at his little joke.

"Now, what about your paper?"

Pickering gave Novotney about five minutes to wind through the complexities of Othello's personality and finally said, "Yes, why don't you write on that? That sounds very good."

"You think so?"

"It could be a very good paper."

Doggett was next. For some reason he had settled himself in the front row and not the back row this morning. Pickering had had Doggett in two other classes and Doggett always, always, wrote on imagery, and wouldn't you know, had discovered light and dark imagery in *Othello*.

"Yes," said Pickering, "but remember, imagery comes in clusters."

"Clusters?"

"Yes. Remember? We've talked about this before. Look also at warm and cold, in and out, high and low, different colors, opposites, you know the kind of thing. Remember your paper on Odysseus?"

"But light and dark is okay?"

"Yes, but just don't isolate it."

"Clusters," said Doggett.

"Clusters," said Pickering.

And, my God, as soon as Doggett left here came Susan Miller through the door, lowering herself into the chair, a blue jumper suit with a bright, white scarf, and her golden brushed hair which she now swept off her face with the back of her hand, and the waft of perfume. Perhaps his theory about her placing herself at the end of the line had been wrong. Certainly. Why the perfume, for example? She had been eager to see him, had been thinking of a way to get near him, jumped at his surprise proposal for student conferences, fought for the first spot at his office door, maybe even thinking of walking beside him on the way to his office, claiming her position, as it were, next to him, but he had had the bad sense to run up the stairs and Novotney and Doggett had closed the gap. But, now, thank God, she told herself, she was here.

"So, Miss Miller, and what have you decided to write on?"

"I think, Desdemona."

But what was that? A glance at her watch?

"And what about Desdemona?"

"Well, I haven't really decided yet."

Was that another glance at her watch?

"But for example, what aspect of Desdemona?"

"I'm sorry, Dr. Pickering, but I had no idea you were going to cancel class."

"Well, to be frank, I wasn't entirely sure myself."

"It's just that I could use this time to my advantage."

"Ah," said Pickering.

"So, I mean, could we cancel this? Just for now? I could come back some other time. This Friday, maybe, during your office hours? Two to three, right?

So he had seen her look at her watch.

"Yes, of course."

He pulled out his appointment book and looked, but naturally he always had office hours between two and three on Fridays.

"I'm sorry, Dr. Pickering. It's just that something came up and I'm in a bit of a hurry."

Although he wasn't sure why he was doing it, he came around his desk and opened the door for her, and then discovered why. He had wanted to look at the rest of the students. There they were sitting along one side of the wall, their books out, most of them studying, not wasting time, and there at the end of the line, yes, at the far end, sat Miss Chenery.

Considering that, he was quite pleased with himself at the attention he gave the others. And Eddy Mirrielees, the second to the last one, actually seemed to have an original idea about Cassio. At least the idea was new to Pickering. He couldn't recall reading about it anywhere before. You never knew about these Addison students.

"I'll be most interested in your working that up. I mean that."

"I'll do my best."

"Good luck to you."

Then Mirrielees was gone and he was sure from his counting that she had to be next. Had to be. But when she came in he was at first disappointed—or perhaps relieved. For one thing, seeing her for the first time, really, outside the classroom, more as a person and not just a student sitting in the front row morning after morning in his class, she was a bit shorter than he had remembered, and for another, even though she was wearing a different sweater and skirt, blue this time, not green, essentially it was the same outfit, or at least gave the impression of the same outfit, she had on in class last Friday. Also her short cropped hair hardly flattered her face.

"Shall I close the door?" she said.

"Yes, why not," said Pickering.

Yes, why not, indeed. And as he half-way watched her sit down crossing her legs under her skirt and adjusting herself on the chair, he thought, no, it had all been some kind of terrible mistake. Not a terrible mistake, exactly, that wasn't the way to put it, since nothing irretrievable had happened, thank God for that, but a mistake nevertheless. It meant that he would have to look elsewhere to find the source of his happiness. Or perhaps not look. Maybe Monday and Friday before it had only been an aberration, some shard of his past intruding into his present, a whistling from a bicycle, now disappearing forever again. In a way, too bad. And in a way, not too bad. Good riddance.

"Miss Chenery, do you mind if I ask you a question?" He had just seen the man's class ring hanging from her necklace down between her breasts. "I couldn't help noticing, I noticed the ring. . . ." For some reason he couldn't complete the thought. So he indicated with his hand at his chest where the ring was.

"This?" She took the ring in her hand and pulled it out from her sweater.

"Yes," said Pickering.

"This is my boyfriend. I mean," she caught herself, "it's his ring."

"Ah," said Pickering.

"He's a senior at Swarthmore. He graduates this year."

"I see," said Pickering. "And . . . ?"

She understood his question. "Yes, we're going to be married. I'll be moving back east this summer."

"Ah, I see," said Pickering. Then he added, "So you'll be giving up your schooling here?"

"Yes," she said. "For now."

Wasn't that a trace of sadness when she said, "For now"?

"And how did you meet him?"

"Well, actually, we grew up on the same street together. In a little town called Media."

The trace of sadness?

"So, then, you were childhood sweethearts?"

"Yes, in a way. We dated in high school."

"That's interesting and very nice in this day and age. And when did you decide to get married?"

"Oh," she said, "I think we always knew we were going to be married. Sort of, right from the beginning."

"Well," said Pickering, "I find that rather pleasant. In this day and age." Hadn't he used that phrase before? Maybe it was because he was trying to be encouraging. "Now, perhaps we should . . . ?"

"Of course."

She brought out her notebook and Pickering was just getting ready to ask her for the subject of her paper so he could get all this over with and perhaps get back to work on more important things such as his article on *Moby Dick*, and even caught himself veering off thinking about the title, "The Reactive Image . . . ," and wondering if "The Reflective Image . . ." wouldn't say it better, when he unmistakably felt a tingle, a thrill, a dance, go up his spine. She had touched him. My God! How could she? No, no, she hadn't. But— and it had to be deliberate—she had rested the toe of one of her shoes on one of the feet of his swivel chair. And, my God, he was getting an erection.

"Now, Miss Chenery. . . . Peggy, that's your first name, isn't it?"

She was looking at him; he was looking at her. They both dropped their glances.

Get a hold of yourself, get a hold of yourself, he told himself. Go on with the business at hand. My God, what if anyone discovered him? Say, Irwin?

"Now, Miss Chenery, have you decided what you are going to write on?"

"Not entirely."

"Perhaps images. Clusters of images."

"Yes, I could," she said, with her head still down.

"The concept of clusters is the important thing when writing on images. Anyone can find evidence of hot or cold, up or down, or in or out. It's really a question of coordination, or more correctly, of assemblage." Assemblage? Was that a word?

"Yes, I see," she said.

"One must relate everything to everything. That is the important thing. Nothing by itself has meaning. Only in relation to other things can, as we say, the truth be divined."

"Yes," she said.

And she pulled her shoe away. It was almost as if, no, not as if, an electric current had been shut off, and, thank God for that, his erection began to fade. Still . . .

"So, I'll look forward to your paper."

"Yes," she said.

"Just a minute, I'll get the door for you."

He got up, no problem, the erection gone, passed her, but when he reached the door she was beside him, not just beside him, but inside his space, a violation, really, a wonderful violation. He could have opened the door, but he didn't. She could have made for the door. But she didn't. He took a deep breath (another cheap novel, so what?) and looked down at her. The sense of void. The edgy dizziness. She looked up at him, that oval face, the eyes so sad, the skin so smooth. But mostly the eyes. Don't do it, don't do it, he told himself as, not believing it, saw his hand brush against her cheek. The rest he would remember forever. Her arms around his neck, her body fitted in against him.

HiS

CAROLYN BANKS

"Ask your boyfriend about Marcy Dunn," the voice said. I would have answered, "You have the wrong number," but she hung up.

"Who was that?" Rinn asked. He didn't look up. He was sitting in an overstuffed chair, naked except for the white cloth robe hanging loosely around him, one leg propped on the cushion. He was trimming a pesky toenail. I heard the blade of the clipper going click!

"Just some nut," I said, pulling my shoulder beneath the cover. I'd been in bed reading, lying on my side, when the telephone had rung.

Rinn walked over to the bed, bent over me. His hair was long and it veiled the lamplight. He looked feral, but his voice was soft. "And what did this nut have to say?"

I squirmed, wanting him under the covers beside me. The proximity of him was all that it ever took. "Nothing. Come on, get in here."

"I might could do that," he said, lips brushing my forehead.

I tried to lift the covers cautiously, but a mass of chill night air came in with Rinn. I shivered. "Brrrr," I said, pressing every press-able part of me against him.

"Mmmmm," he answered. His toes were like ice as he ran his foot up and down my lower leg. The edge of the fresh cut toenail cut into me.

"Ouch," I pulled back.

"No, come on," he said, suddenly still, his arms like locks now.

I always like it when Rinn traps me in his arms. I never struggle, because it's clear there would be no use. That describes, pretty much, my role with him. It is one of surrender. I am incapable, with Rinn, of any other response. But then, what he doles out, al-ways, is pleasure and who would mind surrendering to that?

"It'll change," my friend Camilla told me. "It can't always be that good."

But it has been, and it is: two months, three days.

It is pleasure that he gives me now, his voice beside my ear. "You're so pretty," he says, stroking my cheek with his lips and his beard and his mustache. "Such a pretty little thing."

His voice is deep and he twangs when he speaks, West Texas. He doesn't try to hide or change it. "This is the language that my momma used," he once explained. "This is the way she said, 'I love you, Rinnie. You're a good boy.'"

"I love you," I told him, "You're a good, good, good, good boy."

Rinn never says he loves me when I do. He says it when I'm wholly unaware. Like he'll be driving off to the liquor store, say, and he'll have the pickup running, even turned around.

I'll be standing there, maybe weeding or something, maybe bringing in the wash off the line.

I'll wonder why the truck is sitting there, idling, and I'll look up to see Rinnie grinning at me.

"I love you," he'll say, and he'll floor the thing so that the wheels churn and gravel gets spit everywhere.

And me, I just sit there and churn too, churn with wanting my arms around him right then. Wanting to close him off inside.

The telephone rings. He reaches out and grabs it before it can again. "Hey," he says.

I can hear the edges of a voice, the barbs.

He hangs up while the voice is still going on. Then he gets out of bed, undoes the jack.

I squint up at him.

"I guess," he says, his weight settling on the bed beside me, "that I'd better tell you about Marcy before you hear it from somebody else."

She was crazy, he says, underage, a runaway. There was, as he puts it, "just no getting by her."

My body is stiff, tight. "You mean you slept with her?"

I feel him nodding, yes.

"When?" I ask him. I'm amazed to find my voice.

"I don't know," he says. "A year or two ago."

"Oh," I start laughing, even looking up at him. "I thought you meant now. These past few months."

But he isn't laughing with me. He's shaking his head no and he's rubbing me through the thick shield of covers, rubbing hard. "No, now there's just you. But I still think maybe you'd better hear what I have to say."

"I don't want to be in bed with you and hear about someone else," I tell him, and I roll away.

He stays where he is. "Well, all right then," he says. "Okay."

We are like that, still and apart for a while, and then I feel him edging near.

I roll against him so quickly that it seems like an attack and he laughs and grabs me up.

And then it's just like always, soft and sweet until it isn't either anymore. And his eyes are shut and his head is hurled back and he feeds on me, almost, growling and hissing like an animal that is taking what's his.

When Rinnie comes I can always feel it, it is hot and thick and pro-pelled. He always stays inside while the come trickles out around his soft dick. And then he pulls free, stands and says something pointedly dumb like, "I think I'll get me a beer."

I remember whimpering the first time he did that, and I re-member, too, the way he laughed at his own joke. And the way he dropped atop me, rubbing his face in the come he'd left, spreading it across my thighs and my clit and my belly with his face and then licking through it and around it and over it until I'd come too.

This time he doesn't say anything. He just stands there and looks down at me, his head cocked to one side.

"Come here," I say, tugging at him. "Come here and then you can tell me whatever it is you have to about her."

"I couldn't get away from her," he said. "I couldn't get free. And I had to, I knew that I did and so I packed up everything I owned and I rented a trailer and I . . ." he shrugs and stops to look at me.

I am horrified. I suppose I look it. "That seems so excessive," I say.

"And it was. It was excessive in every way. It was . . ." he looks pained, remembering.

And I feel ancient, a crone, thinking of him with this girl who was underage. She was fucking his brains out, probably. "I don't think I want to hear the rest," I say.

And he pulls me up against his chest and shakes me once, twice, really hard. "But you're going to," he says.

His fingers pinch into my arm so hard I know that I'll have a bruise.

He was married then, and his wife had rented Marcy Dunn a room. "And then she left me, went to Georgia. Left me in the house with this girl."

"Whose idea was it?" I asked.

"Oh, I don't know. Everybody's probably. We were pretty nearly always high."

I am never high. I don't do anything, no drugs, not even alco-hol. I think of how tame I must seem.

"It was a weird time," he says. "A very weird time."

I get out of bed. I slip into my robe and I pad toward the bathroom. I am freezing cold, partly because of the air and partly because of the dread. I sit on the toilet and I pee and when I wipe myself, my skin down there, even my skin, is sore.

I am still slick with his come inside me.

I think I might cry and I wonder why, why? This Marcy Dunn was way before we met. But it isn't Marcy Dunn, it isn't. It is the life he led.

And then he is in the doorway. I am staring through the gap in his own robe at his body, its strength and its promise.

"I don't want to hear about Marcy Dunn," I tell him. "I don't want to hear about anybody."

He squats down, lays his arms across my thighs. His hair spreads out over them and I stroke it, bend down as far as I can.

I can smell myself, smell me, my cunt, on his face. And all over, too, his forehead and his nose and his cheeks. His beard and his mustache are thick with the smell of me and my love for him right then is excruciating.

He looks up at me. His eyes are tired. He kisses my knee. "Then let's get out of here," he says. "Let's just pack our stuff and get out of here."

It is tempting and, given our circumstances, easily done.

He leans on my thighs and stands up. The light in the hall makes a halo around his head. I feel very small, very his, but willingly so. "We can leave right now," he says. "Tonight. Or we can get some sleep."

"Whatever you want," I tell him.

And then I wait.

Holding Your Hands Up

EDWARD KLEINSCHMIDT

Come in past the green bushes, your blue shirt
Filling the white spaces. I've been watering
The dogs. They have grown six inches since
Sunday. Soon they will be like balloons caught
In trees. But the trees are impatient with brown
Dogs. The trees spill out down their branches into
The varnished air. The two bluebirds on the highbacked
Chair will never fall off. You are here and you lie
Down like thirst. You bring down your hands. They
Find your knees, the cups hands can bring up. You found
A flaming sword in the fields of sheep. The tame goats
Butt at the old post. We put the bones in the cupboard
With the china. Now we know where to find them.
We can choose doors. We can pick locks. We can
Picnic by the dam and dive into the water. Swim
To shore and wring ourselves over dry bushes. Tie
Our hair to each other and easily pull back each other
To ourselves. This is what we have and why we want it.

 Say So

EDWARD KLEINSCHMIDT

Meaning that I love you, your repetition,
Your back arched, mouth open to me,
That your hands can untie the tight
Laces of my body, that you fill
Vacuity say always yes always,
When the second moon in one month
Breaks through clouds, shows itself all
Day, that the rise of your nipples
At night, the silver chafing dish
On the table, when we are uncovered with
Linen I want to say so, stay long inside
You that you might truly hear me say so,
That we might pick the ripe pear, eat it in
The afternoon, after sex, after no one is alive
But us, changed with the loud large
Tympani of love, bathing afterwards, rubbing
And rubbing and rubbing ourselves clean, and
On the Persian rug in the study, where we
Speak love to ourselves, the guests we
Welcome as our bodies, hosts of love, and making
Bread, its third rising, the cry that tells
Us the bread is sliding up the sides of the slick
Pan, and our hot fingers, our tongues telling all,
The hair we're twirling, curling in this furnace, and
Now that you know again, your face loveliest loveliest.

if i Could

PETER KUNZ

I would carry you through this darkness
to where there are stars,
the meadows are clean of decay
and the one note of the saw whet owl
stabs at its throat
not in pain but in the pure dark
coat of night

There is nothing to explain to you,
no trick to this desire.
I cannot own you.
I cannot save you.
There is no door left open but love

Now I lie in union with you
here under the simple roof of want
and my body in yours is an oar in a lock
and it is rowing us, slowly, a stroke at a time
through the long and unsolvable night

if the Rise of the Fish

JANE HIRSHFIELD

If for a moment
the leaves fell upward,
if it seemed a small flock
of brown-orange birds

circled over the trees,
if they circled then scattered each in
its own direction for the lost seed
they had spotted in tall, gold-chequered grass.
If the bloom of flies on the window
in morning sun, if their singing insistence
on grief and desire. If the fish.
If the rise of the fish.
If the blue morning held in the glass of the window,
if my fingers, my palms. If my thighs.
If your hands, if my thighs.
If the seeds, among all the lost gold of the grass.
If your hands on my thighs, if your tongue.
If the leaves. If the singing fell upward. If grief.
For a moment if singing and grief.
If the blue of the body fell upward, out of our hands.
If the morning held it like leaves.

July Lover

D. NURKSE

I was cutting flowers
in my kitchen, I felt
my hands become sticky,
I listened and for the first time
all week heard no music—
then you appeared in the door
and closed it behind you
put on water
for herb tea afterwards
and began undressing

explaining calmly
how the traffic made you late
—though when I last saw you
you'd said you were marrying someone else.

Kathy Soffia, Kathy Soffia

J. DUNNE

"Situation: Her and I, late at night, in bed."

(Perhaps the third of my letters)
All is quiet now, I lie beside her, under the covers, it is warm, but we feel each other so we do not mind. The shades are drawn, the room looks blue and I stroke her hand. Along the index finger, around and over the knuckle, the top of the hand. She lies quiet, but not asleep. I am tired but not asleep. Once, a long while ago, I thought I had fallen asleep, just shallow, but definitely asleep. The covers are blue and a little wet. I can not see the color of her skin, but I feel it, and I remember it. Smooth porcelain, not tan, olive, cream. Her eyes are closed. I roll her over. They are still closed. I kiss her brow. She opens her eyes. Now, they are a pure, dark color, not masked, but a pure dark sensation.

She being brand . . .

She seems perfect. I do not smile as she looks at me. I am not frowning, I think it might be a questioned look. Then I kiss her. Not in any way I have before. Hardly touching her lips, many kisses, like in many school girl poems:

City of lovers . . .
State of wishes . . .
Seven hundred kisses . . .

She puts her arms around me, she feels my skin, I do not remember what that felt like, but I can guess. It is warm though. I can compare that to a day a long while ago. I stepped out, and it was warm, and I felt the heat. I also held her then, and I can clearly remember what that felt like. She had asked me to hold her, and I wanted to, jesus how I wanted to. She sneaked in under me and I raised myself a little above her. The cross of my rosary lying in between her breasts. I kiss her, I kiss them, the rosary did not break.

Time passes.

It was over again and we lay closer together. Her skin is moist and mine is the same. I touch her womb, it quivers under the delicate pressure. A thought comes to me, it is fleeting, I do not think I will write it here.

Kites!

MARILYN SIDES

A brilliant pink banner cracked and snapped on top of a dune. I pulled the car over, and my wife and I staggered up through dune grass to see what was going on. CAPE COD HANG GLIDERS HANGIN' IN, the banner read, and under it a bunch of men and women stood staring down at a woman kneeling in the sand, a woman tied to a giant kite. Thick blue straps came down between her shoulder blades and fastened to thick blue straps reaching up from around her hips. Her hands gripped the side bars of an aluminum triangle attached to two long wings, curved, spined, pointy pterodactyl wings, wings barred blue purple yellow, wings lifting lightly in the wind.

"I can't," the woman cried.

My wife touched the wing of another giant kite tethered there, a giant kite rocking in the wind, pulling at its ropes. Next to the woman, a man crouched on his hands and knees. "Now, remember what we talked about in class. Fear's there to make you focus. Breathe. Slowly. In and out. Breathe. Now let's stand up! Breathe. Now let's get ready to fly!"

Locks of the woman's hair stood up against the wind.

The instructor frowned and squatted back on his heels. "O.K." He looked around at the others. "O.K. Roger can go on and go." Freed from the kite, the woman slunk away to the other side of the dune and sat down. The class turned their backs on her to help Roger get into harness. A low chant began: "Go Roger Go!" I watched Roger go white, clinch his hands on the bars of the giant kite. A kick of sand and Roger is running across the dune, Roger's feet are treading air, Roger twists his head back to grin at us—

"Pay attention!" the instructor yells.

Roger sails slowly out, descends gently to the beach below, he's skimming the beach, oh no! skimming the waves, heading out for sea—

"Push out!" the whole class cries with the instructor.

My wife leans over the edge of the dune—

Roger pushes out, the glider stalls, drops him into the surf. The wings float flat on the water. But where's Roger? There's Roger bobbing in the waves, waving to the cliff! Everyone cheers. I looked over my shoulder, the woman sitting on the sand put her head down on her knees.

Catching my wife's eye, I nodded and we slid back down the dune. In the car, I scribbled out the details of the scene: the banner, Roger's flight, the giant hang-gliding kites, the weeping woman. Terrific—maybe?—opening for an article, exactly what I had come to the Cape for. Maybe I'd get two articles out of these kites, a newspaper feature about perilous sports on the Cape and a travel piece for a hang-gliding magazine, someone somewhere must put out a hang-gliding magazine. Hang gliders must want to know where to fly, where to eat, where to sleep on the Cape. That day, instead of insisting "You could put in that, but you should put in this, didn't you see how he—," my wife waited silently and looked out the window.

My wife and I had lunch in Chatham at the *Sea-Inn*, recommended to me by a friend. We ate outside on a deck overlooking the beach. We didn't talk much. We watched three kids hopping up and down around a man in baggy pants and rumpled sweater as he gassed up a model plane. The plane went up with a loud buzz, a smoke trail—one moon-faced girl shrieking, "Dad, Dad, it's too high"—then the plane turned and crashed into the sand. The kids screamed and went running after it, their father crying out to them in comical and desperate reassurance, "That happens! That happens!" Again and again, the father launched the plane, it crashed, and the kids, tireless, fetched the plane. "That happens!" I heard the father still calling as we left.

Walking back to the car, my wife abruptly began, "I'm thinking about looking for a job. Something part-time. I'm—"

"But we agreed."

Three months before, my wife had been laid off. Her job was not a great job. From seven-thirty in the morning until seven at night, six days a week, she, by profession a structural engineer, made the palest of shady deals with the city: if they passed her on an ordinance, her company would plant trees along Boylston and hang holiday wreaths. Sometimes, if she got lucky, she got to inspect new employee cafeterias and bang food trays against the walls to test the paint. But her severance pay was generous, and I had just sold my latest big travel piece, "Ancient Monasteries of the World," so we agreed to get along without her working for a while. She would just rest for a while, let her body fill out, she had become so thin, her bones showed. Rest and boredom would be the richest breeding ground, we hoped. So we had agreed to be a little poorer for a while and then there would be riches beyond measure, our child.

"I'm tired of hanging around the house. I eat too much, I'm getting fat."

"Fat? Just fat?"

"One hundred percent, pure, grade-A fat. Just fat."

Before starting the car, I made a note: the *Sea-Inn*'s famous fish stew smelled like KitKat cat food and I'm sure that's what KitKat tastes like. I added an extra spurt of curare—SERVICE SLOW.

Back on the highway, I looked over at my wife. My wife had her arm out the window, hand out, curving palm riding the wind. My wife loves to feel the wind under the palm of her hand.

"If you wanted to, you could help me with this article. Here's your big chance to get in from the very beginning of a piece. We could even write it together if—" We had also agreed that I would stay closer to home cultivating my own garden, as it were, try to do more local New England stories—though they don't pay as much—and not run all over the world in my usual style, pathological traveler style. Helping me out with these local pieces, that would give my wife something to do.

To the road ahead she said, "A part-time job won't hurt. Something fun. It'll be something I can quit on short notice."

Her shapely hand cleaves the air.

Is this breeding time a brooding time?

We stopped for gas before heading onto Truro. As I was paying, my wife, who had been prowling—aimlessly, yet still very much prowling—the aisles of the convenience store attached to the gas station (such an old-fashioned, polite word convenience—marriage of convenience, apartment with all the conveniences, "at your earliest convenience"), my wife found that her convenience that day was a kite stuck in a cardboard stand. In the mirror angled to catch shoplifters, I saw her take it out, one of those old paper kites wound around sticks, stiff as a tightly furled leaf. A moment later, the kite lay on the counter and two fat balls of kite string came clumping down next to it.

At the restaurant where we ate dinner, I glimpsed our hang gliders in the bar. The gliding refusenik, sheepish but grinning, sat with them. Had she earned her wings at last?

That night we went back to our "housekeeping cottage." I have always been attracted to the Cape's colonies of "housekeeping cottages," like the cottages of Leprechaun Cove scattered in a grove of slanting stunted pines, or like these Above Tide Cottages in Truro, tiny shack houses lined up in a prim peaked-roof row along the beach, all of them alike: white with trim of pink and green. Toy house, toy kitchen, we were setting up house in a housekeeping cottage, the thinnest shell of shelters, would the sun show through chinks tomorrow morning? I thought I'd try to get them into an article somehow.

Lying on the lumpy bed, I sorted out my notes. My wife had claimed the wooden table and was busily unrolling her kite. I looked up. She looked up. She grinned, "You can tell your readers the tables here are just right for making kites!"

Her happiness an unexpected gift. I could breathe again, had I been holding my breath all day? I got up to take a look at the kite. I hadn't seen such a kite in years, but my fingers instantly remembered the soft warm smooth splinteriness of the balsa wood spars, the thinness of the crackling paper. I wouldn't have guessed they still made these paper kites. Most kids' kites these days seem made of plastic with cartoon characters on them, zoomorphic or extraterrestrial. I flew this exact paper kite when I was a kid, this plain white paper kite with thin red and blue stripes, *High Flyer* emblazoned across its face.

I lay back down on the creaking bed and flipped through my notes. Looked up again at my wife. Her long hair fell over her face, curtaining it off, cutting me off again. I love it more when she wears her hair pulled back. The volumes of her face are displayed, the high planed cheekbones—landing strips for my kisses I used to tell her—the sheer drop, the hollow beneath them. The long winged eyebrows, the black eyes. The small potato knob on the end of her nose that makes her thuggish, with a riffraffishness that compels complicity, and at the same time she's like a young nun, sweet and young for all her thirty-five years, so easy to make blush. And when she blushes and beams at me, I know what it's like to be looked at with love, the simplest, plainest love.

Her face was hidden, but I could see her hands, long, pale, graceful hands gifted at corporal benedictions—these hands now picked at a stubborn knot. My wife can swear most foully, too.

The kite is done. But what to do about a tail? My sister and I used to beg old sheets from my mother and tear them into strips. My wife, resourceful engineer, pulls out the plastic bag lining the wastebasket, cuts it into ribbons with her pocketknife, knots the ribbons. "Kite tail!" she proclaims and ties her tail to the kite. Then she is at my side, laughing, tugging at my hair, "Let's go fly a kite!"

I hadn't quite finished with my notes, but she was laughing, I say, and we were only two steps from the beach, and outside a shiny dime moon rising, a wind blowing straight out to sea. Soon, I stood holding the kite to my chest, a faithful page holding his knight's shield.

My wife yelled "Ready?"

I held the kite up by its spine.

"Let go," she cried and the kite went up and up, then nose-dived straight into the sand.

"Uhh," my wife moaned.

Yet the paper wasn't torn, the spine wasn't broken. We tried again.

"Ready?"

"Ready!"

The wind picked the kite up, the string spun out taut and alive, the kite shot up up so high, its plastic tail slick with light, a kite like a monster luna moth. My wife played the string out, more and more string. The kite set out to sea, with that wind so steady, strong and steady, the kite went down the path of rolled silver leading to the moon.

When I saw the ball of string coming to an end, I slogged through the sand to the cottage for the second ball. "Hurry, hurry," she called, as I came staggering back down the beach. I tied the second ball on to the straining end of the first, and my wife let the new string go singing out burning her fingers, until we could barely see our shining kite faraway against the faraway moon.

Suddenly the string snapped. Our kite plummeted into the sea, fell into the sea, far out at sea.

"Oh no!" My wife held the limp string in her hand, so taut and alive one moment, limp and dead the next.

"Lost at sea, lost at sea," I intoned in funereal fashion.

She cried with laughter.

I lay in bed and my wife lay down next to me, turned over on her back, and said aloud to the ceiling, to me, "It was a beautiful day. We had such a beautiful day, even though we lost our kite, our beautiful kite—"

"Lost at sea, lost at sea—"

"I was so happy."

And I, convulsed with tenderness. Brooding breeding silence, now this sudden wind shear of joy. And she had confessed her happiness with such humility and joy, almost childish this thankfulness for one day, this gratitude for one more day, snatched from death, stolen from sadness. I was in bed with a female St. Francis of Assisi. A St. Francis with an edible body, with the rear end of a queen, ample, perfectly designed, very lively.

As we drove on to Provincetown the next morning, a station wagon speeded past us. Two kids hanging from the windows pointed up at—my wife stuck her head out the window to see—a flotilla of hot air balloons. On Cape Cod, everything seems up in the air. Good opening line—maybe?—for my piece.

A month later, I couldn't ever get my wife to look up at me from that sewing machine that whirred stop and go in the extra room, the wouldbe shouldbe baby's room. The room taken over by the sewing machine, by the old ping-pong table she bought at a garage sale and used for cutting out not flannelette, but pieces of kites, kites for the kite store where she now worked.

Tatters of rip-stop nylon in kite bright colors littered the floor. Yellow red blue pink at their brightest purest pitch. Even a black bright like wet paint. As if there weren't any November colors in the world, like right outside the window now, brown leaves, gold grasses, black-red winter berries. Rip-stop nylon is a strange fabric, light and crackling, rustling like tissue paper but so strong, strong enough to withstand fierce winds and sharp branches. I've just become a partisan of paper kites: the art of flying should protect the kite, and if the kite fell, it fell apart, rotted, like us, our bodies. This frightening rip-stop, rot-stop material would last forever wadded up somewhere.

Early one morning, I watched her from the doorway. She is sewing, sitting on that old oak chair with two rungs hanging out of their sockets. Scissors knife up from a tackle box sewing box. A drawer spills green fabric and loops of white nylon line like shimmering spider threads in the sunlight. On the table, stacks of kiting magazines landslide. A needle raised in her hand, her head bent

over a pink kite, my wife is naked, bare, smooth. The only unclut-
tered thing in the room. Demure, desirable.

Crouched on the kite scraps at her feet, his fur puffed full of
light, the cat stares at me. But my wife doesn't look up at me.

I retreated to my study. I said to myself, when I hear her coming down the hall, I will come out of my study, I'll catch her and
press her up against the wall, and ask her softly, would you like to
lie down with me, for just a while? I'll kiss her ear and breathe into
it—my famous Spanish kiss, la paloma del fuego, the dove of fire, I call
it, she calls it the hot pigeon smooch. And if she fidgets and wants
so very much to go back to her kites, I'll show her that I can be infinitely courteous, I'll say to her, "Oh, you are such a good lover.
You know how to make your man wait for you!" Then kissing her
softly, I'll release her.

Minutes later, I know, I'm sure she will appear, suddenly, take
my book from under my beakish nose, and offer to impale herself
on the sword of her Sardanapalus. If only I will let her, be so kind
to her. She'll beg me humbly, all the while her quick hands descab-
barding me.

Instead my wife hurried down the hall, hurried off to work at
the kite store.

The first day I stopped by to see my wife at work, I had just finished an article on a young woman, ex-hippie, long blonde hair,
mongrel dog with a bandanna kerchief, who had made herself into
a local expert on sailing rope. For the one photo I was allowed, I had
my rope lady stand up and I coiled around her her trademark orange rope, thick as an anaconda, coiled the rope around her from
foot to chin, until she looked like a mummy, or a goddess of rope.
To celebrate, I thought I'd take my wife out to lunch and tell her
about the piece. We used to talk over my stories, but I hadn't really
told her about this one, or the last one. She's too busy with her kites.

I walked down the hall of the mall where my wife worked, past
a decorative decoys shop, a mineral jewelry shop, a lingerie shop,
and there around the corner was High as a Kite, a small shop with
windsocks like octopi dangling draping the open door. Through
the front window full of kites posed as if in flight, as if I'd scared
up a flock of kites, I saw my wife. She was leaning back against a

wall behind the glass counter, leaning there in her old black full skirt—worn soft as velvet, that old skirt, my favorite skirt of hers— a faded blue blouse, black sweater, black boots. Above her head played a video on kiting. Against a bright blue sky yellow kites lift off, dart, swoop.

No customers. My wife leaning back against the wall and listening to, it must be the owner, O'Caslin, a wiry rusty-haired O'Caslin, with his hands full of kite line. A thick glass window and a wide glass counter between myself and my wife, nothing came between my wife and O'Caslin, O'Kasbah. I stared at her to make her turn her head, to make her look at me. She didn't look up at me. I was about to walk in, then the telephone rang, my wife answered. O'Caslin, this rusty wirehanger of a man all angles, put down the line and mimed going out to get some lunch for them. For an obvious graduate of remedial mime, he rather cleverly enacted eating a sandwich, holding an invisible sandwich between his hands, biting into it with his small repulsive baby teeth, then chewing. Cupping his hand, he guzzled an airy coffee, raised his eyebrows, and smirked.

To my shame, my wife grinned and nodded her head. As O'Caslin came out the door, I turned to study the bristling conic corsets and lacy but very tensile thongs for Lycra ladies mounted in the window of the lingerie store. My wife's plain black cotton underwear I instantly regretted and wanted to inspect, close up, live, in action. I turned back to the kite store. She had hung up the phone and was unpacking more line. I came up behind her. She turned, saw me—the telephone rang again.

"*High as a Kite*," she trilled and waved me away. "Oh, yes, thanks for returning our call. We want to know if *High Skyers* would be part of the city kite festival in the spring?"

I knew all about this kite championship and kite festival planned jointly for the spring. At home if her foot was off the sewing machine pedal, her hand was on the telephone calling up other kite stores, other sponsors, teams of competitive kite flyers all over New England, public officials for the city park system, and vendors of food, "Hi, this is *High as a Kite*, and we're interested in your barbecue."

I fell in among kites, picked up a box kite, poked aside a bat kite left over from a Halloween display. Found a bookshelf of kite magazines, kite manuals, kite pattern books, and at last a history of kites, which I pulled out and flipped through. Big color photograph of a kite festival in Japan, with red, white, and blue kites sailing above the blue blue sea. Of two kites trimmed in gold foil and tangling in India. Of an immense octagonal paper kite, many colored paper patches, with pretty paper tassels, flying in Guatemala on the day of the dead, taking messages to the dead. Instantly, I could picture an article, an article with large color photographs, what we call a round-up article, a round-up of kite festivals around the world, including Boston, too. It would be a big article, like my best articles, big national magazine, lots of pictures of kites, talks with kitemakers. I could go around the world to Japan, to India. Of course it would mean traveling, going away, again, and we had, of course, agreed, but that agreement she had already broken, really, and the piece would be, after all, all about kites.

My wife hung up the telephone and came over to me. I put down my book, grasped her by the back of her neck, squeezed it to hold her still. I Spanish-kissed her ear—she squirmed and laughed— I whispered my kite tales to her, "Did you know that in Korea they write the name and birthday of their child on a kite, then let the kite fly away with all the evil spirits that might harm the child? And did you know that two hundred years ago in France, there were kite riots? In Indonesia—"

She laughed and, clenching her teeth, pushed me up against the counter with a sudden burst of energy. I slipped my hand up under her sweater—she never wears a brassiere, just a camisole, so sorry corset store next door—up and over her breast, but it was not swollen, her belly, flat, too flat. She struggled, she twisted out of my grasp. She gasped, "Oh Stan, this is my husband. This is, this is Stan O'Caslin."

I bought the kite book. And at my wife's insistence I bought a kite that day, a kite all ready to go, of rip-stop nylon striped pink red white yellow and blue, a kite that packs up into a small pouch. She called it an emergency kite—when the wind is right and you just have to fly a kite.

_____

My flight from Singapore back to Boston took off at three o'clock in the morning. The taxidriver looked like a crew-cut hog. When I said, answering at last his brutal relentless questioning, that I had been married ten years and had no children, he almost stopped his car. "But how can you live without kids?"

At two o'clock in the morning! I answered, "*I can't live*," but was somehow still vaguely alive.

"Why?" he demanded to know with a sort of Chinese nosiness. "Because it is fashionable to live?"

I gave him a tentative, "Perhaps."

He persisted, "Whose fault is it? Yours? Hers? Is it entirely medical?" We were in some suburb whose trees had thick still leaves like glossy leather and wax-like fruits. "I know," he fixed his eyes on mine in the rear view mirror, "get rid of her. Marry young Chinese girl with money. Or computer diploma."

At the next stoplight, I took out my suitcase, my clumsy package of Japanese kites, which I should have mailed from Tokyo, I paid him and sat on the curb. Crushed by a sense of the utter, absolute failure of my life, I could hardly breathe. An aspiring seed planter, I had plowed my wife's furrow, moist and dark, but nothing sprang up. What use was this bulky body of mine, its hidden strength, if I couldn't wring out of it a child?

Thank god the next cab driver only wanted to lament, endlessly, his fate which kept him in puritanical Singapore. I should go to Bangkok, where they have brothels, great brothels where girls who performed acts like *The Living Soap*, and *Tora Tora*,—"Kamikaze girls! You American battleship!"

Maybe the fault was mine. Back in Boston, I secretly made an appointment at a fertility clinic. The doctor unfurled a long list of procedures and eagerly began asking me how far was I prepared to go, how much was I prepared to spend? I asked him couldn't we just begin with a sperm count? A simple sperm count, just to see if the problem was with my male milk? I was turned over to a nurse who shut me up in a bathroom.

My wife and I used to spend a fortune on home pregnancy test kits with their ridiculous names, like *First Response*, a phrase that always made me think of nuclear war. We wanted to be so sure of getting the telegram our child was sending us that we bought three or four kits at a time, maybe this one was defective, maybe that one was not foolproof. And fumbling fools we were at first, yet soon expert enough with droppers, dippers, plastic vials. "I'm going to micturate now, prepare for testing," my wife would announce and I rushed to the bathroom with the official cup ready for her gush. Until it was no longer funny, but sad. She started furtive testing alone behind the locked bathroom door; I saw the boxes in the trash. Finally all testing had been abandoned.

Now I tried manning my pump in this pink bathroom, but nothing happened. How could it in this icy pink bathroom with faded instructions scotchtaped to the wall, with stacks of tattered magazines, their pleated and torn, worn centerfolds of superbosomic models? When I came out empty-handed, the lab nurse smiled in sympathy.

"6:30? You know, the old hands hangin' down?"

She sent me home with a jar, "though any ol' jam jar will do," and instructed me that I had to get the sperm to the clinic within an hour of ejaculation. I turned away as another man came rushing in the door, exclaiming, "I have come to deposit my pollen."

I knew my wife would not be at home when I got home. That afternoon, after closing the kite store early, she had taken off for Martha's Vineyard to try out some new kites with O'Caslin and the stripling, O'Caslin's other assistant, a tall, thin flaxen-haired youth. They would sleep over on the island and get an early start the next morning.

"Do you know where you're going to stay, exactly?"

"With Stan's friends, I don't know their name. On Chappy—"

"Chappaquidick?"

"Well, Stan says Chappy."

"Well, do you know where you'll fly the kites?"

"No, Stan says it all depends on where the wind's up."

Her enthusiasm for the kites had come to seem so dangerous. She could fall in love with O'Caslin O'Kiteland because of the kites, he might become a pretext for the kites, and he might take advantage of that kite love. That was what I feared, the simplicity of this kite love, this love welling up, spilling over onto him, not me.

So I slept that night without my wife cupped in my hands, without her smell. Woke up in the morning without seeing her face half-asleep, almost a child's face again, sweet, her skin the color of quince blossoms, white flushed so slightly with pink. Hot soft skin.

The cat jumped up thumped up on my chest and stared at me accusingly. What had I done with her?

At breakfast, my wife used to chatterbox away, her half-open robe revealing one small breast, pointed, wolfish, a wolf mother's teat, while her hand slipped up my baggy shorts. She'd blush as if surprised to find something quite alive in there.

Now I sat in the kitchen, alone (the cat had gobbled up his food and gone out), drinking coffee made in our old pot that's big enough for a convent. *Caffè di convento*, I call it. I picture us as convent convict escapees, a renegade fat canon who likes his sausages, a nun with graceful praying hands and lively thighs and—I warm to my subject—a lovely quilted womb. For "Green Stone Cities," an article about Oaxaca, Mexico, and several other greenish cities on several continents, I visited the Church of Santo Domingo's rose chapel, whose pink baroque ceiling is covered with gilt rose branches entwined in a latticed bower. I later made it a point to tell my wife (as I couldn't, unfortunately, my readers), this chapel dedicated to the Virgin Mary is in fact an homage to a woman's womb, the squares bounded off by the branches an homage to the quilted lining of the womb, the soft but strong quilted flesh that grips the lover.

Thinking quiltiness, I ran to the bathroom for my jar. I think about my nun's chapel, and in a short while I had my jar of tadpoles, a thriving, crowded, I hoped, school of tadpoles. I jumped in the car to deliver them alive to the clinic, zigzagged through the narrow streets, then shot out on the highway, the road lifting under me and my tadpoles as we sailed up and on.

Twenty minutes later, orange signs appeared: ROAD CONSTRUC-TION,—road destruction—1000 FEET, no exit, 500 FEET, light-bulbed arrows pointing left, herding all cars over into one lane, before me bumper-to-bumper, behind me suddenly the same, and we slowed down, we crept, we stopped. Ahead giant orange Caterpillar tractors jerked along in antediluvian pokiness. I shook the jar gently and whispered to it, "Stay awake you guys!" Rolling down my window, I leaned out to ask a hardhat worker sipping coffee how long—

"Long as it takes." He sipped again, his eyes half-closed crocodilian.

"But my wife is—! The hospital called!"

Hardhat, beetle-shiny hat, spat on the black tarred road. "The Mercedes's kids, *siamese twins*, 're dying. The Honda's sister's dying."

I should have stuck my jar right in his face and yelled, "All my sperm's about to die! Right now!"

But I was too totally defeated. Ten minutes to go before my tadpoles expired. Across the highway, in a field, I saw that with so much rain, such mild temperatures, the weeds and wildflowers were not yet August scorched, the Queen Anne's Lace not frizzled and brown, its silky green stems still lifted up tiny bouquets of white flowers. Beyond the field, the trees' leaves, too, were still the bright green of June. Leaves rustling or leaves moving? My wife would appreciate the difference. She was always looking out our kitchen window at the neighbor's chestnut tree. Leaves moving—delta kites glide. Leaves rustling—bowed kites ride high. Good for something kites are, make you look at the world, think about the wind. Good for something, when I was so obviously good for nothing.

I watched the clock on the dashboard. The tadpoles wiggling slowly, wriggling to a stop. The milky jam turned into clear jelly. Traffic, at last, started up again.

"Good luck to your wife!" Hardhat saluted me as I drove slowly by.

Several hours later, I walked off the ferry at Vineyard Haven, Martha's Vineyard, my binoculars strung around my neck, into the crowds at the dock waiting for the crowds on the boat. I, alone, was unmet. I rented a bike, an old boy's bike with a raveling reed basket and a ring-ling-ling postman bell, brakes that kicked in only if you stomped hard on them. Pushing off, I headed east around the island, skidding in the sand at stop signs and stop lights, nearly hit by a car several times because I was always looking up looking for kites in the sky. My wife was somewhere on this island looking up at kites.

My wife looking at O'Caslin flying kites—but O'Caslin's so wiry and hairy—my wife looking at the stripling flying kites, this tall, tall, blond boy, white shining blond hair, graceful as a girl, smooth, red lips, sweet face. But a man, I could tell, a man as sweet as a girl.

My wife thinks she's excited by the kites.

Bicycled through the ice-cream-cone-clutching crowds of Oak Bluffs and around the edge of the island, stopping and scanning the sky above the beaches and the interior with my binoculars. Nothing but birds and clouds. I pedaled into Edgartown, a town of the thickest white paint, viscous white paint on these wooden columns, clapboards, boxy steeples, white paint made for New England light in fall and winter, thick rich white paint. No kites above Edgartown.

I took the little ferry to Chappaquidick, standing next to my rusty spindly steed. I asked one of hands, a longhaired, teeshirted peeling young old man, "Seen any kites flying today? Heard about any?"

Nope, no kites.

On Chappaquidick, I set off, but soon discovered that the main road only tunneled through woods, the snobby private beaches lay at the end of private roads, and in these trees binoculars were useless. I stopped two other cyclists, in their tight black shorts, clingy nylon shirts, helmets, their water bottles strapped to their elegant efficient bike frames, and demanded, "Have you seen anyone flying kites around here?" It seemed the most outlandish question in the world, asked by an equally outlandish figure in slacks, heavy wingtips, and button-down collar, balancing fatly on a rickety bike. They stared and shook their heads.

Back across on the ferry and down around the south coast of the island, all beaches and dunes. I realized only then, of course, this would be the likely place to fly a kite. I bicycled hard, past cars parked for miles alongside the road, past families trudging coolers and bags and kids up from and down to the beaches. I was so tired, and hot. Even the wind was against me. Maybe I'd head back, take a swim and head back.

One more look through the binoculars. I scanned the sky in all directions and there, there was a bright red kite, bright in the sky, sailing high.

The kite seemed to be flown from behind the dunes. I had to take a road marked for fourwheel drive vehicles. If I could have parked my bike at the bike rack by the public beach, it would have been easy, but I had forgotten to rent a lock. I begin to wheel the bike down the road, and in two minutes, my shoes were full of sand, the bike up to its spokes in sand. Sweating like a pig, I dragged the bike through the sand, I even tried carrying it in my arms. People on top of the dunes stared and laughed. People in four-wheel-drive vehicles powered by and pointed.

Above me floated what looked like a kid's red air mattress tethered at either end and bowed out by the wind. It swayed back and forth, then took a sudden circular swoop down and up again, bright red against the brightest blue sky.

Trudging around the last dune, I saw it was O'Caslin O'Sandman flying the red kite, his left foot back, arms bent and tensed, pulling yawing right hand left hand on the two lines that controlled the kite. My wife held a triangular turquoise kite for the stripling, who was busy laying out the lines. At last he took his stance, and the kite took off, flying straight up, now out at a right angle, and now diving down terrifically fast, with a ripping tearing noise as if the air were silk, and then up up again climbing higher higher.

My wife spotted me and came over. My wife's brown hair gold brown in the sun, her squint against the bright sun made her cheekbones seem even higher. She grinned, "I can't believe you're here—"

"Of course I am here." I was curt and cold. She might recall that I *was* writing an article about kites, and that I *might* think it useful to talk to an expert, *like O'Caslin,* about kites.

My wife's face flattened. She went over to O'Caslin, who came back with her to talk to me about the kites they were flying that day. I nodded, I took notes, made learned references to kites in Malaysia, "ancestral home of most kites, most kite historians believe. Do you agree?" O'Caslin looked blank. My wife stared up in the air at the stripling's kite.

When I could endure no more talk about their kites, about Peter Powell stunters, Phantoms, or even Speedwings, I thanked O'Caslin. I waved good-bye to my wife. With the tragic dignity of the circus clown, I began to haul my bike back between the dunes. Only to promptly sneak up the other side of one dune. For two hours, I spied upon my wife, O'Caslin, and the stripling as they played with the kites.

They performed all sorts of maneuvers with the stunt kites. Pulled by larger kites, they skimmed over the water of a small lagoon. Through my binoculars I see them speed along leaving a lacy wake—if my wife were pregnant, she'd be like a clipper ship, sails big-bellying out, embarked for home, loaded with riches and contentment to last all our lives. My wife, however, steps from the water a slick and slim sea nymph, accompanied by two dripping tritons.

Then the threesome took to the air. Stacking several of the largest kites one on top of the other for more lift, they took turns jumping off a dune, sporting in mid-air—my wife laughing, the stripling hooting, O'Caslin's pale face of a fanatic ecstatic in the air—and at last tumbling down in the soft sand. Everyone watching cheers. My wife trudged up the dune again and again, to jump, jump up in the air.

I could not bear it anymore and slipped away.

Pedaled back slowly, took a lonely swim in my underwear, my bike on its side at the surf line. I did not stay in the water long, for I might have drowned myself. So leaden with gloom and futility, I should sink beneath the waves to hide my shame.

That evening, the cat and I waited on the porch for my wife to come home. She drove up in her little car, rusty car—I should get the rust fixed. She had pink on her cheeks, her hair knotted with sun. There would be sand in her clothes, in the hair under her arms, black and white grit in the creases of her thighs, in the folds of her nymphae, her hidden lips. My prick lifted to play her a hornpipe welcome-home tune, but my heart hurt. Her shining face did not shine for me. It shone for O'Caslin, the stripling, the kites lifting her up, weightless. When I wanted her earthbound, gravity's creature, gravid.

I wanted to say to her how sad I was, tell her how much I hurt. Instead I just sat there, a ball of silent suet. The screen door banged behind her, the fickle cat leapt from my lap and skipped in on the door's rebound. I stayed on the porch a few more minutes, then hid myself in my study and busied myself with sorting photos for my article. Later, when my wife passed by my door, I called her in. I began to pitch my kite talk at her: do you know—guess how this *pakpao* kite is made? I always used to tell her the story of whatever article I was working on. Telling her the story out loud helped me get all the pieces in the right order. And when I finished a good draft, she was my reader, all readers implicit in her—mother-muse, giving birth to the world of readers for me.

That evening, I had to make her listen to my kite story. She could not keep not seeing me, not paying attention to the matter at hand, her kites *and* my kites, our bodies, in conjunction, conjoining, here in this house. This house with a roof, a house with windows and doors fastenable tight.

That night, however, she sat right there, in my desk chair, very still, very polite, but her face had paled. She seemed to be paying attention, absolute attention, yet she was not there. I was looking at a memento of her propped up in the chair, a life-size dry-rot cardboard cutout of her. I tried my best to move her, quoting to her the Japanese poem about kites that I might use to end my piece:

> *A kite—*
> *in the same place*
> *in yesterday's sky!*

Yet she seemed preoccupied, absorbed in some other thought. Some thought at the end of a line she held concealed from my sight, but to whose every tug she was alive. Before she left, though, she did look at the three prints I had picked up in Japan. In one print, an old priest approaches a temple, while behind him fly two kites over the gray roofs of Edo. In another print, a boy lashed to a kite is flown by his father off the island on which they have been exiled. The last print is a black and white forest scene, with a red kite caught in the branches of a leafless tree.

Then my wife returned to her sewing machine, her whirr machine. The new kites she and O'Caslin had designed were selling well. She told me she would soon need to hire an assistant to help with the cutting out and the filling of orders. When it was time to go to bed, we each spent a long time in the bathroom and by mutual mute consent each clung to his and her side of the bed.

Until I smelled the sea salt on her, dwelled upon in my mind the sparkling fine sand sure to lie between her breasts, in the curling hair between her thighs, and I turned her over, she turned over to me. We made love, fiercely, in the dark, out of our estrangement, as strangers. She was faceless to me, she closed her eyes and masked her face, made a mask out of it, so that she seemed any woman, nameless and multitude. And I knew she closed her eyes so that I was any man, in the dark, a man she used any way she liked, she held that man with her nails, thrusting up at him, pulling him into her wide, deep pelvic bowl.

It was like being visited secretly in the night by an unknown lover, a sign from whom you seek everywhere, in everyone's face, all the long day long.

Do others, I suddenly wondered, do others like O'Caslin, see us as almost "separated"? Where was that parallel set of footprints, leading back to that elusive two, the two of us? The two who used to walk together, side-by-side?

A week later, I went alone to the city's kite festival, *Kites Over Boston*, the big event my wife had helped organize and that I was to feature in my article.

As I came up from the train station, over a hill and into the park, I looked up and saw hundreds of kites in the air. Suddenly I was so happy, I began to grin and felt like crying. Families, couples, groups of old people, of kids, had brought their old paper kites, box kites, dragon kites with long whiplash red tails, fighter kites, so many kites! For my article, I took photographs of children assembling kites, becoming initiated into the tangled life of string, then launching the kites and promptly crashing them. One Muslim woman, like a walking laundry basket in her layers of veils, struggled to keep a plastic Superman kite up in the air. A man and his two kids flew a small homemade kite, octagonal, and painted in a bright design, Africana colors, Africana design, the father told me. When the kite came down, they posed for me with their pretty kite. The laughing boy, black eyes turned up with laughter, ducked behind his father the moment the shutter clicked; the girl looked straight at me, bright pink ribbons fluttering from her braids.

Up where the kite festival turned kite championship, the rigging of the kiting club banners pinged frantically. My wife sat at the *High as a Kite* table, command central for the official kiting events. Around her milled the teams in their nylon team uniforms emblazoned with their team names: SKYSAILORS in lime green hats, SQAIR DANCERS in pink, KAPITOL AIR KORPS in black hats and jackets.

My wife's voice crackled and spat over the loudspeaker, announcing the next event, the kite duo competition. The reigning champions, the DUODRONES, in blue, were ready to go.

My wife's voice, in bed, in the dark, is like granite water, the water that seeps through granite, pure cool stony-tasting water.

I went to tell my wife I was going home. Tapping the ground with her foot as she always does when she's excited, she's all kite talk with the others, they talk about kite ballet and kite skiing— "*Parapente*, in French," my wife informs the others, her pronunciation execrable.

"Good-bye,"—all she had to say to me.

In bed that night, my wife lifted up to me in a quiver, but she was not my mare anymore. Not my dark-haired, handsome mare with her mare's croup, who used to nuzzle me, bend her head against my neck, as I stroked her spine, two pools of perspiration in the hollows on either side of her spine, at the end of her spine, little lakes. I dipped the tip of my tongue in them.

My wife was a kite on a string—the string is taut. Then it snaps, falls limp in my hand.

That Sunday, a Sunday at the end of a long, long spring, I was still trying to finish my article on kites. I was almost finished, but overwhelmed by the despair, the doubt that often grips me right before I finish a big piece. I lose all my pleasure in the work, I sleep too much, wander around and around the neighborhood, come home recline decline into the sofa. All this somehow necessary to deliver myself up to the finishing of the piece, to rise up and take it in hand, to look one more time at every word every sentence and say yes, that this has a bit of joy, that this is filled with the simple joy of looking up in the air and seeing a kite, yes, kites!

I sat at my desk. Unfortunately I had already straightened my desk up, so that very useful bit of procrastination was gone.

Had already eaten lunch, drunk too much coffee.

I walked around my study on a small pilgrimage to the souvenirs of past articles. I rolled in my palm a Tibetan bone bead, I studied a reproduction of an old Spanish map. I even pulled out and inspected my emergency kite for the first time since my wife had made me buy it. Out of its pouch, the kite seemed not so small after all.

I lay down on my sofa. Somewhere in Japan, someone makes a kite as small as a postage stamp and flies it with a long strand of human hair. I couldn't find that tiny kite anywhere in Japan. If I had that tiny kite I could fly it here in my study, lying down.

Chasing after kites in Japan, I had been strangely happy. *Tako* means "kite" in Japan, and *tako-kichi*, "kitecrazy." North of Tokyo, I saw the whole town of Shirone go *tako-kichi*. Two giant kites, each flown by dozens of men, meet over the waters of the canal dividing the town. Now the kites' lines entangle, and the fight begins. The kite with the fierce warrior's face tries to pull to its side of the canal the kite with the white cresting tidal wave. The wind turns sharply and both kites begin to fall. The men pull even harder on the line. The kites rise, hover a moment, then fall into the canal. The thick paper melts, and the bright colors bleed red and blue and black into the water. The bones—they call the bamboo frame the bones—free of their flesh, are pulled from the canal to live again, next spring, in another kite.

At the Hamamatsu festival, thousands of kites in the sky. Along the long beach of black sand, kite flyers in short black jackets, cigarettes drooping from their lips, attack an enemy's red-white-black kite. The kite lines saw away, one line snaps, and the defeated kite drifts out over the blue Pacific. "Lost at sea, lost at sea," I intoned, alone among the crowd picnicking on the black dunes.

At Hamamàtsu, I learned, kites were first flown to celebrate the births of sons.

For my daughter, if I had a daughter, I would fly a kite. I would have liked so much a little girl, a girl like my wife. Corinna, I'd name my little girl, Corinna such a ringing, tinkling, clinking name. I'd bedeck her with the jewelry my wife's stopped wearing now. I'd pin brooches on her, fasten bracelets around her wrists, slip rings on her ten fingers and tell her to make two fists so the rings don't slip off. Send her into the living room to surprise my wife, surprise her with herself. My wife would laugh. We would all laugh and be one with love. My wife always said—before we stopped saying these things—she hoped for a boy with a crooked front tooth like mine, a bookish bespectacled boy like me. But I never wanted that. I couldn't bear to see my ugly self as in a living mirror. Yet she was, once, fierce on the subject, to have another me, a boy coming out of the womb laughing and woeful at the same time, telling her a ridiculous tale while still tethered to the umbilical cord.

A tiny Japanese kite. I only had an Edo kite, a large rectangular kite painted with the dark face of a green-eyed demon. The old, old maker of my kite told me that his father had loved making kites, that he himself loved making kites, but since kite makers are always poor, and now everyone in Japan wants to be rich, his son will not make kites. Soon no one will make kites anymore.

If I had a tiny kite, I could fly it here like a moth fluttering in this room. I could finish my piece, if I had a tiny kite.

I did have a sheet of Japanese paper somewhere around that I had bought to wrap a gift for my wife. I found it underneath a stack of magazines—I'd forgotten what a pretty piece of paper it was, busily printed with fans, butterflies, flowers and waves and whirlpools, a busy little world, in lovely worldly colors black and maroon, dark blue, olive green, and creamy white. The paper felt soft, like soft cloth. Clearing off my desk entirely, I cut out a rectangle the size of a regular playing card. For the frame, I went to the kitchen and broke off broom straws from the broom and trimmed them to the length and width of the paper. I had my own bones. I laid out the straws this way, that way, glued them together, glued the paper to them. From my wife's sewing box, I picked out the finest thread. My wife had had her hair cut short this winter, so no good going to her hairbrush. I attached thread lines to the two top corners of my little kite, to the middle of its face, tied them to a long line coming off the spool. Attached streamers at the lower corners to steady her.

Up from the basement came a dusty fan. On Hi the kite spun wildly, but on Lo the kite lifted. My tiny kite lifted and hovered steady as a hummingbird. What a pleasure the gentle tug of the thread at my fingers! I laughed out loud to no one. No one here to see I had gone *tako-kichi*, flying this tiny kite all my own.

I flew the kite from my sofa, and I began to think about my wife. In the last months, we had come to live peaceably enough with the strangerliness between us. I sat in my study, she sat at her sewing machine, or in the kitchen packing up mail-order kites with her new assistant, long and lanky Liz—Liz Lizard, I call her, because she always looks like she's sunning herself. The best was when I had the house to myself, like that day, my wife off at the kite store, or off kiting with Liz, with the rest of her kite friends, I assumed—I didn't ask anymore. The sewing machine quiet, Lizard's loud laugh long gone, and I didn't have to listen to the maddening rustle of their rip-stop nylon pants and jackets.

With my tiny kite sailing on high, suddenly I pictured my wife stepping from the shower that morning, wet and sleek as an otter. My flagpole idly stirred. I wondered, Could I fly the kite with an erection? So I worked on it, poring over my wife's body as I had seen it that morning. Round brown-tipped breasts. Behind, the sacred spheres. Yet something was different about my wife that morning. Was it that her face seemed browner than usual with sun, those scraped elbows and a knee, or her waist so curiously chafed a rashy red? This was my wife, whom I used to know like the back of my hand, my wife, whom I had held in the palm of my hand.

I saw her again, in detail, this morning, stepping from the shower, her breasts surely filling, her belly swelling, an indefinable but certain welling-up. Maybe. It wasn't fat, I'm sure. Her face still lean, her arms still firm. Maybe.

I heard the front door open, shut. My wife was at my study door, watching my little kite fly back and forth. I had forgotten how she could grin, all teeth, gums, a grin like a holiday. What could I say to her? She lingered there. Did she have something to say to me? Something important to say to me? Almost shyly, she turned away. It was as if we hadn't yet been formally introduced, and we couldn't find the right words, the right moment, to begin the conversation, to stop being strangers.

But, then, my wife turned back to me. She asked me nervously, bravely in a rush, my wife asked me if I would help her go kiting. She wanted to go kiting, but O'Caslin couldn't go, and Liz at the last minute couldn't go, but Liz had lent her her truck. And she wanted to go while—she looked at the tiny fluttering kite—while the weather was perfect.

From out of nowhere, the cat leapt at the kite, batted it down, pounced on it, and rolled back and forth, clutching the kite to its belly, shredding the paper with its hind claws.

"Bad, bad cat!" my wife scolded, and got her hand scratched trying to get my tiny kite back, all in all making a big fuss.

All in all, it was finally so easy for me to give in.

Up north of Boston to Plum Island we drove and then down the island's narrow road between the dunes and the marshes where the birds flitter. We parked and from the back of the truck my wife picked up a pile of folded kites, line, and a harness. I lifted out a winch with a reel of orange rope. We wound around the dunes to the long, curving deserted beach.

I helped my wife fasten the winch to the concrete pylon of a lifeguard's station. We checked the teeth and the mechanism for reeling out, for stopping the rope and cranking it back up. I took some time to make sure the teeth caught, did not slip.

When I looked up, I saw my wife poking her head into a Styrofoam bike helmet. Next, she clasped the harness around her waist—swelling waist. Yes she had her jeans safety-pinned at the zipper a bit down, as if she could not fasten the top button any-more. To the rings of the harness, she clipped the rope coming from the winch. She tested the clip, pulling at it, standing on the rope and tugging at the clip again. She attached to the harness the two lines that linked the limp kites lying on the sand.

I stand by. My wife comes to me and quietly explains. Now I stand by the winch, though I'm afraid. One more time, I tell myself, I'll let her go just one more time. Picking up the first kite, she angles them one after another toward the wind, the wind fills the channels sewn into the kites, and suddenly she has a red kite, a yellow, a green, two orange, a pink kite, like large air mattresses, all rigged together, rustling and bumping on the sand, coltish restless and ready. She grabs for the two handles attached to the kite lines. The kites roil, buck, they lift higher and higher, they line up six kites one on top of another, the lines tighten. My wife tenses her arms.

Now my wife is up, too, lifting up, the loose rope snaking up behind her, and now she is moving toward the dunes. The rope straightens out, is taut. I unlatch the catch on the handle of the winch and begin to let out more rope slowly, slowly. My wife hovers in mid-air, flying the kites. She pulls at the kites and flies to the left, then to the right. She goes up and then down, all in mid-air.

And I, with one hand on the winch crank, one hand on the rope, I am flying my wife.

The white crinkled soles of her tennis shoes dangle over my head and fill me with terror.

At the same time, I begin to see that her sweetness and her thuggishness, which I had always prized and had sorely missed and had finally almost forgotten, seems the lowest next-to-nothings of her compared to this discovery of her. She is no longer my mare, my riffraffish girl, my Saint Francis. She is a swan queen taken mortal form. She is—with my help—empress of her element, air.

Slipping off my jacket to free up my arms, I tied it to the pylon as high as I could, away from the teeth of the winch. In the sharp breeze, the jacket snaps out like a blue banner.

Here came three tugs, one tug two tugs three tugs—meaning, let out more rope, and I let the rope reel off up into the air. Breathing slowly, in and out, I was terrified, I was excited, but had to stay perfectly calm, I was in charge of the rope.

Two tugs—put the catch on—and I did. The kites so bright floating almost over the dunes, I had to trust in them. I told myself they were the best kites, she was an expert now, she knew what she was doing. I had to trust in her knowledge of the wind and of rip-stop nylon and nylon rope and winches and hopefully of her husband, some knowledge of him, some confidence in his equipment.

One tug two tugs three tugs. I let out more rope.

She was right over the dunes, the wind steady, remarkably steady, a straight blow in from the ocean. It has to keep blowing and blowing.

The rope quivering—one tug—reel in—or two tugs—put the catch on—or three tugs—more rope? More rope, I was sure it was three tugs—yes, give her more rope.

Think of all she was seeing now! Think of all she would have to tell our child! The birds lifting off from their nests, the soft-furred does bedded in the dunes. The early hay greenish silver, which later in the summer would be gathered into giant wheels standing singly in the field. Rusting tractors and cars a bit of mirror glinting, white farmhouses behind a line of leafing trees. Rivers and streams emptying into the sea, highways, maybe the skyscrapers of Boston. To the east the gigantic Atlantic and to the west the hills and ranges of the continent lifting.

When my wife flew in front of the sun, it was hard to look at her, hard to see her for all the glory obscuring her outline. Yet I exulted, I had that light too on the end of my rope, the whole bright world was pulling my rope taut.

One tug—reel in.

I felt her tug again. But not yet! I couldn't help myself—I loosened the winch, I let the rope out. Let her out just a little bit further, past the sun, beyond the dunes, out of sight, or maybe swing her out over the sea. Let her out to see even more of the world, I had to let the rope out to show my wife my child the whole world.

Thinking, all the time thinking, I'll let them out and then reel the whole world back to me.

Love

PHILIP MEMMER

All night we hadn't slept, expecting
something more. What were we missing there?
The sheets tangled under our bodies

like a Rorschach, so we took our best guesses.
An artichoke? she laughed, meaning of course
that something valuable was being hidden from us

under those folds of linen. *A camel?*
she tried again, *No, No, that vase*
in your parents' bedroom, that awful vase!

and by then I was getting angry, because
all I could pick out was that old
Chevy my friend drove in high school,

the one we'd speed off in after class
let out. *I can't see it*, I said,
Move your leg. She giggled, dragging

the whole mess to the floor with a single
curled toe. She had to be crazy. *Kiss me*,
she said. So I did. I kissed her.

Make Me Dazzle

CAROLE MASO

There is something so simple really, so lovely here: this longing woman walking down the beach that flanks the bay in winter . . .

little seaside town

little seaside star   off season

floating

. . . recalling water: She dreams remembering the way her eye hugged the river on the passing train—long after the ride had ended . . .

like the lip lingers.

like the lip cleaves to the clitoris—long after, long after.

clavicle, lilting world.

It's a long, narrow beach (blowing, salty air, sand flying, a great expanse of gray and blue, etc., without beginning or end), and if one's vision is good, and hers is, one can see a long way, far. Far enough to see what from here is only a blur, then a human figure, then a woman—

Bending, picking up stones or shells, small collections of something . . .

Wind blown, sea ravaged in winter she walks more quickly now toward—

Two women approach each other on the otherwise empty beach.

She picks up the relics of a sea creature. A shell shaped like a clavicle. The sound of bells.

The moan of the lighthouse and roses.

The relics of love. Bones bleached on a beach.

Battered by desire and the sea now she sees the other woman nearing.

fingering moonstones

singing little sea songs

(The long boarded walkway away. This long beach in winter. This long walk away from you now.)

Land's End—
leaving all else behind.

The professor on holiday. She doesn't have to teach anybody anything she doesn't want—the woman on a well-deserved break, walking, walking faster now.

Race Point.

She thought by walking she might dispel certain things.

The woman nearer—

(As you turn to go—but hesitate for a moment and turn back slightly . . . As if changing your mind . . .)

(Now as you go you hesitate, and make an odd half turn back. And I am startled, offered hope by the incompleteness of the gesture.)

She bends and reaches for something.

Their bones, thousands of years from now, glowing on this beach. Recalling pleasure, the hidden sexual residue of their lives, pulsing.

While the woman, still collecting bits of this and that, shells and seaweed and driftwood and small sea creatures comes closer. Then is right there.

"You're right here."

She nods, smiles, bows her head. She sees her neck.

The motion of a hand already moving through that tangled hair and how now looking away she sees that motion—a kind of downward stroke in everything. The woman's head now tipped back slightly.

her mouth slightly open.

her lips slightly chapped.

her head tipped back.

"Hello."

She closes her eyes for a moment and sees her ankles already around the woman's neck. Back arched. Hips slung.

hips slung.

back arched.

like an acrobat

like a woman in a water ballet (the sea pulsing behind them)

like a dancer

like an ice skater
As a child she loved to go ice skating.
As a child she loved to go to the Ice Capades with her mother.
Sea whipped. Sea frenzied. Snow, now, on water. Cold.
Nods. Smiles.
"Hello."
Like the lip cleaves
Like the eye clings
ankles
downward stroke
"On a holiday."
Her knees slung over her shoulders.
Sea drunk and snow they can barely hear each other over the
moan of the lighthouse and the ocean and roses.
downward stroke.
The drag and pull of the tide.
Nets dragging on the ocean's floor. Sweeping . . .
Her teeth dragging over—
Water lapping.
The way the rose clings . . . lip . . .
As they try (unsuccessfully) to get to the end of the sentence.
Water lapping.
The moan of the night already pressing on them.
Water lapping. Night lapping.
She can already imagine them . . .
The moan of the lapping women.
Everything meets in this little seaside town off season.
She sees her ankles already crossed
like the river clings—
taste of water—
taste of—
and sticky . . .
(You brought a bucket of flowers to that tiny room by the sea.
We made love on the beach in spring. Fucked on the pier, the
Hudson glittering, the Hudson River singing and our humming
. . . Unforgotten. Bright sun.)

Taste of—

"How about a coffee or a drink?"

As bleary, delirious, the sound of bells, they make their way to the bed at the end of the long beach and sentence, far.

Exultation is the going
Of an inland soul to sea—
Past the Houses,
Past the Headlands,
Into deep Eternity—

She's got a lovely laugh . . . clavicle . . .

She takes her hand in winter.

The large strong hands. The muscled arm. Biceps, tendons, the soft pillowed breasts.

"Fuck," she whispers, smiles, shudders.

"Huh? What?"

Is it the madness then, the extravagance of roses opening in December in this place that makes them want

"Fish Fry Friday night," a voice calls and the sound of bells.

"Huh?"

"A cup of coffee? A hot toddy or a beer or tea?" (her hips slung) "What?"

Above their sexual static (downward stroke)
and the fury of the sea.

Her legs clasped—
Glistening and ravaged
"You're driving me, you're making me"—
The sentence hard to reach. She stutters.
hard to breathe
hard to talk.
"You're making me—crazy."
At any rate who will save us? "You're making me—
fucked up"

In the little seaside café off season they focus on the maps and tourist brochures, trembling.

Hanging from her teeth (acrobat)   Backward and strung up (sill blurry)

Come to me.

(I am finally speaking about you—if only to myself. It was inevitable, I suppose. I am speaking about you. I hope not in a bad way.)

(Your capacity for wildness . . . your perversity . . . I miss you)

They study the swollen map together. Bells ringing. "Where shall we go?" she asks.

And then, "Pearl Street."

"Or," (her hands so large and strong and—) "would like . . . would like . . .")

"What?" looking at the map.

She nods, "yeah."

"To fuck you on Mechanic Street. To fuck your eyes out on—Bangs Street."

"Easy now," the professor smiles. "How about on School Street?" They're already shipwrecked. Sea soaked, drenched.

She takes her hand and puts it—

like a mechanic

"Race Point," they say deliriously.

You're making me—

Slow down a little then:

First Encounter Beach. They smile. Shhh—

Cool Down. Slower:

Two women walking opposite ways on the beach. Two women finding themselves on the same beach in winter. Two women, lovely, lilting, free a little, on this remote tip two women, of land, strip of land, spit of land, imagining: stranded.

Two women listen to the moan of the lighthouse and ocean and roses as they approach one another—

Sandy beach.

Two women, strangers, pass each other on this wild, windswept tip and bristle, stopped by something glinting, wayward.

At any rate, who will save them?

Two women find themselves, desire driven in waves and wind and fierce and dazzle.

Stranded, high high, driving each other—

crazy

Straddled on her gorgeous mouth. Head tilted slightly back. Or: knees over her strong shoulders. "Teach you . . . "

The tongue poised just a fraction of an inch from—

"I'll teach you . . . "

 She feels her breath and oh

And dazzle.

They smile at each other, "hello." And oh and moan. She's dizzy, frightened. She sees blur and pink and moan and moving— sucking mouth and hollowed cheeks and gloving bones, oblivion stranded aureole—circling and the lapping waves of the seaside town and beach—

dizzy dazzling spit and foam and aureole and

"Hello. My name is Aurelie and pleased to meet you and shall we now go for a drink?"

It's like a miracle then, again, sprung like this from one an- other's longing and desire flung and fucked and oh and oh and au- reole and mouth and straddle

Two women in a cafe, having tasted, glimpsed:

A deep deranging of the sentence—disorder.

Her hair draped now on the woman's thighs. She teasingly hanging above her trying to make words. "What—

"What do you want?"

"But you don't even know me . . . perfect stranger . . . huh?"

Two women in a café imagining

Going at each other, as their bodies draw close, approaching. Focus:

Strong, capable hands and muscled arms, perfect back and ten- dons, shoulders, thighs like a vise: "You are an athlete then?"

"How ever did you guess?"

Having glimpsed, having imagined:

The press of the Watermark. The pressure of her hand—one at the small of her back, the other in front, a little lower, there, just below the stomach. The press of the—

looking at the map.

"Crown and Anchor. Shankpainter."

Almond skin. Dirty blond hair in tangles. Large bones. Those hands. "You are an athlete then?"

They're fucked up, sea soaked, shipwrecked, stranded, drenched.

She laughs and says, "Land's End." Says "Far Side of the Wind. Yeah, I'll take you here."

"Ciro, Pucci, Pepe, Napi. The Mews." Meow. Front Street and Back. I'd like to fuck you on—

The *A* House throbbing—

—God you are hot God you are gorgeous.

spit of land.

world's end.

dazzling night.

The moan of the fog and the cat's cries.

(The long walkway away. The long breezeway. Where I imagine you're OK)

Up the wooden steps and through the blue door press and hurry oh.

Pearl gray light and night approaching and the cats stretching and scratching and asking,

With you up against, rubbing up against—

Hurry.

Sea salt and rough tongue and—

Watermark, White Horse, White Wind—

Up the wooden steps through moan and salt and swim and shudder

devouring

"You're driving me crazy."

"Good"

little seaside town off season

lilting rosy pearl in the evening light.

God, you are gorgeous.

You who guide wide ships through treacherous night, guide me . . .

eternity.

(I am finally beginning to talk about you—if only to myself.

You thought you were just a sex toy. I suppose I don't understand the word "toy" in that sentence, or the word, "just."

And was it always only about sex? Or was it our way to keep

me far, dismiss me when necessary? Diminish what we had, if it got too painful. When it got too painful.

As you turn now. And I lose you again in the azure of a perfect summer night on a beach.

You turn away.)

Prolong this. They build a fire. Prolong. She closes her eyes. "God you are so gorgeous." Two women having just met—and at the threshold of all possibility, all-everything, imagine eternity—

imagine swollen, sticky endless night

"Triathlete"

Her flex and reach and pull and dare. Her arch and skill and will and brave and true.

Lift and open. Ankle. Wrist and reach.

The sound of waves deranged and lapping at their swollen sea door. She presses her mouth and throb. At the blue of wild ocean night.

floating   humming
at the end of the world caught
caught in her pearl
caught in her pearly net
At this glistening altar. Her mouth now moments from oh
"Athletic girl."
"And I'd like to ride you . . .
I'd like to ride you like a porpoise . . .
Ride you like a saint . . .
I'd like to ride you like a mermaid . . .
I'd like to make you sing
Like a siren
Moan like a rose
Scream—
like a siren. Luring others to our ocean bed and door."
Delicious ship.
Most delicious ship.
Guide me. Make me dazzle.
Grinding
Glowing bones to stars and salt and sea, guide me.

Show me

And hip to hip and grind and straddle, ride and yeah, good girl.

Two women scratching, begging up against each other, frantic. Clipped or pierced perhaps and oh and oh and

"fuck."

Scream like a siren.

Fuck like a sailor. Fuck like a siren. Fuck like: two women . . . sudden heat: you put your mouth on my clavicle

She puts her mouth—

And fast and hands, athletic girl and more and suck and come and

Like a siren . . .

"They can hear you at Ciro's, Pepe's, Nape's, Pucci's. They can hear you at the Pilgrim Monument,"

she smiles. Now slower this time.

(This is a message to you: not so embedded in the text after all—I could start now right where we left off.

Talking to you even now, after all this time. Imagining, after all this time, your half turn back—that turn that might set us into animation again.)

Luminous, glowing oyster pearl and—

"Hey there—take it easy, Hon."

Oyster, Carmelite and scratchy urchin, clam—

Her hair now draped. She's dripping on her inner thigh and tease and please—

"What? Come on, tell me what you want."

The moan of the fog and the cat cries.

Shhh and slow and—

rocking on her hips

rocking like a baby on her hips

rocking on a woman's hips like the ocean

rocking on the ocean's hips

"oh, yeah, honey . . . "

riding on a woman's delicious hip, guide me.

Delicious ship.

Flushed.

like women dreaming next to water.

Guide me like a Carmelite.

Sudden heat. You are flushed. A broken pier in summer. The raging West Side Highway at our side. We are lost in a sea of men wanting men. You pretend to want to be them. You take me from behind. My head pulled back. My hair wrapped around
your fist.

I wanted you the moment I saw you. Your look—that of a deranged Carmelite nun, a fallen cheerleader, a mischievous child.

And how you made love. Sometimes like an innocent. Sometimes like an expert. Sometimes like a foreigner, insisting you really didn't like girls. Like a scientist, performing experiments.

With your homemade crucifix, your slingshot. Little tomboy. A toy gun, a water gun you would shoot into me. How does that feel?

Your plastics and latex and shower caps.

And I lose you again in the azure of a perfect summer night.

Now as you turn, now as you traipse with combat boots and negligee into that good night. Away. But turn, for one brief second, back.

Adieu. It seems you've gone to God—or where? Though we lived in the same city, I never saw you again.

Or though we live in the same city, I have never seen you again. Even now, I give room, for some future sighting, hope. Anticipatory. In love with revision, amendments. You turn, with hesitation . . .

Our unhappy love affair. All your friends urge you to get out, but you can't. And I, the impassive temptress, riveted to you. My sin: that I loved others as well. Though nothing compared to you— that is, isn't it, how the song goes? Your touch. Your particular finesse. I have not forgotten.

This time they force each other, they hurt each other, a little. Grinding hard and deep and gorgeous face and teeth and cleave—

Triathlete!

When she's American she says "oh baby, oh honey, tell me what you want."

When she's French she says: *dérangement*.

Sound of water lapping. Sound of—

Water logged. Sea soaked. Floating. Downward stroke. Fucked (so beautifully) up.

In my revision, my fantasy, you whisper, you tell me you turned back to me and fully, but that I was already gone.

And then that tentative reconciliation, unseen by me, shifted, becoming a half turn away again where it became resolute, turned to stone, irrevocably away and engraved and forever.

If you would let me kiss just once those stony feet, just once now with the mouth that—

The mouth that

Let me kiss your feet and the stone boat of your body with the mouth that—

Two women. When they are Italian they say "*ecco*."

Two women. Their hair plastered to their faces.

The sound of water at their door.

Open sea. Never ending. Eternity.

When you're a sailor you say, "Hey and Hidey and Ho."

She takes her hand and puts it:

When they speak of the blue fin, the yellow tail, the great red, the fishermen's eyes haze over seeking something far off—

glistening.

She imagines her in a fishermen's net now and she begins

her slow, fevered suction cupped a little pressure a little more pressure.

Trying to get at

madly

frenzied descent. Chewing. (a chewing sound)

"I need to taste you."

Luscious, pulsing pearl.

Little rosy pearl in the evening light.

Caught in her pearl. "God, you are fucking gorgeous." hard to breathe.

Licking her strung up—

If she could fuck her only one way . . .

Licking her strung up through the net now. Caught in this dreamy net and plan and trying—tired and strung out.

"come on . . . fuck . . . you can do it."

"huh?"

"trying."

Who at any rate will save us?

Humiliated, you wanted to leave me before I left you. But you were sex-addicted, addicted to our bodies together and so you kept putting it off, angrily. Growing to despise us both.

And how you made love sullenly, silently, enraged, lost in your fury and the betrayals and sadness yet to come.

You made me love desperately then.

muttering   buzzing   humming   strange words

For fun the women keep at their bedside a writing tablet. Or else they used their sheets to scrawl—

and crawl and scratch and come

If I only had one sentence to seduce you with. To get you back. To reach you.

One glistening sentence.

She takes her hand and puts it—

She sucks on the woman's fingers. Her ear next to her aureole or clavicle or wondrous shell in sleep where

she hears her dreaming. On the lip, on the edge

of the known world, remembering . . .

as a little girl she used to like to go—

Summer lingering.

Like the lip cleaves and clings

Like the gull hangs in air—

You thought you were of no consequence. You thought you were just part of a larger pattern, a dizzying design and it made you feel sick.

You were part of a larger design. But you were never inconsequential.

Our sad history. I loved others. I wanted others. You could not see how you were any different. Or if you were, then why I would not stop, change for you. Be someone new.

Heat and light and gleam that longing beach where they've teased each other into furious, delirious—

Make me dazzle.

There is something so simple, so lovely here, really. Where I wait for you.

She'd like to coax the sand that's lodged here and draw from her in long slow pulls with tongue and gum and teeth and skill— and if they're lucky, secreted round a grain of sand, a pearl, you gorgeous oyster girl.

sticky   "a lot of practice"

Sudden heat. A broken pier. You take me from behind.

The Hudson River glistening.

"Stand up. Don't move."

Obedient, she stands on wobbly sea legs and she fucks her now, like this.

like this.

Then on all fours. Front Street. Back Street.

The *A* House throbbing.

She swearing like a sailor now

Past the houses,

Past the headlands,

Into deep Eternity.

Far and deep.

And sleep a little.

You made love to dispel emptiness and fear. "What's that?" you'd whisper in the night frightened. And I'd check under the bed and reassuring you, you'd come down to see for yourself and fuck me there. And still you were afraid.

Past the Headlands . . .

a dream where she is being pulled with great skill and ring, with touch and look and a few trembling words—

far out to sea, where she's

stranded now. The pull of the waves and the dark—

Far . . .

Untitled

DAVE HOWELL

Making love

Every few minutes, a flock of starlings flies overhead
toward the evening sun. One flock follows the other.

⊚

Embracing the gentleness of the roan's neck

She leans on my torso, I am familiar with this touch
yet will never understand it.

Like her neck on the horse's thick neck,
calming the froth from his mouth.

⊚

My wife sleeps on one shore, along with the wives of
      other men,
just as the wives of other men sleep on the other shore

The other shore and back, this was my want,
but the darkness was so thick I could not see my hands.
I looked beneath the water, they were not there.
Just the dark and current of the river.

⊚

Whenever the unbelievable visits us, we fall in love

I saw the roan coiled in barb. My wife was in the shower
when I screamed to her, and she did not even stop
      to dry off.
Not that it mattered, it rained.
Her body arriving to pull at the rust could do nothing.

It happens every evening and for every summer
we've lived here. I do not know where they go, and
they only have so much light to help them.

Mother of Pearl

DONALD RAWLEY

Los Angeles is bursting with bad men named Hector, Felice, and
Paco, with eyes like a glass of Kahlua and sharp teeth. They have tat-
toos of mermaids, and crossed knives above the word "MIEDO," and
their arms are muscular and scarred.

They are men at fifteen, corrupt at eighteen, sometimes dead at
twenty. They have moist lips and a way of walking that clears sidewalks. They are perfumed with Jockey Club and Aramis, and they
hold the scent of limping women on their fists.

And they'll hustle you out of everything you've got. Because
Los Angeles is a town built by hustlers, for hustlers, and left in wills
to hustlers, bad men with loins so stiff they have to dance and fight
to keep them down. When they finish with you, whatever room
you might be left in reeks of them, whatever room you're crawling
out of with wobbly legs from too much sex and a dry throat that
won't disappear.

They like fast cars, late nights, guns and knives. Girls named
Suzy who swallow, with fishnet stockings and a real American accent. Sometimes they'll want a man who's got money, who's de-
bauched enough to do as they say. And sometimes they want a kiss
that lingers.

I cannot give any of these things. I am forty-five, a pretty young
man who faded in middle age. Now I am poor, shy and lonely, living in a small single apartment with a view of an alley. The doctor
tells me there is a shadow on my lung. How I've wanted a strong

man to wrap his arms around my skinny shoulders until I can't breathe. How I've wanted his come to shimmer on my chest, every slow thrust an innuendo and a trance. How I've wanted him to promise me his soul.

But I have nothing to trade. Watching the bad men strut like parrots with their wings clipped, I know nothing comes for free. Something is taken. As I see their heads crooked for sex, I say never for me. No, not ever for me.

I am taken to a welterweight fight in East Los Angeles, past an overgrown park and a graveyard where hibiscus is growing out of graves. It is in an ancient two-story warehouse. Felice Garcia versus Angel Jesus del Toro. Past Cuban cigar smoke and grime, past men with gardenia oil in their hair and dirty white polyester suits, I see Felice Garcia on his stool, his mouthguard in place. He's staring right at me. His eyes are a sable brown, and I cannot catch my breath. He is too beautiful, too young, too pure for me.

His arms are very muscular and there is a small tuft of black hair on his chest. He smiles at me, in the second row, scratches his nipple and wipes the sweat on his purple satin shorts. He shifts his legs as he thinks I might be able to see up his shorts. I cannot, but I pretend I can.

My friend Henry hands me a paper cup with bourbon in it. I hand it back.

"I don't drink," I say quietly, not taking my eyes off Felice.

"What DO you do?" Henry asks with a leer. "You into Mexican food? You into big hot burritos?"

I turn and look at Henry. He is seventy-five and obese, with pink skin and a penchant for ex-cons. One shot at him and missed, another stole all his furniture. Someday, I know, he will be murdered. He's dancing towards it with glee, and he frightens me.

I am ashamed to be here. I am too effeminate for this crowd and I have to guard my gestures, make sure I don't cross my legs the wrong way. Straight men generally sit at games with their legs spread and shoulders slightly hunched, as if they're sitting on the toilet. This is the posture I assume.

Angel, with a pug's face, a crewcut and bullet hole eyes, walks proudly into the ring, holding up his arms. The crowd applauds. Over an echoing loudspeaker an announcer, speaking in a velvety, rapid Spanish, introduces the fighters and the bell rings.

"If you want to see real blood," Henry says to me, "in two hours there's a cock fight. Two mean fucking roosters. You've never seen anything like it."

"Why do you think I want to see that?" I ask, annoyed. Henry shrugs.

"Because you like danger," he shouts over the roar of the audience.

"No, I don't," I say to myself, watching Angel Jesus del Toro hit Felice so hard blood trickles out of his mouth and slides over his nipples, some of it getting caught in his chest hair.

Felice must be about nineteen, I reason. I like how his thick hair shakes as he does the boxer's hop. And how his muscles are tense and lean.

The crowd begins screaming invectives at Felice in English, then in Spanish. Two middle-aged women behind me are in a rage over Felice. They sound like bluejays fighting, cawing in a Castilian lisp.

"No. I'm sorry, but I don't like this at all," I say as loudly as possible to Henry, who glares at me and turns his attention back to the fight. I know this is the end of our friendship, which was a minor one at best. I get up to leave, but at this moment Angel punches Felice with such ferocity the oil from his hair flies on my face. I am suddenly flushed, my eyes bright.

It is the most singularly exciting sensation I have felt in ten years. I run my hands along my face, and watch Felice, who, as he crumples to the floor, smiles at me and closes his eyes.

"You took quite a punch," I murmur soothingly as Felice comes to on a rickety cot. It is close to midnight. I have waited in this dim room for four hours. Felice had been thrown in here after the fight, then just a few minutes ago, an ancient Mexican with no teeth and an Elvis Presley toupee threw water on Felice and broke an amyl nitrite ampule under his nose.

The boxing hall is empty, as is the old warehouse. Elvis Presley nods to me as if to say, "I'm leaving now, *maricon*. You take care of the bastard. You lock up."

Felice has been stripped out of his purple boxer shorts. He is wearing a red jock strap. I'm amused. I wonder if he keeps leopard skin bikini briefs at home.

"You. Come out of the shadows. I can't see you." His voice is deeper than I imagined.

I am not sure if I should walk into the light of the bare bulb in this makeshift locker room. He will see that my hair is falling out, that I am thin, white skinned. A stutterer, a whisperer. Ready to be picked over. Like a corpse in the desert.

I walk into the light. Felice's pubic hair is flaying out of his jock strap. He wiggles his feet and smiles.

"What lonely eyes you got, baby." He wipes some dried blood away from his ear with a curious expression, then wipes it on his cot.

"Where did you learn English?" I ask.

"El Paso, Texas. I saw your lonely eyes. You're bad for Felice."

"I should go. I was worried," I say quietly.

"But they're pretty eyes, baby." Felice tries to yawn, but it hurts. "Oh shit, that dog fucker hurt me. Son of a bitch has no dick, thinks he's a big man like me."

Felice looks at me with a satisfied smile.

"You want Felice, don't you baby? Felice is expensive." He gets up stiffly, in a sore heave.

He stands in front of me. He is exactly my height, but he seems so much taller.

"What time is it?" he asks, touching my cheekbone. His hand is thick, almost rubbery. I look at my watch.

"Ten minutes to midnight."

"Jesus, you stay here all that time for me? You must *really* want Felice."

I realize now I have gone too far. I should sink back into the shadows, find the door leading out with the back of my hand. I should find my friends, others with shadows on their lungs and broken hearts. I should try driving at night, to no place at all, with my doors locked and my windows rolled up.

"What's your name?" Felice asks, running a finger along my chin.

"My name is Claude."

"You French?" Felice asks, cocking his head.

"No."

Felice shakes his grogginess off and gestures towards a filthy sink.

"Take that towel, wet it. You rub the blood off me. Okay? You're my new friend, right?"

"Right," I say.

As I rub his shoulders and chest the light bulb flickers above us.

"You take me out for tequila tonight, okay? And hamburgers. Loser don't pay, loser never pays. I saw you got a watch. I lost my watch."

"It's a cheap watch," I murmur. Felice grabs my arm and looks at it, then takes it off my arm and puts it on his.

"It tells time. You got some money for Felice?" His voice is reptilian.

I stop rubbing his chest and look into his eyes. His eyebrows are spiky and black. One eye is beginning to swell up.

"No, Felice, you probably have more money than me."

"You old whore! *Viejo puto!*" He coughs, spits some saliva and blood into a tin can. "Okay, I pay for tequila and hamburgers, but you do as I say. Later, you make Felice come. Okay?"

I nod my head slowly. I don't know what to say, and I start rubbing his chest again. I imagine Angel is with his manager and his girlfriend, plump, with teased red hair. Angel Jesus del Toro won't remember Felice Garcia tomorrow morning.

"Where are you from?" I ask. My questions sound high pitched, like a nervous woman. One loser confiding in another.

Felice doesn't mind the question. He smiles at me, then closes his eyes and licks his upper lip.

"I was born in a corral in Tecate and walked to Acapulco when I was ten. Open those doors." I walk over to a set of heavy, industrial cast iron double doors and open them. They swing out to a second floor fire escape.

Below us several Cadillacs and El Caminos are parked near a liquor store called "El Bambino." I can hear salsa playing from not one boombox, but two or three. Same song and channel. I can see a crescent moon, peach colored in the dank Los Angeles night, and a sky punctured by stars.

"What are you looking at? Get back here, lonely eyes."

I turn and walk back to Felice, who looks at me coolly. I begin rubbing him. He wants to talk.

"There was old men and young boys like me, little baby horses. I was the most popular. I stay at the El Presidente, at Las Brisas with the guys. There were coins to dive for. There were old gringos with white shoes and flowers on their shirts, big wallets. There was a boat, I know, ready to take me away."

"To Hollywood?" I ask archly.

"Yeh, baby, Hollywood. But first El Paso, Dallas, then Ensenada. Yeh, Felice *es muy popular*. Going to be a movie star." He laughs.

I suddenly imagine Felice in a tourist villa at the top of Las Brisas, twelve or thirteen years old, hair just beginning to grow under his arms, holding a candy cane from Christmas. He's sucking it carefully in the Mexican sun until it's a sharpened spike, then puts it in his jeans for later.

I see him dive naked into a tiny round pool as baby cockatiels test their wings and banana leaves quiver.

"You gonna finish me?" Felice asks, grabbing the towel away from me. "You dreaming, huh, lonely eyes?"

I step away from Felice and stare at him in silence. I am too frightened to say anything foolish.

Felice is built like an attack dog. When he moves he crunches his shoulders like a wrestler, little man with big balls. I bet he comes all day and dances all night, snapping his fingers at waiters and pimps. And I cannot stay away.

Looking at Felice and seeing bruises suddenly appearing on his hips and shoulders and arms, I want to kiss him. I realize I am the imprint on a shroud, my face's oil and sewn lips only leave a hard metal mark for Felice to decipher.

Felice balances himself as he stands up and stretches, then pulls his jockstrap down, kicking it off with one foot. Lazily he knocks the lightbulb and it swings on its cord.

"You like Felice? You like big Felice?"

I nod my head. He walks over to his cotton pants and takes a penknife out of his pocket. I lower my head. So this is the trade. A watch for a knife. A blow job for a stab wound. I become frightened.

"Don't back away. Touch it. Touch my knife."

Felice ambles up to me. I can feel his penis against my leg. His knife has a mother of pearl handle and it is warm in his hand, in front of my face, doubled up like a fetus, its handle glowing dully. I can smell Felice, and it is overpowering, like sewage and rose water and heavy fog.

A mambo is drifting up from the street. Felice clicks the blade out, and rubs the handle slowly on his chest to make it shine, then tests with his thumb the serrated edge of the blade. Then lightly rolls it on my neck, my chest. He cuts two buttons off my shirt, and whispers in my ear.

"I cleaned abalone in Ensenada with this knife, faster than anybody. You gut it, one cut and it flips on this big wood table. Then it doubles up, no noise. Just like a heart. Just like loving me, lonely eyes. No noise. Like a fish out of water that dies, when rainbow comes up on its scales. I washed a thousand shells in river water, sugar and sun. The mother of pearl rises, shining like your eyes, old man."

I realize there are tears in my eyes. If this is my last embrace then I will fall into it. Felice raises and cuts off a lock of his hair. He throws his knife at a cork bulletin board, empty of bulletins, where it sticks. I feel like I'm going to pass out. Felice takes my waist with a swollen hand; with his other hand he throws his hair on my face and shoulders like confetti, laughing.

"Now you belong to Felice. You never leave."

The mambo from the street has gotten louder, rapider. It's Tito Puente and Celia Cruz. It's playing from open windows in crowded apartments where the smell of mole sauce drifts past the palm trees and stars that dot my peripheries like talismans. Felice's cock is pressing against me like a mariachi's golden guitar, pulsing like a high tide. Like a winded sunset in the desert. Like a heart.

"You like to dance? Felice will teach you how to dance, *el baile*, baby." I see how welts are rising on his head and neck. Such black curly hair he's grown to make him a man. A vein leads from his loins to his hard belly. Next to it there is a li'l devil tattoo with a baby's ass and a tail, pitchfork and smirk.

Felice undresses me and it dawns on me that I am naked too, old, unkempt. I cannot decipher what will happen, but I tenderly put my hands around Felice. I am careful not to touch his bruises, but he still winces in pain.

"You wrinkled old man," Felice says, breathing heavily. We are pressed together, moving our hips slowly, and I know Felice does not see my sad little chest, my scrawny legs. I put my hands further down, around his buttocks, and look up into his eyes.

It is midnight and I am not poor and sick and old anymore. I am moaning. Felice is listening, his teeth clicking like a rattlesnake and his hair is still on my skin.

"See, lonely eyes, when you dance, *en el baile*, you got to hold the girl close. Like this."

My Shadow Has Blond Hair

DEBRA VIOLYN

I

I keep finding fragments of her. I'll find a sheaf of lined papers in, of all places, a suitcase of mine. The movers must have mixed everything up when they put all of my extra boxes down here in the basement. I find thin blue onionskin wedged in a window to keep it from rattling. Everything covered with the long thin scrawl, always in black ink. I'll look in the back of a cupboard and find a stack of papers where yesterday, I could swear, the cupboard was bare. I feel that as I am inhabiting this house, I am being inhabited by another being, her presence like a thin music, caught just for a moment now and then as I turn a corner, like one long blond strand of hair in the corner, catching light against the dark wood, dust motes taking form, then proving an illusion. Maybe.

I finally find a house for the rest of my life. Big enough to work. Big enough to play, to grow roses 'til they become big and unruly, to grow an almond tree 'til its trunk looks more like an old man than a youth. Room for all my books, a pleasant view for when I look up from editing, room for a pond where I can sit and blur my eyes and listen for the songs of birds. I've always dreamed two dreams, over and over: I am always finding a house, in one of the dreams it keeps having rooms I didn't even know were there, in the other, I can see the water. This house is both dreams.

But as I am putting my cans up on my shelves, there, as I set down a can of tomato soup I see a tiny slip of paper:

> "I have not yet gone to see the man who had called me to his side—over and over again he has called me but I feel I cannot go—not yet. What am I waiting for? Maybe I am too young—my nipples not yet the sheer astonishing defiance of gravity they will be one day soon. Maybe it's the shoulders, still subtly hidden in the shawl of childhood, not yet wide, freckled and gleaming with the muscles of their own possibilities; or my hips, filling but not filled."

and I must get down from my stepladder, and sit down and read it over and over. Who wrote this? How old was she? How did she come to write it? And how did it come to be in my house?

II

The presence of this young woman considerably changes my settling in. It's like someone else is here. Or perhaps someone is. I can't quite determine, for sure, if these things were here when I moved in and I overlooked them, of if someone is sneaking in and placing them in my cupboards, on my shelves, between my books or in my as-yet-unpacked boxes.

And I must say, I'm meeting my new neighbors with perhaps a different perspective than I might have if it were not for the notes. Shirley down the street has a daughter, but she's gawky and still just twelve, with short dark hair cropped close to her head. She rides the bicycle back and forth up and down the street. I can't imagine anyone "calling to her," and besides, no blond hair.

No blond hair either at the other end of the block, the girl, and her mother, are black, a thick ponytail doubled back on itself tied with multiple rubberbands sits atop the daughter's head. Hardly the portrait of delicate angst and self-absorption of the girl, the young woman?, leaving me notes.

Then who was it? Sometimes my cordless phone picked up young voices before the dial tone kicked in; suddenly every young voice struck me as a possibility, and I looked forward to every encounter with a new person as a possible clue to my secret visitor.

> I know what womanhood looks like. They bring me along and think I do not look, but of course I do. I'd be a fool not to look. In all their richness they sit about the kitchen table, thick sweaty breasts half-visible in the opened blouses, legs up for comfort, the thighs thick and sweaty too, the tight underpants up the middle, a child under the table—who even notices. Who cares what she sees. They think I'm still a child. The length of my child bones fools them, the thin gallop of my blond hair.

III

Unpacking, "settling," though it should be called "unsettling" for all the craziness, is mixed—I am nowhere, my whole being is convinced somehow that I'm still somewhere else, but I'm creating something new. Every opened box contains something I'd forgotten I had, one box can take all afternoon to unpack as each item reminds me of a trip to Japan I took, or a love affair, or a part of myself I'd lost and have found again.

But these secret notes added a whole new dimension, I was finding someone else's story, and it led me to my own memories. Maybe this was some playful friend of mine, maybe some new form of therapy.

My mother.

I see my mother in a white triangle headscarf, she's smiling, the sun is on her face and the wind is blowing. We're at our summer cottage. I love her so much at that moment that I never want to leave her.

When you're a child, you never see a whole parent, you see the freckles on an arm or spread across a face, you see a coat that is your mother, you see a mass of honey-brown hair. Little girls love their mothers desperately as long as they are allowed to, which isn't that long.

Did I sit under the table looking up the skirts? No, of course not. I don't think so. My mother never gathered with women around the table. Where was she, I wonder? Where were the other women? Who is this girl who has inhabited my life, and where are her women?

I telephone the man who used to own this house but can only leave him messages. He never answers the phone. He's young, was left the house when his grandma set the corner of it afire, and herself as well. He's off finding work, he's never home. He wants to be a spy. Is applying for spy jobs. I finally hear from him, he doesn't know of any blond women, well, not any young ones, just his sister used to be a cop, with her two kids, and no, he's sure she never wrote any poetry or anything remotely at all like that, he's sure.

I begin to find scars on my arms I never noticed before, I wonder where they came from, where the notes come from, where I come from.

> I look most at my mother's. I came out of there? I think.
> Hard to imagine.

IV

For me, this house is sanctuary. A place where I feel safe, where I can lock the door and keep the world away. A place where I can sit in my armchair with a thick manuscript to edit, feet up, glancing up now and then to catch the sun's golden light playing in the leaves out the window.

This is a place where the quiet rings from wall to wall, where my cat purrs on my lap, where birds sing at every window. This is a house where you can hear the wind. This is a house where I see trees from every window.

This is a house where I can feel protected at night, where no one can hurt me.

And now suddenly it's like I'm having an affair, and there's no one else here. I don't know which I fear more—to find or not to find another letter. I don't open a single cabinet or drawer or closet without wondering if somehow she's managed to slip in again and leave a strange epistle for me to read.

> When I was 14 I first discovered the losses of how a woman loves: you lose your mind, your dignity, your armor. Not that I was innocent before then. I don't think I was ever innocent. Too young stripped from the breast of my mother, I sought items to suck from a very young age. I sucked my blankets and my thumb, I sucked fruits so hard the cleaning ladies my mother hired were shocked and sickened at the shriveled and browned carcasses I returned to them from the plump fruits they had served. I wanted to suck everything out of everything. One life at a time was never enough, I wanted two, three, simultaneously. I wanted to suck from both ends, I wanted engorgement in every direction possible. To frustrate these impossible longings I took to sucking peaches in the bathtub, my eyes covered with damp towels and my ubiquitous blue-jeans waiting to be replaced on my swelled and flushed skin.

Her notes were unsettling me. I made a systematic tour of the neighborhood, in the guise of introducing myself, to every house. The Yashimotos, the Burnses, the Greenes; no one was even remotely like whoever wrote these, was writing these (which was it?) notes. Could she be slipping over the back fence? And why had she chosen me? I went door-to-door on the next block, and then on the one over on the other side. They were probably afraid I was canvassing for something, but I made it very clear, "Hello, I'm the new neighbor. I hope you don't mind, just wanted to say good morning and be on my way. Oh? Come in and meet your family? Well, thanks, then. Maybe for a second."

Also, I must say, I was becoming aware of how sexual the notes were, increasingly so. Maybe I was looking for the wrong person all along, maybe this was some kind of deliberate hoax, a harassment, a seduction?

I go downstairs to do the laundry; lifting the blue and white striped towels folded from the dryer I find under the stack this:

> My father would complain; he would wait outside the door of my bath, touching himself at the sound of every shift of water, every sucking of the peach. He'd meet me as I exited and tell me I needed clean clothes for my clean skin. He'd slip his large hot hand down the front of my bluejeans, my skin still humid from the bath, "Such clean skin," he'd say. "Such soft. . . ." I met his eyes. He didn't fool me. I let him linger there for an instant longer than I should have, then shift my hips away and down the hall as he watched me, younger and blonder than anything he ever had.

I decide that perhaps I've been going about this in all the wrong way, that what I need to do is get to know who she is before I go out looking for her. What struck me so clearly, perhaps attracted me, even, was how different we were. I was envious of this unknown person. Thoughts of her began to interrupt my work, my sleep.

She was beautiful and I wasn't. Long and thin with pale blond hair. The opposite of me. I'm small and thick and dark, too quiet. My hair is unmanageable, my eyebrows too thick. When I was young? No. Not even then. I had youth, but not beauty. To the great disappointment of both my parents, and often myself.

Did my father wait outside my door? Only with impatience, only with anger.

V

There isn't a day that goes by that I don't spend an hour or two out back by the pond, just sitting; there's always something to look at, some new thing I haven't seen before. The way the water looks, black sometimes, bottomless, viscous. The opening of one kaemphari iris, the curling of another. A path of ants. A mockingbird moves closer to sing so loudly he blots out every sadness of the human race: just listen to his song. A Mourning Cloak butterfly, a Brown Towhee, an Anna's hummer. I never leave this place unhappy. I never do not hear the flame-headed House Finch, the Steller's Jay, the Chickadee. The light never fails to amaze, the wind off the ocean in the trees.

Everyone makes choices, and if they're very lucky, their choices suit them. I'll admit, when I open a newspaper I wonder about everything I miss to sit out by the pond, to turn out my lights early to hear the single night mockingbird sing, to smell the blossoms on the lemon trees, to see the stars. Sometimes when I visit married friends I wonder why it's my choice to be alone, but that is my choice.

And that's what's so unfair about this, I have finally found a place away from everything, my own place, I have finally found it. And still, someone is disturbing my peace.

> Many years later, when I was covered, down there, with a thin wisp of honey-blond hair, as I lay on my back, hands wrapped around the posts of the brass bedstead to better arch my back, my gray-haired lover, one year older than my father, forced my legs open farther, then farther 'til I popped open like a pod of peas, and he sat at the end of the bed and stared, getting up now and then to look closer, to smell, and then sitting down again, all I could think was that this was the view my father wanted all along and never got.

Then I found the longest note of all.

> But perhaps I am not really so young anymore. I long to answer him. He calls so quietly. His call is like thin silk around my shoulders, it bristles against the back of my neck. He makes me curious. I walk by frequently, and stop only when he is outside. I say very little, but he hears me answering him. Eventually I find myself walking by more and more often. I say little, nothing to give him any hope, but hope develops anyway. I wear thin cloth-ing, he always watches my body respond to him. I feel a roiling where my legs meet my body, but I am unwilling to open my legs to anyone. Unready. Unwilling.
>
> One day, I accept an invitation to drink some cold tea and I never leave. But still for many months we never touch. Over that time the spaces between us grow smaller and smaller. We have our own chairs; each day they draw closer to each other by one-hundredth of a breath. He gives me my own room. I start with the door closed when I sleep, and each day it is left one-hundredth of a breath further open.

After many months I realize he has been standing outside my door the entire night the whole time I have been there; perhaps he never sleeps. When the morning comes I let him in.

When he makes love to me he cries. He is far too old for me, he is one year older than my father. He cracks my egg, he blurts himself into entire bowls of fruit, he devours anything I have and seems to invent on my stomach even things I don't have. He turns me over and over and over, every crack and opening a cause for intense scrutiny, he sucks me as though pearls will eventually come sliding down my cunt, he sucks my clit like a hard olive. He devises ways to keep me open and displayed for one hundred hours at a time. When he fucks me it is only the outer inch of my vagina, he dips in and out one hundred times with the speed of a young hamster, when he wants to go further he uses his whole fist but never his penis, I never know why.

Every time I read this, besides feeling aroused, I also somehow feel myself just wanting to cry. I am really at a loss as to what to do. Who is doing this to me, and why? I can barely work, I feel I'm in a dark place locked with this girl. I both do and do not wish to leave this closet.

He has stopped going to work. He can't do anything but me. He takes me to the country to live by the ocean. All night I hear the waves and they remind me of his grief. He suddenly turns into the old man and the sea. He has turned into the creaking of the redwoods at night. He has become an embarrassment. I can't stand him to touch me. I can't stand him to look at me. I shave my head for the first time in my life. At last I repel him. But then he comes in the middle of the night and fucks me the whole way, all the way, all the way in. I am fucked with the cock of a horse, a stuck pig, an entire bushel of apples. He fucks me like he wants to throttle a complete Cossack army. He fucks me like he wants to bring rain. He fucks me 'til he rips off my breasts and his dick comes out the top of my head. I am fucking him like an entire grange of wild horses. I disappear the next morning.

I understand why reading this makes me so sad: there is no heart there. How can she be so beautiful and yet so removed from her soul? I can't understand this, on some profound level. Maybe it's what I was taught, the only worth was beauty, it was somehow lent depth by association, though none existed. Skin as illusion of depth.

It's as though I've been raised to believe that soul was inferred from without, a gift from one's admirers, a bestowed quality rather than an intrinsic one. Beauty was the key to existence; without it you were invisible, therefore non-existent. You lived the perpetually ignored life of the unattractive, assumed soulless by everyone.

And yet here was surely soulless beauty, speaking to me, in what seemed to me to be a private performance. The ultimate irony: the body of disembodiment. No wonder I was sad.

But, to be truthful, I was no better. Where she didn't love, I loved too heavily. I grabbed after the sleeve once the arm had been removed. I deliberated and obsessed, while she simply offered herself up, or danced away.

Where was she now? I had simply retired from it all.

VI

I'm sure I haven't completely portrayed the sense of strangeness I felt during these days. No matter what I was doing, I thought of her. Why I wasn't more alarmed, I can't really say. I guess on some unconscious level I believed she wouldn't hurt me. It was more like being encased in a game, a personal, engaging game. Maybe on some level I'd grown to believe that when she was ready she'd reveal to me who she was.

I took to the business of earning my living, painting my walls, hanging my curtains. I planted my garden. Every act was interesting in itself, but every act was made even more interesting by the arrival of the notes.

Then something happened that changed everything:

> Jack took ahold of both of my arms from behind, gently, dick pressed against my back, while Bird fingered each nipple between a thumb and forefinger. Then Bird went for the underside of my exposed underarm, a tongue running from my forearm down through my armpit, then down across both nipples, one flick of the tongue and no longer, then started on the other arm. Then from behind, Jack pried me open like good bread while Bird entered me inch by inch. He fucked me like Miles Davis playing "All Blues" on a slow horn, and we all watched as he went deep into me. Then out. Went deep in, and

*then out. Until none of us could stand any longer, and we fell back, finishing
on the bed behind us.*

I knew this event. This was something that I remembered—
how did she do this? Was this a friend playing an elaborate hoax,
some writer I'd edited too heavily paying me back? Suddenly I felt
like I'd discovered the secret of the hoax—only a writer could pull
this off with such panache, such eloquence! Yet she (was it even a
she?) had taken it to a whole different level. The drama of the
game heightened. Yes, I still felt a touch of fear, but it was also
more delicious.

This was from an event in my own life (whom had I told?!), but
I remembered it differently. Yes, I had met Jack on a plane up to the
Bay Area from Los Angeles, long and blond with a guitar. It was the
"Midnight Flyer," an old mail run that used to fly between the two
cities at midnight. It was an hour flight for $10, no reserved seating.
You'd arrive at the airport and get into a long line of those willing
to fly that way, usually a long queue of hippies with motley packs
and parcels, bare-footed, stony-eyed, long-haired and friendly.

My seatmate (had I planned it?) turned out to be Jack. I think it
was deliberate when I looked him over, long-haired and lean in his
striped pants, and complained out loud that I had nowhere to go
that night when I got back to San Francisco.

"I'm staying at my friend Bird's house; I'm sure you're welcome to stay there."

Bird turned out to be blue-eyed with a long, thick braid down
his back. He was very happy with what Jack had brought home.

I assumed, with very little reason or provocation, that we three
would remain a family. I bought patterns and began to plan infant
nautical outfits that I would knit.

If this were the same event she was reporting, and how else—it
would be too great a coincidence to find both the same names—
her perspective certainly was different from mine.

I think I should name her. Even if I find out later who is really
doing this. Allegra. Allegra and Tristesse. That's us, the masks of the
theater, acting out some as yet ill-defined drama. I wonder if she

knows what *she's* doing. At this point, if I were only one whit less uncomfortable I'd be flattered.

As the three of us, Jack and Bird and me, roamed the hot streets of Berkeley I could tell they seemed to be wondering when I was going to leave. I felt displaced. I wondered what had happened to the family we had begun. There was no family. Allegra, whoever she was, had it right. It was very hot. It was very short. And it was a week at the most. Funny if it had just been a coincidence that she had used those names; without the eyes to see, her vision was clearer than mine.

The next one could even less have been a coincidence.

> Richard was like honey, like bluebirds, like physical music. Loving Richard was a trite set of scales strung with robin-song, airborne, a pretty, silly falling. Richard did everything perfectly. He kissed me perfectly. He knew the exact moment to push and when to pull away. When he fucked me it was like we had been schooled from the same chordbook. One kiss lasted four hundred days, contained seven lifetimes and filled and emptied our pockets with gold a hundred times over. One kiss contained every orgasm either of us would ever have. And when we finally, finally did make love two and a half centuries later, new bird species were created and all of the Lord's angels composed symphonies based on our inspiration.

I found this out on the table I keep by the pond, and I had to sit down. I felt that thin blue feeling of being about to cry, but it didn't break. I sat there feeling that way, my eyes on the verge, but never filling with tears, for a long time. I had loved Richard so much, all that Allegra had said was true, but it left out everything.

It left out that he didn't even want me to stay the night. It left out that, when I later asked him, he said that no, it hadn't really been anything special for him, his every move was practiced. It leaves out the month that followed when I couldn't look at anything beautiful and not begin to cry, with both sadness and confusion. Do you begin to understand why I require a chair now beside a pond?, why my quiet cove is my one shelter? Why I've needed so much to come to rest.

This was too uncanny. No one could have hit the names and the emotions so precisely. But instead of wondering, I found myself looking up, leaning back in my rocking chair, and not caring. I would know when I would know and that was that. Let Allegra come. I would wait.

I receive a letter. An actual letter this time, not one from Allegra. Well, hers are actual, but you know what I mean. A cousin from Paris has died. She has left me something, but I must go there to collect it. It is a necklace of Lalique beads like I once saw there in the Museum of Decorative Arts. Lalique's beads look like they have moonlight blown into the glass; no human has ever made anything so lovely. I don't seem to be able to go. I don't even seem to be able to answer the letter.

I listen to The Goldberg Variations, trying to decide which version I like the best, Andrew Rangell versus Glenn Gould, heart versus brilliance.

I sit in my window, watching the mockingbird dance on the grass. I feel split apart; maybe a new moon will sift through this opening.

I lie in bed at night: there are bats at the windows, there didn't used to be bats in the windows. I have begun to have dreams where everything is dark, just a heavy weight pressing down upon me.

Sometimes I see a whole family of finches take after a crow who has threatened their nests. They don't have a chance.

VII

I am now behaving very deliberately. Sometimes I'm near crying. Occasionally I'm not. Sometimes I'm blond in my dreams, more often I'm still me. Everything is slowly unpacked. Everything has its own place in this new house. It is furnished plainly, but with beauty. I no longer think about who is doing what. It has all become very internal. But that there is another presence here is without question.

I feel her when I sweep the floor, when I pull aside the curtain on the shower or raise the blinds. I will sometimes feel her under my step when I climb the stairs, as though if I turned around swiftly I would see her but of course I never do. Mornings before I open my eyes she's there.

I take on the grace of a woman in love. I find myself staring out the window for an hour at a time. I hum.

But at night I feel that weight, a pressure, pinning me to the ground. At night I sometimes feel a beating, a clamoring, around my head, and I pull my covers up to kill the sound of everything until I fall asleep.

VIII

Suddenly there are more notes. I can no longer work.

> *"When I first saw your face," Daniel later told me, "I wanted to cry, it was as though my mouth had been ripped from my face." I couldn't look at his hands without wanting them on my breasts. I could feel him inside me the first time I looked at him. Daniel came to me on his knees; Daniel made me hollow. He never made love to me without crying. He swallowed each leg whole, he entered me feet first. Daniel curtained his house in red so no one could see in. Daniel took me from behind. Daniel did not allow me to wear clothes except for short white stockings, curled to the knees. Daniel had a name for each of my pubic hairs. Daniel kept his head between my legs for 17 days. Daniel fucked me like 100 bears. Daniel sticks his tongue up my cunt and his fingers up my ass at the same time; I come like a wild piano stuck to an oncoming train.*
>
> *And how quickly I forgot him entirely.*

And in reality I left the country, seeing his face on every changing wave of the Mexican shore, he was the heat and the salt in the air; he was the cry in the throats of the gulls that gathered anywhere they were not wanted.

Because I had met Aliana.

How I had wanted Aliana.

How Aliana had wanted me.

IX

I decide to stop reading the notes. They intrude too much. I can't take it. They take me over. I can't quite understand why, but they keep me awash in memories of all sorts. I came here to feel safe; I came here to be away from all that, to be away from everything, I want, yes, to be alone, and she will not leave me alone. I am feeling persecuted, badgered, assailed, from within and without. Not only her constant stream of letters, now cached away in a stack in the closet, but, for some reason, an equally constant stream of memories of things I do not want to hear, over and over again: Let me be!

My parents, though they're dead, still count the ways I am unlovely, my eyes too close together, my nose too big. I take to wearing lovely clothes, growing a garden. I surround myself with beauty, train the eye away, willing others to look elsewhere, and not at me. I give them ample opportunity for loveliness, while silently I grieve, and sing, "Look at me, look at me."

When I was twelve, I went away to summer camp. Every night I dreamed about my mother, I couldn't bear to be apart from her. On the first visiting day, I made her take me home with her. How can one not reciprocate love that strong? She found her ways.

It's lost in memory now, what started it. Night after night, now, I wake up pinned to the ground. My mother is hitting me in the head, with a shoe. Then I am above the door of the room looking down, watching a savage man and woman tear at this little girl. I can remember it like it was yesterday. . . . I can see them hitting me, but I can feel not a single blow fall. It is like I am two people, an invisible one who remembers only the strike of the shoe, and myself who can remember watching.

X

When I pick up a note again, I am undone.

Pin me. It's okay, pin me. It's what I want. Please, pin me down.

Everything appears to me like it's shot through an infrared camera. Bright fuzzy green lights on a scratchy backdrop.

I look up at him, straddled across my hips, with half lowered eyes. "Fuck me, Daddy," I say. "Fuck me harder." He gets angrier and pins my wrists to the ground and my mother howls and strikes me harder and harder in my head with my sister's brand-new shoe.

You see, I can't get up. And if it's ever happened to you once, you can't get up. They give you home and shelter then pin you to the floor and you can't get up, and they're—stop! They're beating me in the head with a—can you stop?! They can't stop. They can't hear me—the shoe comes down, again and again. . . .

It's always the same—the shoe comes down again and again—and I cannot move, and then suddenly I'm lingering above the door of the room, looking at my sister still sobbing in the corner, look at my parents pinning that poor girl on the floor, savagely beating that GIRL, pinning her to the floor and beating that girl's HEAD. It's me, but it can't be. I'll never be that girl. I'll never be that girl again. I can't return. I am going to stay here forever, because if I ever go back, they will surely kill me.

Hit me daddy, hit me harder, harder daddy, hit me daddy. It gets you so nice and hard.

XI

When I look in the mirror now, I see the two of us. How lovely she is. I must give her care now, and be very gentle. I must be grateful to her; look what she took for me. I will add her to the list of what I care for. I think I'm not as smart as she is, I'll take to listening. Maybe I'll love her. I love yodeling and accordions and delphiniums and mockingbirds. I love the wind, and Earl Grey tea with milk in it. And I love you, little Allegra. Thanks for sticking around, in all your sad, glorious, and pathetic ways. You're a mess, it's true, but a mess I really need. After all, loving isn't about judging or proving anything, it's about being gentle on someone. And from now on, I'm going to be gentle on you.

Allegra and Tristesse, she calls us, time to wise up the girl. She thinks she's going to take care of me from now on, but I got news for you, honey—it's me gonna do the taking care of from now on. Get up off your ass—save that pond for later. Allegra is running the show now, girl, and kid, I ain't ready for it yet.

New York Public Library

JILL MCDONOUGH

When I woke from the last orgasm with you
there behind the open stacks
I thought I'd find your sleepy head on my breast,
    but instead
there was the library assistant just as she pressed
her left hand and forehead to my sternum
and slid her right hand in and out of my
    well-greased cunt,
her thumb, warmed up from years of flipping
    through card catalogues,
flicking my clitoris from table of contents to its very index
and back again and again and again, faster
than an accusing whisper, stronger than her grasp of
    the Dewey Decimal system,
and she was sighing "shh . . . shh . . . shh . . .
    shh . . . shh . . . "

The Story of Joe

JILL MCDONOUGH

In bed he asked me after I came he asked me
    what I thought about the
size of a cock, not his cock specifically since we
    didn't really know each
other that well, just cocks in general, since
    he'd heard recently three
inches was enough, and I said well hell who knows
    what "enough" is
'sposed to mean and I said well it's really the width
    that matters more than
the length I mean you could be long-but-slim and
    I couldn't feel you but
you could be three inches by three inches and make quite an
impression. And he said what do you mean you
    couldn't feel it I mean
maybe the cock's not too small, maybe you're too big,
    and I said sure,
maybe, but I can squeeze, and he said really and I said
    yeah here put
your fingers inside me and he did, he put his fingers
    inside me and
pushed up without hesitating or questioning and my
    head slipped back
and my mouth opened and I squeezed and bit my lip
    and his eyes got
wider and I said that's why I like you, because you
    just do what I tell you
when I tell you. Oh he said you like me because
    I'm subservient and he
kept moving his hand inside me and we were quiet
    and I said yes I said
yes that's what I like.

On the River Road

ROBERT WRIGLEY

The full moon newly risen made the skin
of the river real, every wave
a dark, continual tongue. Ten miles from town
we still kept the truck windows down,
the wind through them breath warm
and redolent with a high summer musk.
Lit so clearly, that narrow, treacherous road
nearly lulled me to sleep. How else can I explain
her sudden nakedness beside me,
how she guided my right, shiftless hand
between her legs to awaken there,
wind warm and river wet?
I could not take my eyes off the road,
off the swell of her breasts pushed in
and up by her arms. She had my hand
in both of hers, her two middle fingers on mine
making it her tool, her half-possessed appendage.
For miles I drove that way,
the summer air awash with her scent,
—the truck's cab lush with it and calling
all the night-prowling animals in our wake,
until she came and we came
to the bridge for home, where she let me stop
the truck but not move—middle of the span,
middle of the river—until she had kissed dry
my hand, each finger knuckle by knuckle sucked,
when she placed my twice-anointed right hand
on the back of the seat and turned,
in the light from the moon and the tick
of the engine growing cool,
her full attention to what was left.

Post Coital

JOAN LOGGHE

All day post coital, you reverberate
both man and woman. Even our therapist
says you look handsome. I'll name you
Mr. Deluxe, which means of good quality.

I'm storing up for winter. There's
always another winter and an Egypt.
Tear out the raspberries, the Pyracantha,
the goat's heads, the locust, the rose.

anything with thorns. Last night half
a white moon planted asters, half
a dark moon sobbed. I came from coal dust.
You came from milk. We met in Chicago.

Even Kaballah has a place for your leg
a place for my leg, rungs of the same ladder,
branches of the same tree. We were flying up
all night and we were climbing down.

We held hours before action, it was less
Italian and more Viennese, that is to say
waltz and not tarantella. My mother met
Your father and flirted. Your mother baked

a pie for my father. All night was a washing
as if the leaves cleansed with rain before
a meal. I only saw you once since morning.
You said my lipstick accentuates chamisa.

Your head is still on my breast. My hand
around you. Throb is a word more autumnal today.
Aspens throb as much as quake. Hearts vibrate.
Seasons migrate like geese or grown children.

If I weren't so happy I'd be forlorn.
Like her eyes under the word divorce.
I'll go there with widows and divorcees
and men with AIDS avoiding Fire Island.

The Dalai Lama has never felt this. I have
no system for this loving, except the four
seasons and the four chambers of the heart,
the four emotions: joy, fear, sadness, and pity.

Grace of last light on roadside wildflowers.
Graves at the Jewish cemetery need tending.
My own grave, an image on your chest.
the miraculous shroud where my face stains your shirt.

Pushing Me into the Past

RICHARD ZIMLER

Someone to teach. . . . I didn't know it, but I think what I was really looking for when I returned to Europe was a man or a boy with an open heart and mind, who wanted to learn. And yes, I admit it; I was probably looking for an open mouth and rear end, too, if they offered me the most direct route to his brain. And I wanted someone who could teach me, too, because I think I'd learned all the wrong things when I was young and needed to unlearn them.

So I began to instruct António in the ways of the guitar. António, who's got the crystalline hazel eyes of a cat and who leaves a line of whiskers below his nose because he fears slicing off a nostril.

Keys always jangling as he lopes down the street.

Tight jeans contouring thighs made muscular by soccer and gymnastics. His hands tucked into his front pockets.

Thick white socks that soak up his boy-sweat until they stink like garbage.

Curly, dirty blond hair.

Sitting at my feet and begging me to read anything in English to him *just for the sound of it*.

Biting his cuticles.

Teaching me Portuguese curse words like *piça, pito, cona, cabra* while rolling on the ground at my grotesque pronunciation.

Asking waiters about the vintage of the Coca-Colas which I order at dinner so that they'll smile and we can laugh together.

Hopping on and off curbs downtown.

A nest of brown hairs at the center of his chest which is the best place to tickle him and make him fight you and then kiss you as deep as he can.

Nipples rimmed with a circle of delicious blond hairs which I once trimmed and then placed in an envelope marked, António's Nipple Hair, October 22, and which I've kept under my pillow of late to remind me that there is someone alive who has learned something good from me and who needs my help.

Memorizing new pieces so fast that I wonder if he isn't an alien in human form.

Concerts he hopes to give in Carnegie Hall and the Paris Opera and even the Antas Stadium in Porto before a soccer match between the home-town team and its Lisbon rival.

António, who will be famous and honored and warmed by the kindness of strangers if . . .

When he entered the practice room for his audition with me, I knew none of this, of course. I had no idea that he would help me regain some sort of purpose in life. Although I knew right away that he was gay. He sniffed me out, too. We exchanged that needful vampire stare that is the natural handshake of our kind, and then he looked down and away toward safety. His hair was cut so close to his scalp that he looked like an army recruit ashamed of the soft halo it might give to his face.

As I say, he was wearing his ever-present jeans and ratty leather jacket when he came for his audition. There was no doubt in either of our minds that he was horny and willing, but I hadn't traveled nine time zones from Los Angeles to Portugal to wind up with a fledgling surfer boy looking for an excuse to come out, who'd then run off at the first sight of a perfect wave curling over the shore. Besides, I'd always considered students off limits. So I didn't think we'd ever share the same pillow.

I was also still afraid of venturing forth into the sexual world after two years of right-hand pogo sticking.

Nevertheless, I desperately wanted to slip my tongue into his mouth and lick all the way to his brain.

He fixed me with the stare of a sweet but hard-edged boy wondering if he'll get serviced by an older man. In a language which approximated English, he said, "What do you want that I play, Professor?"

"Anything," I answered.

"I no understand."

"Play anything you like that takes less than five minutes and which isn't too loud. And please, nothing Spanish. I just got here from Spain and if I hear another mock bullfight for guitar I'll throw up."

Sweat beaded on my prince's forehead. He took off his jacket, folded it, and placed it on the ground by his chair. In those gestures, I saw years of his mother nagging him to clean up after himself.

He was wearing a neatly ironed white shirt. He leaned over to take his guitar from its case and lifted it onto his lap. It looked like it was made of balsa wood and purchased at the Toys-R-Us across the river from Porto in Gaia. The action on it was terrible; the strings were a centimeter from the frets. It was going to sound like a ukulele. He took a deep breath, as if he were preparing to swim a 100-meter freestyle. He sat up very erect.

As his hands took their positions, he flashed a self-conscious smile intended as a disclaimer for what was to come and said, "Me nervous."

"Me Tarzan, you Jane," I replied.

"What?"

I smiled. "Everything's going to be okay. Just play."

"Me very nervous."

"Let's just see what happens. Come on. Don't panic, just go ahead."

He stared at me as if I were expected to say something which would take away all his anxiety. When I didn't, his eyes grew glassy. I leaned back in my chair and folded my arms. I looked away. Amazing that I didn't realize just how important this audition was to him.

He wiped his nose with the back of his hand. I coughed.

Finally, he started to play the first Gavotte from Bach's Sixth Cello Suite. It was excruciating; his right hand fingered the tinny strings of his Toys-R-Us ukulele as if he were plucking out feathers from a turkey's ass. I nodded for him to go on out of perverse curiosity and a need to ruin someone's day. But António, God bless him, actually settled down. Considering the quality of his instrument, he played with admirable technique. And, more importantly, he put notes together into recognizable phrases and never lost his tempo.

"Enough!" I suddenly shouted.

He looked up at me. I frowned at him. Tears welled in his eyes.

I watched the water caught in his lashes and thought of my brother saying good-bye to me. "Put that toy guitar down!" I ordered.

He placed it atop his jacket.

I was free to say what I wanted since he wouldn't understand the more complicated English words: "Now get up, you little beast!"

He sat there gaping.

"Up, you beast." I raised my hands like a lion tamer. "Stand up!"

He stood. He wiped his eyes and his nose. I walked to him, took his cold hands in mine and squeezed them. "You've always thought that these were just the mittens of a little boy from Portugal," I said. "But these are the magic wands of a sorcerer. Why? Because they can summon the music of Bach across two centuries. When they touch the strings of a guitar, we can hear the composer thinking in his study in Leipzig and writing down the notes as quick as bunnies humping one another in their lairs. Can you see him there with his feverish quill?"

"Me no understand," he said.

I undid a button on my shirt and put his hand against the brown fur over my heart. "You feel that, my prince? Can you feel my faulty metronome?"

He started to breathe long and heavy, like he might faint. He nodded as best he could.

Our faces were only a foot apart. I said, "When you can feel Bach's heart, you will be playing this piece correctly. You understand?"

Of course, what I was saying was crap. But it was my performance which counted.

He nodded again. Gay kids have no resistance for affection from even moderately attractive older men, so I gave him a bear hug. At first he stiffened, but then he hugged me back and melted into my arms.

Never let it be said that I take advantage of a desperate little boy, however; before it could go any further, I pushed him away and held him at arms' length. "If you're going to study with me, you've got to know something—I'm an asshole." He didn't understand. "Me asshole," I said, pointing to myself.

"Asshole?"

I didn't yet know that *chato* would have been a good translation, but I knew the words for "crazy whore" and figured that that would suffice for now. In point of fact, of course, it was more accurate. "Me *puta louca*," I explained.

He laughed, then gave a big sigh.

"Watch . . ." I said, and I pointed to his toy guitar. "This is shit, pure *merda!*" I stepped on top of the damn thing. Strings groaned and snapped, wood splintered. I crushed the life out of it. António gasped and gaped. I handed him my guitar. "This, on the contrary, my little prince, is not shit. This good guitar. Good guitar." I petted its neck as he held it, then took his hand and made him stroke the deep contour by its sound hole. "One must be gentle. Treat it like you were playing with yourself on a warm beach." I made a motion with my hand imitating masturbation. "Like you are abusing yourself. Your cock may be hard, but it's fragile all the same. Take it easy." I sat down. "Now start playing again. And try not to pick at turkey feathers with your right hand."

He launched into the Gavotte. After a while, I stopped him because I realized that the biggest problem we were going to have was his inability to listen to the notes as he played them; everything was too disconnected, too staccato.

"Sing it!" I ordered.

"Sing what?"

"The Gavotte . . . the melody."

"The melody?"

"Just do what I say."

He sang like a prissy Lisbon faggot afraid to wake his granny up from her siesta. I ordered him to shut his trap. I sang for him, angrily, from my belly, linking all the notes together as if I were trying to forge them into a chain around his wrists. When I came to the end of the first long phrase, I said, "Now you sing like that."

Like most of you pitiful Portuguese, the boy was embarrassed to actually express himself. He acted as if his voice were trapped like a nasty little raisin at the very top of his throat. It was going to take some time to get him to listen to the music he produced. Was it worth my trouble? As he stared at me, I began to finally see in the clarity of his pale green eyes how much he wanted to study; I'm a thick son-of-a-bitch when I'm angry and horny at the same time.

"Where did you study before?" I asked him.

"I teach myself," he answered.

"How long ago did you start?"

"There are two years. Before that also . . . also . . ." His English faded to frustrated silence.

"And how well do you read music?"

"I no read music."

"What are you telling me?"

"I no to read music," he said emphatically.

"Then how did you learn the Gavotte?"

"From the *disks*." He pointed to his ear. "I play what here enter."

"You hear all the notes you played?"

"Yes."

If that were true, then he had a one-in-a-million ear. I got that tingle in my backside I get when I meet someone really talented or handsome. "Are you fucking with my head?!" I demanded.

"I no understand."

"How old are you?"

"Twenty-one."

"Most students enter here when they're eighteen. How come you waited?"

"I work with my father. We no money."

"So tell me why you want to study music."

He shrugged. "I want . . . I like. I no know." He licked his lips nervously, and his frightened eyes followed me as I put my guitar back in its case. "May I study with you?" he chirped suddenly.

"The audition isn't over," I said. "I want you to come home with me."

"Home?"

"Yeah. To my apartment, *meu apartamento*."

"Now?"

"Don't worry. No fucking." I made a hoop with my left thumb and index finger and stuck my right middle finger through it. I spoke like Boris Badinov: "Teacher and student no screw. Just music." I pulled him to his feet and put my hand up against his chest to feel his heartbeat. I rubbed his pectoral muscles and slapped his belly. "I crazy whore. Not you. You prince . . . dirty blond prince. You do nothing you no want to do. I no be mean to you. But I no promises make because I big crazy whore. And you . . . you try never to hurt me on purpose. Okay?"

He didn't know what I was talking about, but he said, "Okay."

"What my guitar?" he asked.

"I've got an extra guitar at home. You'll use that for now. Now step on yours once more for good luck. Crush it good!"

"Now?" he asked. When I nodded, he jumped on top of it and grimaced comically, like he'd done something delightfully naughty he was hoping nobody would notice.

We took a taxi to my house. He sat stiffly next to me like I might bite. I complained about cod fish and unreliable people and traffic jams. He nodded and kept his hands trapped between his legs. Once inside my apartment, I cleared a space for him on the couch by tossing Fiama's laundry onto her bed. Then I put on Edith Piaf records, one after another: *L'Accordioniste, Milord, La Vie on Rose, Les Trois Cloches* . . . Piaf's not a great technical singer, of course, but she's got vibrato that kills entire orchestras and legato which strings the words of her songs into the most lovely rusted iron chains. António had to learn the meaning of vibrato and legato right away or we'd never get anywhere. He sat with his hands still locked between his legs without saying a word, however, like he was an anxious little boy freezing to death outside his parents' house. I didn't want to watch him and looked out the window. Finally, when we'd had enough examples, I knelt next to him and said: "I want you to sing any song you know, but sing it as if you were Piaf. You understand?" I demonstrated with the chorus of "Just Like a Prayer," your favorite Madonna song, Carlos. Remember?

"Now you," I said.

"Same song?"

"Anything."

António took his hands from between his legs and braced them on his knees. His eyes closed. He sang the Portuguese national anthem. He had a lovely voice, a masculine voice buried deep in his gut, a voice far beyond his years.

"That was great," I said. I caressed his cheek, and his eyes opened wide. "Very good," I said. I was strangely excited and was thinking that maybe I was so happy only because I wanted to sniff his every crevice in bed and obviously had him seduced. I hadn't yet realized that something more was happening. I picked up my guitar and played the first eight melody notes to *Les Trois Cloches* with overdone vibrato, then sang it the same way so he'd see the connection: *Village, au fond de la vallée* . . . I told him that vibrato is not just an embellishment but serves to keep the true pitch of a note. He nodded. "And no space between the notes," I emphasized with my index finger wagging. "No space, because space *mucho* bad. Now, you do it." I handed him my guitar.

António had heard *Les Trois Cloches* only once, but could play all the melody notes in tempo without a single error.

Do you know how unusual that is, Carlos?

He has the best sense of pitch of anyone I've ever met. He's one in a million.

As he played, I showed him how to relax his left wrist and jiggle it to create the proper vibrato. I cajoled and yelled and pleaded. He took deep breaths to steady himself. After a half-hour, he was doing well.

While I fetched some wine from the kitchen to celebrate, he played *Les Trois Cloches* and added harmonized bass notes. I thought: *hee hee! He's a natural. He's got more talent than anyone I've ever met. And he's a fucking vampire, just like me!!!*

As I walked back in with the bottle and two champagne flutes, I said, "Now stand and sing the 'Gavotte' again."

António placed his feet apart like he was bracing for a blow. I licked my lips.

The boy channeled the Gavotte up from his balls into his chest and through his mouth. He was so proud of himself and so abandoned to the melody and now had such a nice semi-hard erection down the leg of his pants that I loved him as much as I could just then and even felt tears of pride knotted in my throat. I closed my eyes. Behind the darkness of my eyelids, I was standing at a train station watching everyone at whose deathbed I'd sat depart across an impassable checkpoint. I was the lone survivor. *I'm alive,* I was thinking, *and I've met a boy with greatness in his fingers!* It was the contrast that made me both sad and happy; here I was, left behind but listening to the sweet voice of a Portuguese youth who hadn't seen anybody he loved die yet and who had his whole future ahead of him. When he finished, I told him he'd learned well, then gave him his wine. "To António, who will know greatness," I toasted.

He smiled shyly. We sipped our wine. We stood there eyeing each other like two acrobats before a performance. We were wondering if we could trust each other without a net below. I said, "If I don't take the leap I'm going to explode."

He stared at me and sipped his wine.

"We have to do it before you become my official student," I explained. "We won't be able to do it afterwards."

He kept staring.

"Take a sip of wine, but keep the liquid in your mouth," I told him.

He did as I asked. I walked up to him and placed my chest against his chest and put my hands on his ass. I kissed him and took the liquid from his mouth. He moaned as if he were hurt. His cock swelled against me. I pulled away from him. His eyes were open and frightened. "You're a muscular little beast," I said.

After that, we simply *devoured* each other. There's no other word that could express our sexual hunger. In the living room, he opened my corduroys and fell to his knees. He groaned like he was being beaten. He licked and mouthed and nipped at me as if he were a slave trained from the age of two for this one activity.

A natural, I thought to myself again.

I rubbed his hair and caressed his shoulders and fell over his back like a cape as I came.

Yes, Carlos, he did what you always felt was disgusting and swallowed my offering. Greedily, I should add.

I freed him from his clothes and saw he'd concealed a dark cucumber with a blooming purple flower in his pants. "Lovely," I said in admiration. "Where'd you get it?"

"She is too big?" he asked.

"She is just fine," I replied. "And neither rain nor sleet nor snow shall keep me from my appointed rounds."

I did the best I could with my mammalian, unhingeable jaw, gagged a few times, but didn't give up; I wanted him to free himself in my mouth because I knew it would be over quick and the second time I wanted him to take me from behind and wanted him to be able to hold out for a good long while. Turns out, the kid had more bitter seed than could be stored in any normal set of balls. He grimaced in pain as he shot himself out. I kissed his neck, nuzzled around his underarms, told him he was beautiful.

After a minute, he started to groan again and breathe deeply. The magic latex of a young man's soul was rising between my hands, and I was holding a divining rod searching for a long-lost spring.

It hurt the boy to get hard again so soon, but we were too excited to stop.

Maybe we were both figuring that for the grand prize of an American rear end with a master's degree from the Manhattan School of Music he had to endure just a little pain.

I slipped a condom over him. "Please fuck me," I said.

But my poor behind was so tight from maybe five years without being sodomized by anything other than a green banana once in a moment of mad desperation inspired by ouzo and an old James Bond movie that it was knotted like an old pair of shoelaces. I had to pry my opening apart with my own forefinger and thumb, then lubricate it with K-Y jelly a half-dozen times to get a third finger in. Then and only then could we get him a little ways inside me. He had to pull out right away, because it felt like a big fat spiny lizard was trying to crawl up my bowel and make an unwelcome home in my stomach. I kept cursing as I pried myself bigger and bigger with my fingers because it was taking so long to loosen me up. António thought I was mad at him and began to go soft. "Not you!" I shouted. "Not you, my dirty blond prince. Me, the *puta louca* is angry at *himself!*"

But I should've had more confidence in myself; another ten minutes and we had his bloom, if not stem, safely inside me. He was squatting behind me, panting with panic and lust, and he didn't know what to do. I told him, "Now, push slowly forward. Not too fast or you'll have to clean up my bowels and a lot of blood. And then the police will come and ask a lot of inconvenient questions about how you killed the American professor without any weapon in sight."

I tugged on his buttocks so he'd know to move forward. Slowly, the spiny lizard started to make its way toward my gut. He was splitting me open, and the pain made me go limp, but now getting him inside me was a question of personal pride—like soldiers taking a hill that is of no value in itself but means everything for morale. Finally, the damn thing was all the way in—flower, stem, leaves and roots. I slid forward onto the bed and took him down on top of me. "Just stay still!" I ordered.

He was nervous that he'd hurt me, and I could feel him going limp.

"I'll kill you if you go soft on me!" I told him. "Start thrusting when you want."

After he took me from behind, I flipped over on my back and put my legs over his shoulders. It was like being cleaved in half, and each thrust of his powerful hips took me back into a past before HIV, when you could let yourself be swept out to sea on sex and give yourself to Neptune and not expect to get beached on a desert island where you were going to waste away toward death. Fuck me! I kept shouting at him. Fuck me, my prince.

And like the sweet kid he was, he obliged.

I sobbed afterward. Like I hadn't cried in years. António's face grew white with fear. I caressed his cheek. I kissed all his fingers and inhaled their delicious scent of tobacco and shit. "Don't worry," I told him. "I'd forgotten that sex was like this . . . long ago and far away, when touching a man could help you heal all your wounds." I placed his hands over my closed eyes. "You haven't hurt me," I assured him. "You've just pushed me a bit into the past."

Rapture

GALWAY KINNELL

I can feel she has got out of bed.
That means it is seven A.M.
I have been lying with eyes shut,
thinking, or possibly dreaming,
of how she might look if, at breakfast,
I spoke about the hidden place in her
which, to me, is like a soprano's tremolo,
and right then, over toast and bramble jelly,
if such things are possible, she came.

I imagine she would show it while trying to conceal it.
I imagine her hair would fall about her face
and she would become apparently downcast,
as she does at a concert when she is moved.
The hypnopompic play passes, and I open my eyes
and there she is, next to the bed,
bending to a low drawer, picking over
various small smooth black, white,
and pink items of underwear. She bends
so low her back runs parallel to the earth,
but there is no sway in it, there is little burden, the day has
    hardly begun.
The two mounds of muscles for walking, leaping,
    lovemaking,
lift toward the east—what can I say?
Simile is useless; there is nothing like them on earth.
Her breasts fall full; the nipples
are deep pink in the glare shining up through the iron bars
of the gate under the earth where those
    who could not love
press, wanting to be born again.
I reach out and take her wrist
and she falls back into bed and at once starts unbuttoning
    my pajamas.
Later, when I open my eyes, there she is again,
rummaging in the same low drawer.
The clock shows eight. Hmmm.
With huge, silent effort of great,
mounded muscles the earth has been turning.
She takes a piece of silken cloth
from the drawer and stands up. Under the falls
of hair her face has become quiet and downcast,
as if she will be, all day among strangers,
looking down inside herself at our rapture.

Telephoning in Mexican Sunlight

GALWAY KINNELL

Talking with my beloved in New York
I stood at the outdoor public telephone
in Mexican sunlight, in my purple shirt.
Someone had called it a man/woman
shirt. The phrase irked me. But then
I remembered that Rainer Maria
Rilke, who until he was seven wore
dresses and had long yellow hair,
wrote that the girl he almost was
"made her bed in my ear" and "slept me the world."
I thought, OK this shirt will clothe the other in me.
As we fell into long-distance love talk
a squeaky chittering started up all around,
and every few seconds came a sudden loud
buzzing. I half expected to find
the insulation on the telephone line
laid open under the pressure of our talk
leaking low-frequency noises.
But a few yards away a dozen hummingbirds,
gorgets going drab or blazing
according as the sun struck them,
stood on their tail rudders in a circle
around my head, transfixed
by the flower-likeness of the shirt.
And perhaps also by a flush rising into my face,
for a word—one with a thick sound,
as if a porous vowel had sat soaking up
saliva while waiting to get spoken,
possibly the name of some flower
that hummingbirds love, perhaps
"honeysuckle" or "hollyhock"
or "phlox"—just then shocked me

with its suddenness, and this time
apparently did burst the insulation,
letting the word sound in the open
where all could hear, for these tiny, irascible,
nectar-addicted puritans jumped back
all at once, fast, as if the air gasped.

Sailing

STEVE MILES

I stand and you climb me,
my hands cradled
under your buttocks,
your feet curled behind
my calves, my eyes on yours,
yours somewhere behind mine
as my back fills like a stretched sail
and the taut shrouds hum
in the pitching sea;
the hull of your spine
bows into the depths
as my fingers open the shape
of a wake above my hips
that scoop and revolve,
forearms lift you
into the crow's nest
then settle you down
around my sex, and your fluid
lips leave no skin untouched,
washing me clean
of sand and scales

and leaving me shining
with blood and quicksilver
and the waves of salt-edged
cries from your mouth,
your breath and breasts
luffing and tightening,
as your eyes fly open
for the first time ever,
startled as a netted fish,
shivers rolling down
as you gasp through clavicles,
ribs suck air like roseate
gills and I dig in deep,
but the wind from your heart
gusts through mine
and fills my back and
the keel cuts toward you
and my sail pulls over
in the windward whorl,
and the mizzen-mast dives
fully into the choppy
sea of green.

Springtime

JESÚS GARDEA, TRANSLATION BY MARK SCHAFER

We leave the room. The yard burns in the afternoon light. The sun
floods the porch and lights up a wicker armchair, the only piece of
furniture left outside. I don't see plants anywhere, not even the
trace of old flowerpots on the floor tiles. The porch is shaped like a
half moon, closed off in front of me by a very high wall that has

almost lost its ochre color. At the foot of the wall is a small pile of bricks. I feel the woman next to me following my gaze. I don't hear her breathing, but rather the subtle dialogue of her spirit with everything that moves through the air. It's as if the air were burnishing the mast of a small, secret boat anchored to her breast. That's what our dreams must sound like. Perhaps the pile of bricks was once a fountain for children and birds, I think to myself. I saw a fountain like that once but I can't say where.

The woman waits for my eyes to return to where we began, the solitary armchair, and says to me:

"It wasn't always as neglected as it is now. We've left it here to be consumed by the indifference of the seasons, but it resists. My mother asks about it every morning. My father, Artemio, sat there with her on his lap, caressing her thighs and breasts until he drove her wild. It will be forty years now."

The woman half-closes her eyes. She is beautiful, even in the dress she has on which spoils her figure. It is her mother's notion that she dress in black and wear high collars. I don't understand how she puts up with the double cage in which she lives: her dress and the bedroom of her mother who is slowly returning to dust.

The elderly woman's room stinks of potions from the turn of the century. While the daughter told her about me, I looked at the shelf where large cups inscribed with golden letters stood. There, as in so many places, the world was rotting away behind closed doors. I suddenly hated the old woman and imagined throwing her onto the porch to die under the sun, drowned at last in the fresh air. If it hadn't been for the daughter who announced that we were about to leave, I would have satisfied my desire.

When the daughter opened the bedroom door, her mother said, in an extraordinarily clear voice: "Artemio was my joy and my flame."

Despite the intense April sun which sears us, the woman and I do not seek the shade. My clothes start to give off the same odor I smelled in the sick woman's room. Feeling uncomfortable, I look at the woman again. But she seems unaware of the rank smell. She is still looking at the armchair. I discover her quiet skin, dark like aging wine.

"You can gather its quality," she says, referring to the piece of furniture, "by what it has withstood."

A woman like this almost inevitably has down on her upper lip. One whose imagination is in love with the things of this world might take that as indicating a lively temperament. One whose imagination is like mine.

"How long did you say the armchair has been outdoors?" I ask her, feigning interest.

"I already told you," she answers. "Forty springs."

The down is blonde like the wicker. Along its edge lies a string of tiny, iridescent pearls of sweat. I would gladly wipe them off with my index finger, letting it linger on the rim of her perfect lip, there to arouse her to love.

"But ma'am, have you examined it carefully?" I ask her again. "Because often with this kind of furniture, it looks solid to the eye but then collapses under the weight of a fly."

Without saying a word, the woman walks over to the armchair and plops herself down in it, bottom first. Her bust trembles as if shaken by an explosion. I think of two doves, unexpectedly powerful. The woman and I look at each other for a good long while. She searches my face for the impact of what she has just done. I am tempted to give her what she desires: to gape like a fool, eyes and mouth wide open, but I won't. She might interpret this as meaning I agree the armchair is in fact worth a fortune. I'm even afraid to blink too much. Business is business. I can't forget that. Though her next glance devastates me, I will stick to the subject at hand. There is one thing, however, I hasten to admit: the woman has grown more beautiful. She is radiant. Immutable, she is graced by the afternoon sun. She shifts her legs under her dress, crossing them lazily. She doesn't take her eyes off me, the antique buyer. I never wear my tie to a sale, least of all when it's hot. I must look in pretty sorry shape.

No, the woman is not thinking about business. She's waiting for me to loosen the knot of my tie and escape the stifling enclosure that is paralyzing me. She pities me. The knot is thick, large as a fruit. My fingers probe it incredulously, burned by the silk whose color I can't remember. Feeling as though I were in a nightmare, I start to take my tie off then and there. It remains a mystery to me why I put the tie on that day and not on any other. The monstrosity of the knot is obvious: lack of expertise in using such articles of clothing.

The woman yawns. It makes sense. Just before we entered her mother's room (she had to ask her permission to sell the chair and furthermore to present her with the buyer), the woman asked that we resolve the matter quickly because she took a nap in the afternoon.

At last I free the damp tie from my stiff collar. The woman has closed her eyes and is nodding off. Weighed down by the sun, I belatedly seek the shade of one of the porch columns, one by the armchair.

The woman is already asleep, making tiny noises with her lips, her legs still crossed. I decide to let her sleep.

I will contemplate her to my heart's content from the shade and then I will go.

So great is the silence surrounding us that I can almost hear the sun crackling in the sky.

I notice that my clothes no longer stink. My cologne and skin lotion are emerging again, very tentatively, to assist the shadows in their beneficial work.

The rays of sunlight do nothing to alter the golden brown of the woman's face. In fact, she doesn't even sweat, except for her upper lip. She sleeps with her face turned to one side, revealing a small ear and, at the nape of her neck, part of her hairline. Naked, this woman would surely blind anyone who looked at her.

I will buy the armchair from her but will tell her that she can continue to use it whenever she wishes, since that is where she receives grace.

"I live by night," she told me in front of her mother, "listening to the passion of my father, Artemio: love, according to the flesh."

The shadow of the wall begins to fall and fill the yard.

I walk very softly over to the armchair and place my open hand on one of the woman's breasts. I am trembling; I don't know what's going to happen. I see the woman half-open her eyes, foggy with sleep. Then she puts her hand on mine and says:

"Come back tomorrow, but early. I will have to present you to my mother again."

Tell Me What it is

EDWARD FALCO

Ten steps back behind a pair of blue tents pitched side-by-side under thick trees on Cape Flattery, the ground ended abruptly at a thirty-foot vertical fall to the Pacific Ocean. A campfire in front of the tents had burned down to red embers. Alongside the fire, two card tables pushed together made one longer table topped with a battery-operated fluorescent lamp and a bright yellow plastic game board and crisp black tiles. Enclosed in the circle of light emanating from the lamp, two couples seated in folding chairs around the card tables were deep into a session of Acquire, a board game involving the placement of randomly selected tiles on a numbered grid. The tiles formed companies in which the players bought stock and either gained or lost money as their companies merged and grew or were taken over and disappeared. It was Barrett's turn to move and he had been staring intently at the board for several minutes. In the intense quiet of his concentration, the others listened to water lapping at boulders and rushing through sea caves that lined the shore below them.

Finally Barbara said, "For God's sake, Barrett, will you just merge Worldwide and end my misery?" She didn't have any stock in Worldwide and was almost out of money. If Worldwide were merged she'd be out of the game.

Barrett said, "What makes you think I have the merging tile?"

"Oh, please!" Barbara shouted.

Adam said, "Here they go." Adam and Adele were the second couple. Adam and Adele. Barrett and Barbara. They lived in adjacent apartments in Manhattan, and they referred to themselves as the alphabet couples, because of the unfortunate alliteration of their names—or sometimes they called themselves the As and the Bs, as in "Barrett, see what the As are doing tonight," or "Adam, see if the Bs want to come over for a drink." Adam owned The Body Works, a physical fitness center, and Barrett acted in "Days of Our Lives," an unending daytime soap opera. They were on vacation now, camping a few days on Cape Flattery, which was part of the Makah reservation.

"Do you think I'm an idiot? Do you think we're all stupid?" Barbara put her elbows up on the table and leaned toward Barrett. She was a woman in her early fifties who looked twenty years younger, easily. Some of her youthful appearance came from the fortune she spent on skin-care products and minor cosmetic surgery, and some of it was genetic. In any case, she looked good. Her naturally sandy blond hair was dyed a brighter blond, and it contrasted strikingly with her pale green eyes. She wore jeans and a sheer green blouse that showed off the shapeliness of her breasts. All of her beauty, natural and purchased, was at that moment however swallowed up by the anger that surfaced in her face. She shouted: "You've been buying stock in Worldwide for the last three rounds! You don't think we know you have the merger? You either think we're all idiots, or else you're an idiot for buying the stock!"

Adele laughed and said, "You guys. . . ."

Barrett placed the merging tile on the board. "Okay," he said. "Worldwide comes down." He smiled broadly at Barbara, his white teeth catching the lamplight. "Bye-bye, Barbara," he said, and he laughed out loud.

"You love it," Barbara pushed her chair back from the table. "Anything that screws me, you love."

Adam said, "Talking about screwing you, Barbara . . . "

Adele reached across the table and slapped him playfully on the head.

"Yes?" Barbara said, perking up. She leaned seductively toward Adam.

Barrett said, "Let's do the merger first. Then you can talk about screwing my wife."

"Okay," Adam said. He pulled the bank toward him and began counting out money.

Barbara said, "I'm hot." For weeks now the Olympic Peninsula had been hot and dry—weather conditions almost unheard of in the region. She stretched, extending her arms over her head and pointing her fingertips to the sky. Her blouse rode up on her stomach. "I'm going to go take this thing off," she said, referring to the blouse, and she walked away from the table. As she bent to enter her domed tent, she pulled the blouse off, revealing a bare back and a quick flash of her breasts swaying in the pale outer reach of the lamp light.

Barrett said: "Too bad, Adam. You missed it."

From inside the tent, Barbara answered: "Go to hell, Barrett."

"What?" Adam looked up from a stack of hundreds. "What did I miss?"

"What did she do?" Adele said to Barrett.

Adele and Adam were a much younger couple than Barrett and Barbara, younger by more than twenty years. Adam had met Adele at The Body Works, where she had started working out at age thirty-two, when her daughter turned thirteen, entered junior high school, and started living behind a locked bedroom door. Her fourteen-year-old son had been living behind locked doors since he had entered teenagedom some twelve months earlier. Adele couldn't blame either of them. She and her then-husband bickered constantly. Their principal forms of communication were the jibe and the insult. Adam, at thirty-four, was also married at the time, also with two teenagers. When he saw Adele, the first thing he noticed was her body—which was worth dying for, and which no one would ever believe had been through the wrenching changes of childbirth. Seeing her in a blue and red Spandex exercise outfit that clung to her like brightly colored skin, he offered immediately to be her personal fitness counselor. A year and two months later they were both divorced and remarried to each other.

Barrett said to Adele, matter-of-factly: "She pulled her blouse off before she got in the tent."

Adele turned to Adam. "And you missed it, honey," she said, her voice dripping mock sympathy.

"Damn . . ." Adam handed Barrett a pile of pink thousand-dollar bills and pale-yellow hundreds. "Why didn't you nudge me?"

Barrett sorted out the money and placed it in neat stacks next to his black tiles. "Haven't you seen her tits before?" he said.

"No!" Adam said, petulantly. "I haven't. And I don't think it's fair. After all, you've seen Adele's."

Barrett and Adele laughed. Barbara came out of the tent wearing a bikini top. "Shall I strip?" she asked Adam. "Shall we even it up?"

"Absolutely!" Adam said. He pounded his fist on the table, making the tiles on the game board bounce.

"Hey!" Barrett said. "You're messing up the game."

"I'm sorry," Adam said. He pouted, sticking out his bottom lip.

Barbara sat down at the table. "You first," she said to Adam.

"I can't," he said. "I have a very small penis."

Adele laughed out loud, and Adam and Barbara laughed in reaction to her. Barrett just shook his head.

"I've heard about that," Barbara said. "Adele's told me all about it."

Adam grinned wickedly.

Barbara said to Barrett, "You saw, didn't you? Are the rumors true?"

"Like a horse," Barrett said. Barbara was referring to that morning, when Barrett had found Adam and Adele bathing in a tidal pool under a stone arch. He had applauded their naked bodies. Adam had looked taken aback for a moment. He had looked toward Adele, as if he might want to cover her. Adele, however, had appeared unconcerned, and Adam had wound up clowning as usual, doing muscleman poses before Barrett turned and walked on. Now Barrett slapped Adam on the back. "Like a damn stallion!" he added.

"Absolutely," Adam said. He touched one of his tiles and seemed to hesitate for an instant. Then he said: "Why don't we all go skinny-dipping?" He looked up at the sky, at a full moon that was about to disappear behind a long line of clouds.

"Fine with me," Adele said. "I love getting naked in the ocean."

"Are you two serious?" Barbara said.

"Sure," Adam said. "This is an Indian reservation, isn't it? Didn't the Indians used to bathe in the ocean?"

Barrett said, "I'm sure the Makah people bathed in the ocean—a hundred years ago, anyway."

"I'll do it," Barbara said. "Except the water's probably still cold—even with all this heat."

At fifty-six, Barrett was the oldest member of the group. He had been married three times before Barbara, and he had one child from each of those previous marriages. His youngest child, a daughter, was in her mid-twenties. He was still an attractive man, but his attractiveness didn't come from being in superb physical condition, as it did for Barbara, Adele, and Adam. Barrett's attractiveness was in his face, which was weathered and leathery, and in his eyes, which suggested an inner intensity. It was a look which many women over the years had found appealing. Women found his size appealing too. He was six-one, two hundred and twenty pounds. He looked up at the others and said, "You guys go. I'm too old and fat."

Barbara said, gesturing toward Adam: "You'd let your new bride go skinny-dipping with this sex fiend?" Barbara and Barrett had been married less than a year.

Adam said, "She's got a point, Barrett."

"You have to come," Adele said. "Otherwise you'll be the only one whose body's still a secret."

Barrett shook his head. He laughed as if he were nervous and a little shy. "I don't think so," he said. "You guys go. Really."

"Okay," Barbara said. She jumped up, rubbing her hands together with anticipation. "He's already seen you two naked," she added, with her back to the group as she ducked into her tent. She returned with two flashlights and tossed one to Adam. "Come on, Adele." She leaned down to Adele and whispered in her ear, loud enough for everyone to hear, "Not that I'm gay or anything, darling—but I'm dying to check out your body."

Adam laughed and Barrett said, "You believe the libido of this woman?"

"You lucky dog!" Adam grasped Barrett by the neck and gave him a shake.

"Come on, come on!" Barbara took Adam by the arm and led him to the path that went down to the shore. "It's getting late and we've got that dumb fishing trip in the morning."

Adele hesitated at the table, looking across the game board at Barrett, who was watching Barbara and Adam as they made their way along the path. When Barrett turned to meet her eyes, she said: "You sure you won't come?"

"Believe me," Barrett said. "I haven't got the body to show off."

Adele laughed, dismissing Barrett's modesty. She smiled warmly at him, touched his fingertips with hers, and then joined Barbara and Adam, calling for them to wait.

Barrett put the game board and pieces away as he listened to the others descending the path to the water. For a long time, he could hear their laughter and the shrill, playful screams of the women. When, finally, the sound of their voices disappeared under the constant low whistle of wind through trees and the white noise of small ocean waves breaking over boulders that rose up out of shallow water all along the shore, when the only sounds left were the elemental ones—the fire, which occasionally popped and hissed, water leaving and returning ceaselessly, wind moving along the earth—Barrett carried the Acquire game into his tent, put it away, and came back out with a flashlight and an expensive pair of high-powered binoculars attached to a black graphite tripod.

Carrying the tripod on his shoulder as if it were a rifle, holding the feet in his right hand while the binoculars bounced along up over his head; and carrying the flashlight in his left hand, its beam trained on the ground; he followed the same path the others had taken, only in the opposite direction, up to the cape, to the point where the land ended and he could look out over Neah Bay to Tatoosh Island and the Pacific Ocean. Earlier in the day, Adele had taken his and Barbara's picture there as they stood on either side of a makeshift, cardboard sign that read:

> THIS IS CAPE FLATTERY,
> THE NORTHWESTERN-MOST POINT
> IN THE CONTINENTAL UNITED STATES.

Now, as he walked along in the dark, he was watching for the sign. When he reached it, he would be close to the lookout point, where he planned on setting up the binoculars and watching his wife and friends as they undressed and went swimming.

Barrett approached the cape amazed at himself. He was fifty-six years old and waves of sexual desire still pushed him along like so much driftwood. Desire swelled in him and still, now, at fifty-six, he couldn't find the will to resist it. That morning, for example, his coming upon Adam and Adele bathing had not been accidental. He had been lying awake in his sleeping bag, looking out at the green canopy of trees through the netting at the top of his tent, when he overheard Adele suggest to Adam that they bathe at the shore. He had waited until he heard them leave the campsite before he got dressed quietly, careful not to wake Barbara, and he went down to the shore, hoping to come upon them. When he first saw them, they had their backs toward him. It was amusing to him that both Adam and Adele, at thirty-five and thirty-three, thought of themselves as old. To Barrett the two of them were luminous with youth. Adam had the body you'd expect on a man who'd made a career and built a successful business around physical fitness. And Adele . . . Adele's beauty extended from the luster of her shoulder-length auburn hair, to the intelligence in her eyes, and the creamy glow of her skin.

When he came upon them, they were standing knee-deep in a tidal pool, Adam behind and to the right of Adele, his right hand on her shoulder, his left hand turning a thick bar of white soap in slow circles at the small of her back. While Barrett watched them, partially hidden by a pair of side-by-side boulders, Adam slid the bar of soap down over Adele's buttocks and then under her and through her legs. She laughed and turned around and they embraced and kissed. Barrett moved back behind the boulders and waited. He looked around, nervous about getting caught leering at his friends. Getting caught would be humiliating and he was genuinely afraid of it—and that mixture of real fear and sexual excitement, that was one of the things that made him do it. It felt powerful, intense. He waited a few minutes and when he looked again, they were kneeling in the water, splashing each other playfully. Then he walked out from between the boulders and began applauding—as if he had just accidentally come upon them, as if their naked bodies were nothing more to him than an amusement, something which of course in his maturity and experience held no real power over him. Adam seemed taken aback at first, but Adele met his eyes and smiled—and then Adam, jackass that he was, began posing.

When Barrett reached the head of the cape, the shelter of the trees ended abruptly. The moon was just emerging from a bank of clouds, and it was bright enough that Barrett felt confident turning off the flashlight and laying it on a boulder. He walked carefully, testing the firmness of the ground with each small step. When he was close to the place where the land dropped away, he crawled on his hands and knees to the edge, where he lay on his stomach and looked down to the beach. Forty or fifty feet below him, Barbara, Adam, and Adele had just reached the water line and were standing in the surf with their shoes off and their pants legs rolled up. Barrett set up the tripod behind some bushes and a small tree, and he focused the binoculars on Adele. He had paid thirteen hundred dollars for those binoculars, and every time he used them he saw why: through their powerful lenses, Adele appeared to be a few arm's lengths away from him. He felt as though he could touch her hair.

After several minutes of watching the threesome talking at the edge of the water, Barrett began to fear that they would chicken out and not go skinny-dipping at all. For a moment, he wished he were down there to urge them all out of their clothes and into the water. But, really, he didn't want to be down there with them. If he were down there, when they were all out of their clothes, he would have to pretend that it was no big deal. He wouldn't be able to leer and stare. He would have to pretend he didn't want to feel the weight of Adele's breasts in his hands, he didn't want to run his tongue over her nipples, he didn't want to reach down under her the way Adam had. The truth was that he wanted to look, and he wanted to look with concentrated attention—not a pretense of amusement. And, if the relationship wasn't sexually intimate, that required distance and anonymity. So he preferred being up on the bluff, behind a tree, with his binoculars.

At home, in Manhattan, on the set at work, he was surrounded by stunningly beautiful women—all out of his reach, by his own choice, because he was married again. The tension was incredible. He wanted those women intensely and he didn't want them intensely—both at the same time. He was fifty-six years old, with three grown children, a veteran of three failed marriages. He was lucky to have Barbara. He knew it. He knew it absolutely. And yet, whenever an attractive woman came near him, something happened in his blood, something over which he had no control. It was as if his blood heated up, the surface of his skin grew electric, his breathing changed. He didn't know if it was like that for all men, all the time—but he was determined, absolutely, this time, with Barbara, to stay in control. He had slept with so many women over the years. And he knew now, knew absolutely, in his heart, that what he really needed to be happy was one woman. He needed Barbara. In the years he was single before he met her, in those years when he moved constantly between one woman and the next, when his life felt like an habitual swirl of movement, he suffered from anxiety attacks, terrible attacks that on a couple of occasions included hallucinations. Since he married Barbara, he had been fine. He needed to stay with her, to stay with one woman, with Barbara. He needed to learn to stay still. He needed to learn to value what he had and to resist the desire to move from woman to woman to woman.

Barrett knew what he needed. . . . And yet, some nights, he still found himself out at Flashdancers on West 21st, where dozens of mostly undressed girls filled the room and the runways. All the women were beautiful, and varied in form: with light skin and dark skin; with big breasts that floated over taut but ample skin, and small breasts tight to the rib cage; with small pink nipples on white white skin, and large oval nipples, brown or nutmeg on darker skin; with asses that were round and asses that were long and flowed into youthful thighs: beauty everywhere on the pedestals of table tops, and what he desired was to look at it, what he desired was to see what was everyday all around him hidden from his view.

In a sense, Barrett's voyeurism was a kind of compromise. He chose looking over acting. He was going to leer at Adele, but he wasn't going to make a pass at her. Adam was a jackass, but he was his friend. He liked betting football and basketball games with him, and playing poker with him on Friday nights, gambling being another source of intensity in Barrett's life. He didn't want to sleep with his friend's wife. Even though his relationship with Barbara had been strained for the last few months, he didn't want to mess up the marriage by sleeping with another woman. But of course he wanted Adele. He wanted to see her, to touch her. He wanted her. He didn't want her. It was maddening and confusing. It had always been maddening and confusing.

Down on the beach, Barbara slipped out of her bikini top, and Adam's loud whistle floated up to the cape. While Adam and Adele watched, Barbara stripped out of her jeans and then her panties, slowly, with an equal mix of seduction and play. Watching from the cape, Barrett felt the familiar tingle of sexual excitement—and it surprised him. He had seen Barbara naked on a daily basis for almost a year now, and he had thought that she no longer excited him—not even when she put on the flaming red teddies, or the exotic black garters, or the Frederick's-of-Hollywood panties with the crotch cut out. Now, here he was watching her secretly from a distance through binoculars and feeling that old, recognizable tingle in his groin. When Barbara was fully undressed, she trotted away into the water, where she watched Adam take off his clothes, her head bobbing on the surface, as if she were just slightly jumping up and down in the water. Adam got undressed quickly and yelped as he dove dramatically into the waves. Then Adele turned around and looked up at the cape, looked up directly at Barrett.

Barrett moved away from the tripod and took a step back behind a tree trunk. His heart raced wildly. He said to himself, "She can't possibly see me." Then he wondered if she had perhaps seen the glint of moonlight off the lenses of the binoculars. Or maybe he was wrong, maybe his body was somehow silhouetted by the moonlight and she knew he was up on the cape watching her. He slid down and sat on the ground behind the tree, and he was filled with wildly chaotic feelings of shame and guilt and anger and remorse. Why did he do things like this? He was a fifty-six-year-old man. He had a career. He had a family. Why was he hiding in the bushes like a pimply teenager peeking at girls? For God's sake, he repeated to himself, and he was filled with a ragged humiliation. Then he told himself he was overreacting. So what if they knew he was up here watching? Hadn't he been perfectly welcome to join them down on the beach? He'd make light of it if they knew. He'd turn it into a joke.

When he went back to the binoculars, he half expected to see Adele wave at him. Instead he found her reaching behind her back to unsnap her bra, still looking up at him, looking directly at him, as if she were engaged in a staring match and resolved not to be the first one to look away. She had already taken off her pants and blouse, and when the bra came off, she smiled, the same warm smile she had given him just before she left the campsite. Then she took off her panties and just stood there for a long moment, looking up at the cape, before she turned around and walked slowly into the water. Barrett watched them all the time they were in the water, and he watched them get out and get dressed, and then he hurried back to the campsite and put the binoculars and tripod away, and got undressed and into his sleeping bag.

By the time Barbara came into the tent, Barrett was almost asleep. He had listened to the exchange of good-nights through a sleepiness that was like being drugged. He heard the zipper to Adam and Adele's tent open and close, and then Barbara was climbing into their tent, almost stepping on him.

"Barbara?" he said, exaggerating the confusion in his voice, as if he were waking from a dream.

"Go back to sleep," Barbara said. She bent over him and touched his cheek gently with the back of her hand before pushing a strand of hair off his forehead.

"How was it?" he asked, turning onto his back and looking up at her.

"Fun," she said. "They have beautiful bodies . . ." She paused and bent to kiss him on the forehead. She whispered, "But I'm happy to be with an older man, someone with character and real strength."

Barrett laughed softly. "Are you putting me on?"

Barbara didn't answer. She kissed him again, gently, told him she loved him, and then pulled her sleeping bag close to his before she got in it and went to sleep.

Barrett was better able to relax once he was sure Barbara didn't know he had been watching them. For a long time he lay quietly thinking about the next morning's fishing trip, trying to remember what was exciting about holding a pole for hours while you waited for a fish to bite. Then he started thinking about himself, about who he was, about his relationships with others. Did Barbara really believe he had strength and character? He guessed she did. That was his image, the image he projected out into the world. He was an actor. He was a man of experience. He had suffered and he was world-weary. He was a man who lived with the knowledge of the nothing at the center of everything. That was the image he had been working on and refining from the time he was a boy. But who he was, who he was really, that was both his image and something more—and that something more. . . . He wasn't sure what it was. It was shaped by the people and places in his life, but it was something more. It was his angry father and the Brooklyn of his youth. It was the wives he had gone through one after the other and discarded or been discarded by because he was unhappy or unfulfilled or unsomething, or she was. It was his children, all grown now and into their own lifetimes of trouble. But it was also something more. It was his experience and his thought and something more.

But Barbara believed in the image within which everything came wrapped. As he lay in his sleeping bag, not seeing the dense bright stars in their patterns so infinitely complicated they were like a complex, visual music, he tried to think about that something more that he never had been able to apprehend as anything other than a feeling, an idea, that there was something under the images he invented and rendered for others—but he wound up feeling as though he were floating loose of the earth. He wound up feeling as though he were drifting. If no one knew you, who were you? And how could anyone know him if he wouldn't stay still long enough to be known? Outside his tent there was an amazing variety of noises as the nocturnal creatures of the local woods began their nightly foraging—but Barrett's thoughts made him deaf to their music long before sound truly disappeared in the genuine deafness of sleep.

At four-thirty in the morning the sky was an unbroken mass of dark clouds. Adele stood in a circle of lamplight staring out over a fleet of fishing boats to the black water of Neah Bay. Adam stood behind her, looking the other way, back to a small building, a glorified kiosk, set at the edge of a gravel parking lot. Through an uncurtained window, he could see Barrett and Barbara standing in front of a desk cluttered with papers, while behind the desk an elderly woman typed some figures into an adding machine with her right hand and opened a desk drawer with her left. Barrett handed her some money, and Barbara took the slip of paper that had issued forth from the adding machine and been ripped off precisely by the old woman. Adam said, "We shouldn't have let them pay for this. It's probably expensive as hell."

Adele grunted softly, a sound that meant nothing beyond acknowledging that Adam had spoken.

Adam went on: "Barrett makes me feel like a little kid sometimes, the way he's always picking up the tab. I think I may have a tendency to let him take too much control. Probably because he's so old."

"He's not that old," Adele said. She laughed quietly, as if to herself.

"Are you laughing at me?" Adam said.

Adele didn't answer. She was wearing white shorts and a bright yellow sleeveless blouse. A hooded, red vinyl rain slicker was folded over her right arm. She had taken the raincoat just in case—even though the weather report had called, once again, for clear skies and a temperature in the nineties.

Barbara nodded toward the raincoat as she approached Adele. She was carrying two Styrofoam cups of black coffee and she extended one to Adele. "You must be psychic, honey. The captain's mom says it might rain."

"Shit," Adam said. "Will we still go out?"

Barrett, who had been following behind Barbara, carrying two more coffees, handed Adam a cup. "We're just waiting for the couple that's going out with us. Captain says they're on the way."

"Is this latté?" Adam asked, looking down at his coffee. "I like a lot of foam."

"Right, latté," Barrett said. "And the captain's serving croissants and apple scones on the flying bridge at seven."

Adele stuck her hand out, palm up. "Is it starting to rain?"

Barrett looked up to the sky, as if he might be able to see the rain falling. "I don't feel anything."

Adam said, "I think it's just misting."

"There," Barbara said, and she gestured to the village's single blacktop road, where a station wagon had just come round a curve. As they all watched, it pulled into the gravel parking lot and a middle-aged couple emerged. The man was shaped like an egg, with a small chest and a huge stomach that sloped down to skinny legs. He was wearing a camouflage outfit. The woman was also heavy, but her bulk was solid and seemed evenly distributed from her shoulders to her feet. She gave the impression of a living rectangle.

"Good God," Adam said, as the couple approached them and the captain emerged from his office at the edge of the parking lot. "I hope this boat's solid."

"Stop it," Adele said, turning her back to the couple and giving Adam a look.

The man in the camouflage approached the group with his arm extended for a handshake. Barrett switched his coffee to his left hand and shook the man's hand. "Joe Waller," the man said to Barrett. He extended his hand to Barbara and he gestured to his wife. "This is my wife, Lady," he said. "Would you believe twenty-five years?" Lady nodded, confirming what he said. "Married twenty-five years yesterday, two kids through college and married, one in college, one in high school." He said this as he shook Adam's hand and moved on to Adele. "Can you believe it?" he said to Adele.

Lady said, "And we're only forty-three."

"No kidding," Adam said.

"Hey!" Joe exclaimed, turning around to face the captain as he approached them slowly, carrying a large white bucket in each hand. "We going to catch some salmon today, Captain Ron?"

The captain was a Makah. His skin was dark and lined with myriad creases and folds. His eyes were solemn and deep. "I hope so," he said, and then continued on toward the boats, the large white buckets dangling from his hands like balancing weights.

Adam said, "I guess we follow him."

"That's Captain Ron," Joe said, putting his hand on Adam's back. "You ever been out with him before? Where you folks from, anyway? The wife and I are down from Alberta . . . "

Joe went on as the group followed the captain down the rickety boat ramps and over the narrow docks to The Raven, Captain Ron's fishing boat. Behind them, the village at Neah Bay was quiet and dark. The only lights came from the Thunderbird Motel, which overlooked the water and was bracketed by gravel parking lots, one of which housed the small rust-red building out of which Captain Ron ran his charter fishing boat business. When all six passengers were on board, the captain jumped off the boat, undid the mooring lines, and then hopped back on and climbed up to the bridge. He backed the boat out of its slip and onto the bay. From below deck a young woman came up dressed in boots, denims, a blue and gold Notre Dame sweatshirt, and a heavy yellow rain slicker. Her eyes were watery and her short, dark hair was pressed flat against one side of her head, as if she had just a moment ago been sleeping. She introduced herself as Tina, the captain's daughter, and explained she was working this trip as First Mate, which meant she'd be the one untangling lines and helping with the tackle. Then she looked at Barbara, who was dressed in shorts and a summer blouse, and said. "You're going to freeze like that, ma'am. Want to borrow a sweatshirt?"

Barbara shook her head, although she was already hugging herself and shivering slightly. "It's supposed to get hot later," she said.

The girl laughed. "Not on the water," she said. "Not this morning." She disappeared below deck again and came back up with a ratty gray sweatshirt, which she tossed to Barbara. Barbara put it on and continued hugging herself and shivering.

By the time the sun came up, everyone was fishing. The captain had taken the boat out past Tatoosh Island, onto the Pacific, and within forty-five minutes everyone had pulled at least one salmon on board. The Canadian couple had each caught two big sockeyes in rapid succession, and Tina was kept busy unhooking everyone's catch and getting their lines back in the water. In minutes the deck had grown slippery with fish slime, and the pervasive stink of fish-smell grew so intense it was as much a taste as a smell. The sun had risen on a gray, chilly, misty morning, and the ocean swells regularly lifted and dropped, lifted and dropped The Raven, as one after the other the fishers yelled out "fish on!" and Tina came running with a net or a gaff, depending on the degree of bow in the pole tip.

Barbara was the first to get sick. Then Adam, Adele, and Barrett joined her. The Canadian couple was fine. They stood side by side in the stern of the boat, and it was as if their mass and bulk created a solid, unmoving place in the liquid midst of a rolling, perpetually moving ocean. They kept fishing away, pulling in salmon after salmon, while one by one Barbara, Barrett, Adele and Adam made trip after trip from the deck to bathroom, from the deck to bathroom. After a while they gave up trying to fish and each descended the short stairway to the cabin below deck, where they lay on benches and cushions, trying to maintain some control over the awful sickness in their stomachs. It was no use. They kept having to carry themselves to the bathroom, where the smell of vomit and diarrhea mingled with the ubiquitous stink of fish.

On one of his trips back from the head, Barrett sat next to Adele, at her feet, and across from Adam and Barbara. The cabin was a tight, dark place with only two small portholes to bring in light. Benches followed the contour of the boat's hull. They were covered with thin, dirty cushions, and the tops of the benches were hinged and apparently opened up to create storage space. Barbara and Adele were stretched out on the benches, curled up into fetal balls. Barrett was sitting with his head between his legs.

"Barrett," Adam said. "Can you die from seasickness?"

Barrett's voice was harsh. "Damn," he said. "What I'd give for solid ground."

"Jesus," Adam went on. "I'm serious. I really feel like my stomach's bleeding or something. I think I saw blood last time I puked."

Adele said, weakly: "Nobody dies from seasickness, Adam."

"How do you know!" Adam snapped back at her. "Are you an expert or something?"

Adele opened her eyes and lifted her head from the bench. "Adam," she said, firmly. "Your stomach's not bleeding. Once we get on land, you'll be okay."

"Are you sure?" Adam said. He dropped his head down between his legs and clasped his hands over the back of his neck. When Adele didn't answer, he asked again, sounding close to tears: "Honey? Are you sure?"

"I'm sure." Adele looked over her knees, to Barrett, who was sitting up straight now, with his back against the hull. When she caught his eye, she shook her head, as if exasperated.

"Barrett," Adam whined. "Will you go talk to the captain? Maybe he'll take us back in."

Barrett was silent a long moment; then he pulled himself to his feet. "What the hell," he said. "It's worth a try."

"Really," Barbara said, opening her eyes for the first time. "You think he might?"

Barrett made a face, indicating that he doubted it, seriously. Then he climbed the stairs to the deck and a metal ladder to the bridge, where he found the captain fiddling with the electronics. He asked him to take them back in, and, as he expected, the captain refused, explaining he'd have to refund the Canadians' money, and that would make the day a loss. Barrett offered to cover the captain's losses, but he just shook his head and looked out over the bridge to the ocean. Barrett returned below deck defeated. Along with the others, he lay around in misery for another hour before the Canadians softened, having anyway caught the boat's limit for salmon, and allowed the captain to take them in. When they finally made it back to the campsite on Cape Flattery, everyone crawled into a tent and immediately fell asleep.

It was late afternoon when Adele opened her eyes. Alongside her, Adam lay stretched out on top of his sleeping bag. He lay on his stomach, naked except for the bright red briefs that clung to him tightly as a tattoo. His body was covered with a sheen of perspiration: a pool of sweat had gathered in the small of his back, and his hair looked as though he had just stepped out of the shower. Adele was also soaked. She ran her hand over her chest and stomach, and sweat ran down her sides in rivulets. She sat up and let herself awaken slowly to the sounds and sensations around her. It was quiet. And it was hot. Very hot. She pulled on a pair of cut-off denims and a T-shirt, and she crawled out of the tent.

The campsite and the surrounding woods seemed eerily still. There was no breeze, and the heat, even in the shade of the forest, was palpable: she could feel it on her skin like standing close to a fire. The only sound was the constant, faraway murmur of the ocean. It didn't take Adele more than a few moments of standing in the heat to decide she wanted to go for a swim. She retrieved a pair of sneakers from her tent and started down the trail to the shore. When she approached the beach, she found Barrett crouched in the surf. He was sitting on his haunches, wearing a blue bathing suit, looking out over the ocean as water rushed back and forth over his feet and ankles.

At Adele's approach, Barrett turned around and smiled. "You believe this heat?" he asked.

Adele knelt alongside him, immersing her calves and thighs in the water. She threw her torso forward as she pushed her hair up over the back of her neck and submerged her face and hair in the surf, rubbing the cooling water into her scalp and forehead and eyes. She came up shaking her head, getting Barrett wet. "Oh God," she said. "That was good. I think I roasted in the tent."

Barrett laughed and wiped the water away from his face. "Are Adam and Barbara up yet?"

Adele shook her head. "Still cooking," she said. "At least when I left they were."

"Poor Adam," Barrett said. "He thought he was going to die out there."

"He's such a baby." Adele turned around so that she was facing Barrett. She sat in water up to her waist. "Do you mind if I ask you something?"

"Go ahead."

Adele hesitated. She was sitting with her legs stretched out and open in a V, and she swirled the water between her legs with a crooked finger. "I'd better not," she said, and she looked away and then back, as if with that motion she had turned the page in a book and was now reading from a new script. "I got so sick out there," she said, referring to the fishing trip. "For a while, out on the water, it felt like I was blind. Do you know what I mean? It was like I couldn't see because nothing would stay still long enough. Up and down up and down drifting moving. . . . Do you have any idea at all what I'm talking about, Barrett?"

Adele was being cute, and Barrett smiled in response. It was an honest smile. "I think I know what you mean. So?"

"So, what?"

"The question," Barrett said. "The question you wanted to ask."

Adele looked down and her expression changed suddenly. Her eyes in an instant grew watery.

Barrett put his hand on Adele's knee. "What is it?"

"Adam and I are not going to last," she said. "I mean, I doubt we'll be together another month after this vacation."

Barrett looked off, past Adele, his face taking on an appropriate expression, a world-weary look of sadness for the unfortunate ways of this world. Inside him, however, the rate of his heartbeat picked up slightly. His mind was blank but his blood was moving. "I'm sorry," he said. "I didn't know things were bad between you."

"It's not that things are bad," Adele said. "I doubt Adam has any idea. It's just that. . . . He's such a little boy. He's sweet, but it's like being married to a child. You heard him on the boat." She looked up at Barrett, as if wanting confirmation. "He was whimpering, for God's sake. I mean, if someone had taped that exchange in the cabin, it could have been a ten-year-old boy talking to his mother." Adele touched Barrett's hand. "Am I inventing all this?" she said. "Isn't that how it sounded to you?"

Barrett rubbed his eyes with his fingertips, hiding his face momentarily. Of course Adam was boyish. It was the way he was. Adele's complaints against Adam threw Barrett back into his own refuse heap of complaints—his wives' against him and his against his wives—complaints that had wrecked one marriage after the other. The problems were many, the details numerous, but after three marriages all Barrett really remembered was the process by which things fell apart, the faults real and invented that led to arguments followed by unhappiness followed by separation. It wasn't that the specifics, the details of the complaints, had disappeared; it was just that now they seemed unimportant in comparison to the process of coming apart, a process he had been through three times already. So Adam was boyish. That was Adele's complaint. What was his complaint against Barbara? There were several, none of which seemed very important at the moment.

Barrett removed his hands from his eyes in time to see the emotion gathering in Adele's face, building second by second as he failed to respond. "Of course," he said. "That's something about Adam. He's like a kid sometimes."

Adele looked up at the cape and closed her eyes for a long moment. Then she turned to Barrett and stared at him intently, waiting to read his smallest gesture.

Barrett had been here many times before, at this moment. It was the moment when he had only to touch her and she would lean toward him and they would embrace. He could kiss her now. He could touch her. She wanted to be kissed and touched by him. This was the moment when it might begin, whatever it would turn out to be: an affair, love, a sexual adventure. He stood up and extended a hand down to Adele. "Let's walk a little," he said.

Adele took his hand and lifted herself from the water. She walked alongside Barrett in her dripping cut-offs and soaked sneakers. Her T-shirt too had gotten wet and it clung to her, the shape of her breasts and the color of her skin almost revealed entirely through the thin fabric.

Barrett looked away, toward the green hills that sloped down to the sand. They were walking toward a place where three boulders formed a semicircle on the beach and three more out in the water completed the circle.

"Can I ask my question now?" Adele said.

"Sure. Go ahead." Barrett answered without looking at her.

"You and Barbara," she said. "Are you going to last? Are you two going to make it?"

Barrett's heart was beating fast. He didn't answer. He looked down at his feet and folded his arms over his chest as if contemplating a response.

They had reached the circle of boulders and Adele stopped and looked around. The boulders formed a small private beach, a place protected from the casual view of others. "I'm going in here," she said, and she pulled off her clothes and waded into a deep tidal pool that was still connected by a flowing stream of water to the ocean.

Barrett had watched her as she tore off her clothes and tossed them in a heap on the sand, his eyes searching out the soft and shadowy places, the slow curves and sloping angles of her skin. He followed her into the tidal pool. When she turned around to face him again, standing waist-deep in water, he stepped close to her, took her hands in his and said, "No. We're not going to make it." When he spoke, he heard his voice change, the timbre turning just slightly more resonant, the tone dropping a note. It was his best acting voice and it had emerged out of nowhere, on its own. It surprised him, as did the tears welling in his eyes.

Adele brushed the tears away with wet fingers. "I didn't think so," she said. "You act as though you don't even like each other any more."

"She doesn't understand me," Barrett said, and he bowed his head and covered his eyes with his hands, and as soon as he did it, the gesture seemed fake to him. He half expected to hear a director yell cut! He pushed on. "I feel empty," he said. "We're married . . . but I feel. . . ." He heard himself speaking, but he could hardly believe what he was hearing.

"I know," Adele said, and she embraced Barrett, wrapping her arms around him and holding him tight against her. She repeated: "I know. I know exactly."

Barrett pulled away and held Adele at arm's length. "I have a question for you," he said, allowing a note of urgency into his voice. "The other night, when you went swimming with Adam and Barbara, did you know. . . . Did you know I was watching you?"

"From the cape?" she said. "With the binoculars?"

"Yes," Barrett said. "How? How did you know?"

"I didn't. I mean, I didn't know—but I imagined it. I imagined you were up there watching. . . . And it was like I could feel you, I could feel your eyes on me."

"But what made you think . . . "

"It's your eyes. . . . They're hungry. Everyone sees it in you. It's just, like, a hunger about you . . . "

"It's crazy," Barrett said, "because . . . I felt this connection between us then. It was like something real between us. I felt filled up by it. I can't explain, really . . ." He leaned forward, as if he were tired of stumbling for words, and he embraced and kissed Adele, his lips pressing hard against her lips, his tongue pushing into her mouth.

Adele returned the kiss, letting her hands move over his back, clutching and releasing his shoulders—but when his head moved lower, to her breasts, and he tried to pull her down to the water, she resisted. "Not here," she said. "Barrett. Not now." She stepped back from him. They had moved, while kissing, into shallower water, and Barrett was on his knees, looking up at her. She ran her fingers through his wet hair.

Barrett took her hand and pulled her toward him. "Yes," he said. "Here. Now."

Adele shook her head and remained standing. "Someone might come by. Barbara or Adam. . . . They're probably up."

Barrett looked at the sky, at the wavering, late-afternoon light. "No one can see us here," he said, and he ran his hand along the length of her thigh. "Adele," he said. He leaned forward and kissed her leg, high, above the knee. "Listen," he said. "There's nothing to life but moments like this. Intense moments like this." He touched his chest. "My heart is racing," he said. "I'm looking at a beautiful woman, and my heart is a drum beat: it's pounding in my chest." He took Adele's hand and held it over his heart. She came down to her knees in the water. She knelt in front of him, her hand pressed flat against his breast. "We'd regret it forever," he said, "if we let this moment pass." He embraced her and kissed her and turned her body around, moving them both toward shallower water, where he lay on his back and pulled off his swimming trunks, and moved his body under Adele's, threading his legs between her legs. He had, then, only to thrust his thighs up slightly and they were joined. Above him, blocking out the bright yellow circle of the sun, Adele's head was lifted to the sky as if in ecstasy or grief, the heels of her hands pressed against her temples, her fingers buried in her hair. She appeared, from the angle where Barrett looked up at her, to be floating away from the earth, attached to nothing, not him or the ground or the water; and in the pleasure of the moment, Barrett too felt as though he were floating—into a place of pure sensation, rising free of the gritty earth. Then he moved his hips, pushing into the heat of Adele's body, and the seasickness from earlier in the day came back with a rush. He felt as sick as he had at any point on the boat trip.

Barrett tried to hold himself steady to let the sickness pass, but Adele was moving rhythmically, the palms of her hands flat against his chest, pushing him down into the sand and water. He held Adele's wrists, and behind him, from someplace beyond and above the boulders, he heard a sound like a rock might make being kicked in the sand. He wanted to turn around and look, but he was afraid of what he might see. He feared that Barbara and Adam were above them on the beach looking down at them in the water. He closed his eyes and told himself these feelings would pass in a moment if he remained calm. Amazingly, as his mind swirled and his nausea swelled, his body kept properly functioning. Adele appeared to have no idea there was a problem. When he felt her hair brushing his chest, he opened his eyes and found himself looking into a rip in the fabric of the sky, a shifting blaze of energy and light. He threw his forearm up over his eyes, and the motion sent him spinning, as if he were spiraling up and away. With his other hand he grasped blindly for Adele, and when he found her shoulders he pulled himself up and wrapped his arms around her.

"What?" Adele said. "What is it?"

Barrett didn't answer. His eyes were filled with a mosaic of color, blinding him to the solid coastline that might have steadied him; and the blood rushing in his ears made him deaf to the music of water and earth and wind that might have calmed him. He was sick. His body was tumbling through light and space. He held on tight to Adele, as if her body could anchor him.

"Barrett?" Adele said. She wiped away the sweat gathering at his temples. "Barrett," she repeated. "Can you tell me what it is?" And when Barrett didn't answer, when he continued mutely clinging to her, she tried to calm him by saying, again and again, soothingly, "Tell me, Barrett. Tell me. Tell me what it is."

The Breeze at Dawn

THOM WARD

ripples the sheets, brings
tulips, magnolia, bradford pear.
When the fragrance enters my lover's dream
her nipples stir. I lick the back of her neck,
leave small, feathered kisses.
The breeze comes again and again
her nipples rise to my fingers
and fall.

Love, you are asleep
in a country where you hunt
a thousand other men. Their musk
is a wind that is not mine.
Yet, would you think me dishonest
if I said it won't be long
before the rain taps the flowers,
before your mouth fills
with the first water, the sweet root
that even now grows toward your flesh.

Barbara

THOM WARD

This morning I wake, startled
by the white river of bed between us.
But since I am a water snake,
I slither, roll on my side and pull
the warm of you to the cold of me.
Now, your spine is sheathed in my chest,
your nape moist against my face, your legs
clamping my knees. All this, balance
on the rim of sleep. I flash
my tongue along your shoulder,
brush my fingers over your hip, slopes
that keep shifting. Your thighs and breasts
could be kames, drumlins,
your nipples the smooth stones
I find along the path, your hair so thick
scouts with compasses would vanish.
Forgive me, it's selfish to act like this
when you're exhausted, to stroke your skin,
clasp the pouch where our first,
in his cumulus bubble, sleeps,
as you are trying to sleep, now
that your legs have begun to ache,
your pelvic bones separating,
two wings loosening for the passage
of this child, who is river and cloud,
snake and bird, yet mostly, you, a woman
numinous as the water
in each cloud, each river,
abiding all that comes to you,
even thoughtlessness borne from love,
a man's gaze, a man's touch, this.

The Cold Fish

ALISON FELL

Once at the Court of the late Emperor there lived a pair of ill-matched lovers. In her childhood the Lady Hanako had been a harum-scarum girl, much given to climbing trees, damming brooks, and the like, and her mother, despairing of the child's torn garments and snarled hair, had comforted herself with the hope that maturity would cure her of her rash untidiness.

In her grown womanhood, however, the Lady Hanako was scarcely more ladylike. If she penned a letter to a lover you could be sure that enthusiasm would get the better of craft, and that ink would blot the page or drip unnoticed on her gown. If she tarried at the lily pond to feed the fish, it was a foregone conclusion that her hem would trail in the mud and her long layered sleeves be stained green with waterweed.

By contrast, Hanako's lover was a man meticulous in mind and habit, as befitted a Controller in the Bureau of Central Affairs with Special Responsibility for the Imperial Wardrobe. If a loose thread hung from his mistress's gown he would scrupulously pluck it out, and if a speck or two of rice-powder dusted her shoulders— for Hanako's toilet was often slapdash—he would immediately brush it off. The Controller brought the same fastidiousness to the business of lovemaking, approaching his mistress's iso-ginchaku with the merest tips of his fingers, and never, to Hanako's dismay, with his lips.

There came a hot and handsome evening in the Seventh Month when the swallows roistered in the eaves and the apricots glowed fatly on their trees like a thousand infant daughters of the sun. Unable to bear the tedium of her indoor duties, Hanako escaped to the lily pond in the Palace gardens to feed her favourite carp.

She had called this imposing specimen Yugure, because it was at twilight that he preferred to come to the surface of the pond to graze on waterweed and lily flowers, but also because of his venerable age, which was now approaching forty years. Yet there was nothing of the dotard in this great fish, who was as long as a young deer from nose to tail, and of a boisterous and manly bearing.

Stirring the water with her fingers, Hanako hummed a song and waited for Yugure to rise from the mud of the bottom and swim up to greet her. After a few moments the great pouting mouth with its four fleshy barbels broke the surface, followed by the green-gold head, the lustrous eyes, and the diamond-patterned scales of the back. Hanako had brought with her boiled peas and grains from the kitchens, and now she offered a little of the mixture to the waiting lips, which closed with pulsating voluptuousness around the delicacy, sucking and smacking at her fingers with a greedy abandon which made her chuckle with delight.

After passing a peaceful hour in communion with her friend, with a heavy heart Hanako informed him that she must return to her apartments to receive the Controller, who was invariably prompt to the second and brooked no unpunctuality in others. With a flick of his tail Yugure showed her his silvery sides, and swivelled his golden eye and watched her go, worrying a little over the mud stains on her underdress, and the fluff of dandelion seeds in her hair, for he was well aware of her lover's perfectionism.

When Hanako greeted her lover she was dismayed to receive not one word of affection, but instead a positive tirade of criticism. Throwing her mud-stained clothes in a heap, the Controller instructed the maid to dispose of them. Then he ordered Hanako immediately into the bath, and insisted on supervising her toilet himself. Every orifice must be scrubbed, he commanded, every last hair tweezed out, every flake of dry skin buffed away with the pumice-stone. A final inspection, however, revealed a residue of fish food under Hanako's fingernails, and those the Controller cleaned out himself, with a special bamboo implement and with much fussing and scolding.

Afterwards Hanako, who positively ached with cleanliness, climbed resignedly into bed and thought longingly of the liquid tickle of the carp, who relished mud and had never turned from her in disdain. Her trials, however, were not over, for, before approaching her *hoto*, the Controller first drew on a pair of cotton gloves, and only then began his hygienic caresses.

As soon as her lover had concluded his scrupulous congress and lay sleeping, Hanako crept out of bed and, carelessly throwing on an outer-robe, ran to the fish pond for solace.

Moonlit apricots fell from their branches with a plop and floated on the water as the lady lay all abject on the muddy bank. Meanwhile, Yugure, the giant of twilight, called up from the depths by the sad sound of weeping, rose to the surface in all his kindly majesty.

Spying Hanako's white hand upon the water, Yugure opened his muscular lips and sucked sympathetically at her fingers, which shed their sadness under his touch and opened out like jasmine flowers.

Under the bridge of the night sky with the air smelling of apricots the great carp scented out another delicacy, and this was the lady's small bare foot which dangled, abandoned, in the sultry water. The small morsels of her toes filled his ardent mouth, and each one he worshiped separately, until Hanako's eyelids drooped with contentment and her long sigh rippled the surface like a balmy wind.

With a spiralling dive Yugure swept his silver belly lightly along the curved sole of her foot, and resurfaced to nudge her splendid calf, which glimmered in the moonlight. All thought of her scrupulous lover was banished now, as Hanako rolled on to her back and, luxuriating in the slickness of the mud, stretched her legs out in the shallows until her robe floated up around her like a giant water lily.

Yugure circled the lady amorously, for on the table of the waters the feast had been laid for him, and he wished for nothing more than to taste her pleasure.

Hanako, for her part, felt the golden head butt gently between her thighs, and she clasped her legs eagerly round his broad girth, for his slippery scales were far less chilly to the touch than the pallid skin of her lover. Her small breasts bobbed like apricots on the water as the great lips closed on the kernel of her, and she cried O O O, and hid her face in her tumbling hair, feeling the four tender barbels stroke her with a touch lighter than lark's breath.

With exquisite consideration, Yugure scooped up water and blew it in spouting fountains upon Hanako's tenderest places, so that when his lips swam back to nibble her they found the lady an-chored unflinchingly to her own pleasure, and swelling up to meet them. And if Yugure's heart swelled also, then so might a gardener feel who has watered his pea-flowers lovingly throughout the spring and now admires them in their glorious unfolding.

With his tickling barbels teasing at her outer crevices, the giant fish enclosed both pea and pod within his noble lips. And there were moments when he sucked, and moments when he blew, and moments when the delicate morsel rolled in his mouth as if it would detach itself from its moorings. The lady's juices flowed saltily, and her limbs quivered, and her belly arched, and he knew that before too long he would be rewarded by the lovely wash and thrash of her.

At last, with her excellent gate open as never before, Hanako cried out in the velvet night and fed her pleasure to him inch by streaming inch, and Yugure drank down her very good essence and held it hotly in the thrill of his fins and the diamond patterns of his belly, for what better accompaniment is there to the lavish feast of love than the intoxicating wine of the soul?

And afterwards she laid her mud-slicked hand on his accom-modating head, and both carp and lady lolled back in the sultry shallows, she heavy-lidded and content, he with his lidless eyes un-wavering under the curious scrutiny of the stars.

The Door

JAY ROGOFF

Either a door is swinging or it's still;
it's open or it's shut. I can imbibe
aromas, I can hear an angel sob,
me, moaning in private prayer as I kneel

holding my breath, beholding through the keyhole
no Degas glimpse of her astride the tub
but full-spread thighs beneath her velvet robe—
"I've already given you my naked soul."
Open to me my perfect one, my dove.
The ushers have removed the last drunk guest.
Feel your heart buck against mine as we clutch—
Hey! Open up! Clocks are striking, let's thrust
the bolt aside, our fingers dripping flavor.
I stand ready, hand trembling on the latch.

The Fourth Child

LINDA VANESSA HEWITT

She went to see the son of her mother's second cousin about her
teeth. That winter afternoon he seemed to her just a big, blond, af-
fable dentist, but on the third visit Helen English looked at him and
saw the golden hairs on his freckled arms. They were little wisps
the color of the thick curls on his head. As he bent over her, she felt
weak from the odor of his scrubbed hands and clove-scented
breath. She closed her eyes. He was family, really, a cousin. It seemed
safe to inhale the oddly sweet smells of his office, and wonder what
he looked like beneath the white smock and trousers.

When her teeth were clean and her cavities filled, Helen regretted that she had no reason to visit Karl Tornberg. As she was leaving
his office, he called after her, "My mother would love to meet you.
We could all go out together some Sunday." Oh yes, she thought. Yes.

He called once to tell her about the benefits of a new Pepsodent
toothpaste, but did not mention the trip to the farm. She began to
worry about the condition of her children's teeth. She imagined
that her husband, Bill, who was in Japan with MacArthur's army of

occupation, would want her to take them for check-ups. It was the spring of 1946. She had not seen Bill since 1944. The children, Billy, five, Amy, four, and Tom, two and a half, reminded her of Bill but as time passed they seemed more like her children and less like his. There had been so many family birthdays without him, so many holiday celebrations, so much life passing.

The children's teeth did not require much attention. When Dr. Tornberg declared them free from dental problems, Helen was again without a valid reason to see him. She was surprised that she wanted to see him more than she wanted to see Bill. In August, Karl's mother called and invited her to Sunday dinner at the farm. Karl and his family would be there, and his sister and brother and their families.

"Karl thinks your children need a day in the country," Mrs. Tornberg said. "And I want to see my cousin Alma's grandchildren."

When Karl called for Helen and her children at nine on Sunday morning, he was alone. It was a two-hour drive to East Bridgewater, where Karl's mother, a widow, lived in a New England farmhouse off a county road that ran between fields of ripening corn. From the front seat of Karl's lime-green Packard, Helen looked back at her children, who were unusually quiet as they watched the rows of wind-blown golden tassels. They looked expectant but slightly anxious. They were city children. They played tic-tac-toe in the alley beside the two-decker where they lived, and chalked hopscotch on the sidewalk. Taking them out for fresh air and vigorous games was the reason for the trip, but Helen sensed that they were as unsettled as she was by the prospect of a day in the country with Karl.

The Tornberg farm was at the end of a long drive lined with tall elm trees. From their drooping branches green leaves dappled sunlight over the grass and dusty driveway. Corn marched in to the edges of the lawn on both sides of the house, which was white, with dark green shutters. Mrs. Tornberg waited on the open veranda, a housecoat over her best blue silk dress.

Helen had not asked about Karl's wife and children but his mother did, even before she said hello to Helen.

"Mama, this is . . . ."

"Where are Lily and the boys?"

Karl waved his hand. "In Gloucester, with her mother," he said.

"She was there week before last," Mrs. Tornberg said. Helen and her children stood in an awkward circle, holding hands.

"Yes, and she's gone again. Now, say hello to Cousin Helen and her little ones."

Helen felt Mrs. Tornberg take her hand as she stepped from the morning sunlight into the dark living room.

"Oh, but you're just a child," Mrs. Tornberg said as she patted Helen's hand. "And three children already." She linked arms with Helen. "I didn't know you'd be so young."

Helen did not understand the concern in Mrs. Tornberg's voice and eyes. "I'm almost twenty-two," she said.

Karl and his sister, Nora, gathered all the children in the side yard, leaving Helen alone with Mrs. Tornberg as they walked through the house. Helen liked its old-fashioned spareness and the smell of kerosene in the cool rooms. It was so unlike the noisy city apartments where Helen grew up, so far in spirit from the top floor of the two-decker in Savin Hill where she and Bill moved when they married.

"Maybe we should wait," Helen had said to Bill two weeks before the wedding. "I'm only sixteen."

"We can't wait. If I get called up we might not have another chance for years—or ever. Don't you want to start a family?"

"Maybe we should wait," Helen said to her mother. "I'm only sixteen."

"You're old enough, I was only fifteen when I married your father."

The day after they returned from their wedding trip to New York City, Helen planted geraniums in a strip of worn earth on their side of the alley.

"Not enough light there, sweetie," Bill said as he dug them up. Helen watched him from the swing as he replanted them in the backyard. She remained on the swing, moving slowly through the summer dusk, long after he went in to wash his hands.

"Come in now, Helen," Bill called from the porch. She knew from the urgency in his voice that he would lead her to the bedroom as soon as she went inside. She would lie quietly on top of the bedspread in the cream-colored satin slip from her trousseau. She would look past Bill and watch the sunset light reflect off the wall of the Kelly house. She often held his head in her hands and wondered at the spasms that shook his body and made him cry out in such a broken way.

Now she was in the house where Karl had been born thirty years ago in the small bedroom off the kitchen. Mrs. Tornberg stood with her on the worn pine threshold, squinting into a shaft of sunlight that striped the carved walnut headboard and brown and white comforter. The sheer curtains lifted gently in the south-westerly breeze. Helen felt excited, as though the wind brought with it some essence of the day Karl was born.

All morning Helen was happy, attentive to everything she did. She knew that at some moment during the day she would be alone with Karl. As they set the table together, Helen smiled at Karl's mother across the white linen and Bavarian china with such intensity that the older woman frowned. She must think I'm crazy to enjoy laying out the table so much, Helen thought.

After lunch they sat with their chairs pushed back from the Mission Oak table. They drank strong coffee and toyed with the remnants of applesauce cake. The children were running from the porch to the yard, shouting, the sound of their heels clicking on the floorboards.

Karl sat in his late father's place at the head of the table, his long legs crossed over an arm of the chair. One of his brown-and-white saddle shoes dangled in a shaft of sunlight. Helen knew what the ankle and foot would look like if she unhooked the white laces, pulled the shoe off and peeled down the brown silk sock. The foot would be very white, it would tremble in her hands. She could smooth the patches of wiry gold hair on the instep and big toe, and caress the veins that bulged blue under the translucent skin. When Helen looked up from Karl's foot, he was looking at her. She looked away—into Mrs. Tornberg's faded blue eyes, which moved back and forth between Karl and Helen.

Conversation and laughter continued around them. Warm air lifted the lace curtains and swirled them over Helen's shoulder. She grabbed a length of fabric, covered her face, and closed her eyes.

"Excuse me," she said, letting the curtain fall from her hands. In the bathroom she sat on the oak toilet seat and imagined Mrs. Tornberg bathing her baby boy in the claw-footed tub. She visualized the mother on her knees on the plank floor, bending into the tub, scrubbing the boy's pale arms with a brown sponge and cake of homemade soap. Young Karl frisked in the tub, evading his mother's soapy hands, and wriggled from one end to the other, his skin squeaking on the wet porcelain. Mother and son laughed and splashed until the image of Mrs. Tornberg receded and Helen slipped into her place by the tub.

She placed the soap in the brass soap dish, the sponge on top. She plunged her hands into the warm, sudsy water and splashed the boy's arms. His high-pitched laugh broke off. His body was still now, he looked at Helen with a question. And then it was Karl, the man, in the tub who looked at her. Without looking away, Helen moved her hands so that one cupped the soft, submerged testicles while the other held his penis. She felt it rise until the tip broke the surface of the cooling bath water.

"No," Helen said aloud and pulled hard on the chain of the overhead water closet.

The family was leaving the dining room as she returned from the bathroom. She picked up the roast chicken platter and followed Mrs. Tornberg into the kitchen. From the window over the sink Helen saw a mowed area and Mrs. Tornberg's clothesline.

When she had dried all the dishes, Helen stepped from the kitchen down to the grass. Moisture from the dish pan slops that Mrs. Tornberg had just thrown out seeped through Helen's open-toed shoes. She looked past the clothesline to the edge of the meadow where a path opened into the grasses and wildflowers. She saw an apple orchard a quarter mile away. She leaned against one weathered gray post of the clothesline and breathed deeply, eyes closed. The air was thick with the scent of sweet grass and new mown hay.

"Such good air," she said to Mrs. Tornberg, who bent over a tomato plant.

"Yes, nothing like it in the city."

Helen thought that later she and Karl might walk down the path, the grasses tickling her legs. She imagined his arm as a circle hovering around her waist. Perhaps he would not touch her at first. Then his big hand would settle on her hip, the long fingers spread wide, kneading her through the seersucker dress. She would stop, right there where bees sucked nectar from fireweed along the path, and turn into his arms, feel his hand hesitate on her hip, then move down over the nubbles of the fabric along her thigh. She wanted to feel him bend so that his cheek rested on her breasts as he caught the hem of her skirt and lifted it. A few yards away the grasses at the edge of the path were matted. They could lie there together where some animal had slept, leaving behind its musky scent. Karl's broad lips would graze her face with kisses. She would feel his bristly blond moustache on her cheek. He would whisper her name.

She imagined his fingertips pressed at her hip and the sensations that would race from them down the roadways of her body. She thought of running ahead of Karl to hide in the orchard. Her back was pressed against the licheny bark of an old apple tree when he found her. She felt open, free. Even as he pulled her deeper into the orchard, she felt no fear or sense of sin. When he spread his jacket on a smooth place under four trees that had grown together into a canopy, she walked behind a tangle of bushes and stepped out of her underwear. She rolled the apricot silk into a ball and hid it in the palm of her hand. When she stepped back into the grove, Karl was on his back. The collar of his shirt was open, his suspenders were down, he was unbuttoning his tan trousers.

The image stayed with her even as she answered Mrs. Tornberg's voice.

"Excuse me?" Helen said, turning her head towards the older woman but still moving towards Karl in her thoughts. If she could hold on for just a few seconds, she would see Karl's hand move inside his trousers as she lowered herself over him, her blue and white skirt billowing over their bodies. Only a few moments more and she would feel warmth, pressure, wetness, fullness.

"I said the wash, dear," Mrs. Tornberg repeated. "Would you bring in the tea towels, please?"

Helen pulled the towels from the line, feeling their sun-warmth as she gathered them to her bosom. She tossed the rough wooden pins into a box by the back step and followed Mrs. Torn-berg into the kitchen. As she put away the dishes, Helen watched Karl and Nora, Dolph and Kitty. They sat in a grove of trees, watch-ing the children play. Karl pushed Helen's daughter on the swing that hung from the ancient maple. Amy pumped hard with her stocky legs and looked over her shoulder at Karl, wanting him to push her higher and higher.

When it was time to go home, Helen mourned quietly in the Packard. The children slept in the back seat under throw rugs Karl kept in the trunk for his own children. As they arrived in Savin Hill it was past ten but the sounds of a city street on a warm summer night surrounded them.

"I'll help you get the children to bed," Karl said as he lifted the sleeping Tom from the back seat. Mosquitoes circled the yellow light on the front porch as Helen led the way with Billy and Amy.

Karl refereed as all three clustered around the bathroom sink to do their teeth. Helen laid out pajamas and sent Karl up to the attic room with Billy and Tom, while she tucked Amy into bed in the lit-tle room off the central hall. Amy fell asleep quickly but Karl was upstairs calming the boys for a long time. She heard Billy's high voice, on the edge of hysteria, and Tom's over-tired laugh. She put the kettle on to boil and sat at the kitchen table.

Her modern kitchen was a gift from her husband. "I don't want the queen of my household making meals in a place like this," he said when they moved into 44 King Street. Helen liked the old double soapstone sink and the wooden ice box but when Bill re-placed them with the latest in electrified porcelain and stainless steel, she just smiled. "Yes, I'm lucky," she said to her friends. Bill planned to convert the pantry into a breakfast nook but she per-suaded him to wait until they saved a bit of money.

She heard Karl come down from the boys' room. When he hes-itated on the landing, she felt frightened that he might leave with-out saying goodbye. She watched from the kitchen door until she saw him step into the hall, then went back to her seat at the table.

She liked the light tap of his shoes on the uncarpeted wood as he tiptoed down the dark hall past Amy's open door.

"A cup of tea?" she said as he entered the bright kitchen. He squinted, a boy coming into the light after a long time in the dark. He nodded, as she rushed to the stove to catch the whistling kettle.

"Don't worry," he said. "They're dead asleep. I told them a story about tantagobins and Dallecarlia horses, one my Uncle Adolphus used to tell. I couldn't remember all of it but your fellows didn't seem to notice." Karl laughed. "I think I bored them to sleep. And I was just getting to the best part."

Helen set her grandmother's Austrian china teapot on a wrought iron trivet. She took two English bone china tea cups from the pantry, filled them with hot water and left them in the sink to warm. Bill wanted a set of the pottery dinnerware like the heavy brown mugs and thick plates his stylish sister set out when they had dinner at her house on the third Sunday of every month. When he came home, Helen would buy a set, any kind he wanted. Until then she would use her bone china.

She put an inch of top milk into each warmed cup. The almost black tea turned tan, then beige as she stirred sugar into it. Karl watched her. He lifted the fluted blue and yellow cup to his lips without glancing away from her. She lifted a hand to warn him but it was too late. His cup clattered in the saucer and tea spattered over the linoleum tablecloth. Karl's fingers tested the place where tea still burned on his lips.

Helen hurried to the sink, wet her handkerchief, then pressed the cool cloth to his mouth. Her hand rested on the shoulder of his linen jacket. He looked up at her, then drew her down to his lap. "I'm sorry we didn't have time alone together today," he said. When she didn't answer, he put his hand on her dress over her left breast. "Is there somewhere we could be together now?" he whispered.

"I don't know," she said. "Not the bedroom." She thought of the framed photo of Bill on her dressing table. He looked out at her with pleasant confidence every morning and evening.

"The bathroom?"

"No," she said. "Amy's next door. The walls are thin."

He kissed her neck near her ear. She marveled that a touch in one place could create such disturbance in another. He kissed down her neck and moved his hand from breast to thigh. "The living room? The dining room?" he breathed.

"No doors, no privacy—if the children wake."

"There must be somewhere, Helen, just a few minutes together." He kissed her mouth. His lips were big and moist and his mouth tasted of cloves. When he reached under her skirt, she let him caress her thighs, wondering how long she could wait before it was too late. He shifted her on his lap and tugged at the waist of her underwear. She pulled back from the kiss and stood up. She would say goodnight now, tell him to go.

Instead, she saw the pantry door ajar and gestured him into the dark room. As she shut off the kitchen light, she listened for her children. She tiptoed down the hall and looked at the sleeping Amy. There were no noises from upstairs. She stood in the kitchen a while longer, listening. Then she stepped into the darkness where Karl waited, closing the door behind her.

Months later when she thought of Karl, she still wondered about his body. From the claustrophobic darkness of the pantry she remembered the feel of the hair on his back, the sound of their coming, the smell of sex and kitchen spices, the tingling, the tremors, but she could not imagine what they had looked like together. She could not *see* it. For awhile it had been easy to believe that it was only a fantasy.

Their hands moved awkwardly, grazing each other's skin as they took off their clothes. She was not sure but she imagined that he had been naked except for his brown silk socks and his white shirt. She felt him toss her dress somewhere in the darkness. She took off her bra and rolled her slip to her waist, while the rustle of cloth nearby told her that Karl was taking off his trousers. She thought about removing stockings and garter belt but he came to her breasts before she could. She caressed his shoulders under the smooth cotton of his shirt and kissed his hair. She wished she could see his golden head and freckled shoulders (they would have freckles, she was sure) against her body. The blackout curtain on the narrow window created a darkness so complete she felt disoriented.

"The floor," he whispered. Her stockinged feet slid along the linoleum as he pressed her down. She managed to lie on her back with her knees up, the crown of her head forced against the ribbed wood door of a cabinet. Karl tried to lie over her but the small square of floor surrounded by cabinets would not accommodate his long torso and legs. He lifted her from the floor and they tried to make love standing up. "Damn, my back," he groaned, as his arms guided her down to the floor again.

They tried to couple sitting down but their knees got in the way. Finally, with desperate sweeps of his arms, Karl cleared one counter of canisters, spices, canned goods, and unknown objects that clattered to the floor.

"Oh God, the children," Helen cried.

"Never mind," Karl hissed. She felt him moving, climbing. She sensed that he was above her now. "Come up, come up on the counter, Helen," he whispered, his arms pulling at her wrists. She used the metal drawer pulls as steps and let him hoist her to the counter, where they twisted arms, legs, torsos on the narrow space, trying to bring their private parts together in the suffocating blackness.

Finally, they managed it with Karl sitting on the edge of the counter, Helen on his lap, her legs around his waist. She felt the cool glass through the curtain where her ankles pressed against the tiny window. Something about the utter darkness of the pantry or the unfamiliar feel of Karl drew all of her consciousness to the sensations in that small, powerful triangle of her body as never before. She rocked back and forth, riding forward, pulling back, confident she would not fall as they dug for every possible pleasure in the narrow valley where they were joined.

As the tremors died, Helen wanted them back, so lovely, so brief. Then her legs began to cramp and she was startled by a moist kiss on her cheek. Holy Mother, she thought. She had forgotten Karl.

They scuttled away from each other like satiated crabs. He helped her down to the floor, where they stood in poultry seasoning and ginger powder and kissed once, lightly. They ran their hands over the floor and counters, looking for their clothes. She recognized his underwear from the elastic waistband and metal snap. She shook the shorts briskly, releasing his scent mixed with nutmeg.

"I'll clean up in the bathroom," he said. When he opened the door, there was a rush of warm air from the dark kitchen. Alone in the pantry, Helen cupped her breasts in her hands. When she pressed a hand between her thighs, she was startled by the lingering tremors.

Then she dressed, pulled the cord on the pantry light, stepped around the mess on the floor, and fetched the broom and dustpan.

Karl returned, smelling of gardenia soap. He looked clean and pressed, except for a faint smudge of cinnamon on his shirt collar.

"I could stay with you."

"No," she said.

"I could be gone before the children wake."

"No," she said again.

"It would be nice to sleep with you. And . . . we could do it again."

"There's nowhere to sleep except my husband's bed," she said.

He looked away. He let her hands fall from his to straighten his tie.

"I'll be going then," he said, taking back one hand to kiss the palm. She let him go down the stairs alone. When she took a deep breath, Karl's scent seemed strong in the kitchen air, although she thought it might be only the odd mix of spices they had released in the pantry.

Not until the next morning did she begin to wonder. She leaned against the railing of the back porch and watched the dawn flush the horizon behind the copper beeches in the convent school-yard across the street. It was quiet, too early even for her children. She remembered the confidence of her childhood friend who had said, "You can't get in a family way the first time you're with a particular boy." Of course they were only twelve then. She was older now and Karl was a man, not a boy.

Her thoughts skidded away to Bill. When would he come back from Japan? She felt suddenly angry at Truman and the Army for keeping him away. She needed him back right now. Fingers of anxiety played in her stomach. She hurried from the porch to the kitchen to find the Sears catalog. It might take awhile to get the pottery dinnerware and she wanted it for Bill's homecoming meal.

The Goddess of Sleep

GINU KAMANI

Babies whose feet don't touch ground in their first seven months escape contamination by bad spirits. That's what they say. When Steven first heard of it he recognized immediately that this described the Goddess of Sleep. She had escaped the malevolence that plagued ordinary mortals, and did not even know it. She was a genius at sleep. In her own bed she excelled at slumber, but even in unfamiliar locations she rested peacefully, suffering marginally if at all. He marveled at this uncanny ability to surrender her body to the abyss.

Her talents as the Goddess of Sleep were masked at first by their shyness in bed. Though they embraced long and lovingly, skin touching skin, they separated before sleep settled in and spent the nights side-by-side. He awoke every night at two or three as was his habit, wishing he could fall back to sleep but too anxious to do so. He would watch her then for hours, watch her peaceful breathing, the stillness of her spread hair and gently curled fists. Sometimes she would open her eyes and catch him staring at her, his breath gentle on her cheek. She would smile and turn away, effortlessly reentering the wave of sleep without a ripple to mark her entrance. His panic would overwhelm him then, as if the bus for which he had been racing had abruptly left him sweating on a windy street.

A month or so into the relationship they found their timing, and the first time he unleashed the powerful ripples of her potent muscle, he counted more contractions than he had ever known in a woman. They prepared for sleep with some haste on his part that night because he sensed the possibility of a breakthrough.

Lying on his side he drew her body carefully around his so they formed twin curves extending from shoulder to heel. In minutes she was asleep, and her soft, unwavering breathing melted his body into a pliant liquid that entered into the vessel of her body and took on the shape of her restful peace. He awoke in confusion with the sun piercing his eyes, and cried with relief at having spent the night in dreams.

They discussed their night with great enthusiasm. She had never fallen asleep clasping a lover before. And he never being clasped. He worked steadily on closing the gap between his Goddess's crowning moment and the passage into sleep they took together now. He willed his fingers to grow, relax, twist with unimagined suppleness. He learned to drape himself around her so he could absorb the racking spasms, and while her body still pulsed from her release, their combined breathing slowed to a gentle roll that slid them effortlessly down the chute of sleep.

So many women had preceded his Goddess—his search for the Sleeping Beauty he could lie down with, break bed with, leach sleep from undisturbed. Instead he had stumbled through years of mismatches—women who misunderstood his mission and faked orgasms for him; women who feared his clutching and had nightmares about him; chronic insomniacs who wanted nothing more than to keep company with him. But he definitely had the Goddess of Sleep this time. She smelled right, emitting pheromones of celebration, not fear. She felt right, her skin soft and smooth, covered with silky dark hair. She tasted like mother's milk. She had never rehearsed a climax. She never remembered her dreams.

Her parents came to visit. Unlike their daughter, they still carried the inflections of their native India in their accent, idioms, and pliant body language. They too slept the sleep of the blessed. Was this then a family trait? They laughed at Steven's question. Everyone in India sleeps, they insisted. No problem. In the heat, in the cold, in houses, out in the open, men, women, children. . . . The Goddess of Sleep assured him that this trait emanated from within the culture. He scoffed at her naiveté, mocking this explanation. The parents rose to the challenge and regaled him with stories of individuals sleeping through war, through marching bands, through doors being smashed in, violent storms at sea, on the median of the most congested urban streets. With every story, he felt his heart beating faster. Sweat poured down his back; he felt like a junkie in need of a fix. He turned to the Goddess with shaking limbs. "Why didn't you tell me?" he demanded, his tongue thick with desire. "Take me there now!"

The Air India flight proved the perfect introduction to his coveted kingdom of sleep. As he patrolled the aisles, he saw the Goddess's countrymen lost in snores in the most uncomfortable of positions. Crying babies did not awake them, nor did chattering stewardesses or announcements from the flight deck. They landed in Bombay in the darkness of predawn. The airport was brightly lit with fluorescent tubes, noisy and crowded with residents awaiting their loved ones. Impervious to the bustle, rows of plastic seats cradled human forms divinely suspended in slumber. On the pavements outside where taxi drivers pushed and shoved for access to passengers, prone bodies lay dissolved in rhythmic breathing, oblivious to those stepping over them. The uncomplicated abundance of sleep brought hot tears of envy to his eyes.

Don't you recall in childhood, mused the Goddess, falling asleep at parties, or at the cinema, or on the noisiest bus or train? We're trained in this kind of chaos. We have no choice but to make lullabies of this vitality.

The hotel was located in a crowded area. By day, hordes of office workers filtered through the streets. Book and magazine vendors spread their wares on the pavement, makeshift canvas stalls displayed imported goods, food stands fried up spicy snacks, all attracting commuters as they hurried between their trains and office buildings and back again. At night, families ventured out for a late stroll, wealthy patrons flocked to expensive restaurants, and pavement dwellers prepared their evening meals and settled down for the night.

But here sleep teased him too; rather than lying awake beside the Goddess, Steven found himself returning to the dark streets each night without her, reluctant to return to the hotel. Close to midnight, revellers still jostled by in groups, searching out a bite to eat. Kerosene lamps blazed brightly at each locus of activity, and within inches of the bustling commerce, humans spread themselves out in sleep.

Even later, Steven watched a solitary old man cook his late meal on a small stove, eat out of the pan, wash it out over the gutter with a cupful of water, then pack all his worldly belongings into a small bag. A body-length rectangle of plastic spread on the rough pavement was his bed, and in seconds he and his bag disappeared under a grimy sheet.

All night the inert, shrouded forms on the sidewalks beckoned him. Never had Steven experienced stepping over and around the various postures of sleep. Many times he paused amongst the cloaked forms, listening intently to their palpable exertions. Each body in trance concealed a body in healing.

The next night he was back to watch his solitary friend prepare for sleep. The old man recognized him and waved in greeting. Squatting on the pavement finishing his meal, he spoke to the nearby stall owner, who wryly translated in English. The foreigner was being invited to share a meal. Would he accept? No thanks, Steven replied, Already eaten. But he had a question for the kind street dweller: Where did he learn to sleep? The stall owner scratched his chin with amusement. He repeated the question once, twice to the old man. Back came the astonished reply: At his mother's breast, where else?

The dark man washed out his vessel with a great show of scrubbing and polishing, aware of being watched. Then he sat back and watched the foreigner watching him. They sat in silence for a while, and the man made no move toward rolling out his plastic sheet. Steven prodded the stall owner and pleaded: The man should sleep, he liked watching him sleep. Thoroughly entertained, surrounded by a gaping crowd, the translator conveyed Steven's request. Back came the irritated reply. In his country, did they not sleep?

The conversation transformed into a communal event, an impromptu convention on a busy street. A barrage of questions in broken English flowed unabated from the growing crowd. Dark eyes twinkled and flashed, hands touched him casually, ascertaining his corporeal nature. A feeling of deep benevolence descended on the American as he fielded inquiries on a vast array of topics. Even as he spoke, individuals thrust out their hands to be shaken, savoring the feel of having gone palm to palm with him. Others ran fingers down the crease of his pants and over the fine leather artistry of his Italian shoes. The crowd closed in on him with effortless coagulation. His skin tingled with waves of contact. His body filled with unfathomable well-being. Soon he had both arms over the shoulders of chatty young men who invited him for a cup of tea. As they left the spot, he noticed that in the midst of his own adrenaline surging, the street dweller had veiled himself and fallen asleep.

Two nights stretched into five, and the Goddess seriously worried about her lover. He stayed out until dawn, then escorted her all day through family visits, shopping, sightseeing. He seemed to have given up sleeping, yet glowed with an unfamiliar light. Something had changed in their lovemaking, too. They made love as before and the Goddess relinquished herself to the depths but he held himself aloof, waiting for the tide of anxiety to wash over him, but it never came. Instead, each night he would feel a vague stirring within him and images of his street friends would dance again through his mind.

The groan of the ceiling fans, the horns of passing cars, the shouts of passersby swirled in a time-tested melody. He felt a yearning to lose himself in the dense crowds, to be ogled by the dark-eyed stares and the impulsive reachings for his skin. He liked the sensation of locking his gaze with every passing individual, of being endlessly consumed by the quizzical masses, of emotionally recharging through the powerful call and response expressed in a look, in a smile, in a posture that invited "Show Me."

Steven gazed a long last time at his sleeping Goddess and knew this was no longer where he belonged. He got up and slipped out the doors and into the beckoning human stream.

The implausible lovely

LEONORE WILSON

The implausible lovely
body of the unfaithful;
the unimaginable
limbs I collapse into
when the blue-black
of night consumes us.
His face of ruin and resentment
because he knows we are not
the shape of strength
but of suffering; we are
what is buried
in the world—
old capsule of indifference
and death. Our helpless
empty is the first thing
in the morning we wake up to;
malice of blankets
tossed off like a secret.
The unrequited aching
of doves
is the knot
in marriage,
the invisible drifting,
the muck
and mire of what we
want and don't
want, not memory,
(memory both
sweet and blind).
We are the long arrow
of flesh,
male and female,

knowledge without peace,
not what is
precious or clear.
We cling because we are
pointless,
two slabs at right angles.
We are the beauty
of coolness, of discarding
and decline. We are
the common
not the excessive;
the continual and continuous,
not the sheen
but the unharmony—
earth
made ungodly in design.

Sex While Driving

LEONORE WILSON

Under the steering wheel
that sang over my neck
like a dark star, I hid my face.
Here I was saved.
Here I learned the structure
of every highway north
(out of the pastures of sunflowers,
out of the young fields of winter corn)—
My childhood faith
crouched in the canyons.
It was afraid.

It knew I would come there.
He would pull me from his lap
into the gully.
Driving was just foreplay.
The earth wanted us;
we were never really locked out
out of the garden.
Its spark was inside us;
we were the season missing
and found. We were the savior,
the one mourned for and benevolent.
The car was only a vehicle,
an instrument;
like a good parent it wanted us
to go further into the world.
We learned our positions first in its belly.
It was not greedy;
it loved its children.
It gave us that permission.
It said run from your mother,
my babies, my blessed ones,
unfurl.

The Life of the Body

JANE SMILEY

I had been going to call my sister Rhonda when the phone rang, and even then, when I heard her voice, I thought that I could just open my mouth and tell her, but when she heaved a blue, premenstrual sigh and said, "So what are you going to do today," I just said what I always say, oh nothing. I thought, another day. Just another day. Then the time will be more right, somehow.

The fact is that I am in about the worst trouble I have ever heard of anyone being in. After Rhonda hung up, the phone rang four separate times. There is no one I dare to hear from, and so I let it ring. If I had picked it up, I would have said to anyone on the other end that I am pregnant, that Jonathan Ricklefs is the father, not Jake, my husband, and that everything inside me is about to be revealed, layer by layer, to Jake, to Jonathan, to Rhonda and our parents, to my son Ezra and my daughter Nancy, to people who care about me and to people who barely know me. What is it that will shame me most when it is revealed? Maybe it is the crazy force of my desire for Jonathan, the full extent of which I have kept from him and which makes me squirm with discomfort even as a secret. But maybe it is something else, something that has not even been revealed to me yet.

I used to have three children. The third was Dory. Five months ago, when she was almost three, she fell head over heels down the stairs. She went over three times, we think. She broke her neck at the bottom and died that afternoon. Various children around the country have her liver, her kidneys, her corneas. There was no one to receive her heart at that moment. A heart is something that can't be saved for very long. She had a little book in her hand when Jake found her at the bottom. It was a habit we couldn't break her of, "reading" on the stairs. Really, she didn't know how to read yet, but she loved to look at the pictures.

I was getting dressed in our bedroom, Jake was ironing his shirt, Nancy and Ezra were eating breakfast. We all heard the long cry of surprise and fear, the thump of limbs toppling and hitting, the utter silence of the house around those noises. All struck dumb, all thinking, *What's that?* all listening. The rustle of buttonholes, stopped, the swish of the iron, stopped, the interior crunch of cereal and toast, stopped.

I can't say what I would have given to have been standing at the bottom of the stairs, holding out my arms to catch Dory. My inner life isn't very mysterious or symbolic. I often dream that I am there, that she is saved. Some part of me, in the dream, always asserts that even if the last time was a dream, this time it is true. It isn't.

Jake wouldn't let me speak at the funeral. He was afraid I would say something outrageous. I might have. I might have said, What right do I have to grieve, having lost only one? Isn't the society of mothers who have lost some many times bigger than the society of mothers who have kept all theirs? I would have said a lot of contradictory things, since I was very confused. Instead, we thanked God who took her away for giving her to us in the first place. That was Jake's idea. He is a religious person, more so now.

Jonathan is a fatalist rather than a providentialist. Things come and go. Forces arrange themselves so that he will, for example, eat granola instead of a peach. When I think of the way he sees himself, I imagine a kind of pinpoint at the vortex of a whirlpool. Blakean swirls above his head. Streaks of light moving through darkness. He is not a very hopeful person. I used to tease him about it. When I tell him I am pregnant, he will nod slowly, his expectations of the worst confirmed.

Maybe that is what I hate most about this, all the suspicions confirmed, especially the suspicions about me that everyone seems to harbor—that Dory's death has made me crazy, that Jake and I have never gotten along, that I would do anything to tie Jonathan to me, that I wanted to replace Dory at any cost, that women are by nature evil, irresponsible, and deceptive. What does it say in the Bible? *And I find more bitter than death the woman, whose heart is snares and nets, and her hands as bands: whoso pleaseth God shall escape from her; but the sinner shall be taken by her.* All that stuff. Once on the *Today* show, I saw a man who had written a book about the Dionne quintuplets. When they were born, their mother was ashamed. She said, "People will think that we are pigs." So much intercourse revealed to the world. Well, I was never proud of my pregnancies. Just by looking at you, people knew what you were thinking about.

I could have told Jake last night. I could have told Jonathan last night, too, when he brought over some lettuce from his garden. It doesn't make it any easier that this will be the first news Jake has had of my affair with Jonathan. Jonathan talks well to Jake. Not many people do—Jake is antisocial and impatient, and his idea of a serviceable conversational gambit is "What do you want?" Someone else who talks well to Jake is Rhonda. I am tempted to tell her, and let her tell them all. She is a great moaner. "Ooooh, Sarah. Ooh, Sarah." That is how she listens to confidences, moaning those word-less cries that you would like to be moaning yourself. "Ooh, Sarah. Ooooh Sarah." I try it out, out loud, but it isn't the same. I know I should be finishing the sentence, "Oooh Sarah you shithead," which is something Rhonda would never even think of doing.

There is the crunch of wheels in the driveway, Jake returning from work, as he often does. He will find me standing over the sink, as he often does. I get up and position myself there. He comes in and runs up the stairs. There is the slamming of closet doors up-stairs, the thump of his heavy feet. He really has forgotten something, he always really has, but he never did before Dory died. The manifestation of his grief is more than forgetfulness, it is perennial searching. Though he gave up smoking years ago, his hands wander his pockets in search of cigarettes. He is always making sure he has his keys, his wallet, his checkbook. I find him in closets looking for sweaters and pairs of slippers and magazine articles we threw out years ago. He turns over the cushions, puts his hands in the cracks, comes up with pennies that he gives to Nancy. He calls his mother and asks if his old yearbooks are at her house, his swimming trunks from high school, his old Bo Diddley records. We are patient with this searching, his mother and I. Even Jake knows what he is searching for, but he can't stop just because he won't find her.

He appears in the kitchen doorway. I have my hands in the water, as if I were doing something, and it might be that, not look-ing at him, looking out the back window at the peonies blooming in the yard, I will say, "I'm pregnant." I know the words, I've said it before. But of everyone in the whole world, Jake is the only other person who knows that we haven't slept together since the week before Dory died. It is also possible that I will tell no one, just wait for them to notice, and ask. It may be that social nicety will prevent most people from asking. It may be that fear will prevent Jake from asking, and even greater fear will prevent Jonathan from asking, and a year from now I will say, in a cocky voice, "Ever wonder where I got this baby?"

Jake says, "I forgot the reports. I can't believe I actually forgot the reports."

"It's okay."

"Of course it's okay. That isn't what I'm talking about. I just can't believe it. I'm just remarking on that, is all."

"I know."

"What are you going to do today?" He asks suspiciously, because he thinks that my grief is to loiter around the house for hours, then hurry and clean up just before Ezra and Nancy get home. It was. Lately my grief has been to go to bed with Jonathan Ricklefs as much as possible, on every flat surface in his apartment. I say, "I'm going to go to Rhonda's dance class with her again, then I'm going to order meat at the locker, then bake cookies with Nancy for the day camp birthday party. How about cooking out for dinner? It's already getting hot enough."

"Will you make potato salad?" He glides up next to me, kisses me on the neck, as if bribing me. I turn and put my hands on his shoulders. I smile, as if being bribed. "I'll boil the potatoes as soon as you leave."

"The day camp counselor thinks Nancy seems fine. She's playing with everyone, and the shyness has worn off completely. She's making a belt in the crafts class."

"Good."

"Ezra is being more reserved."

"Ezra is more reserved."

"How much more?"

"Sweetie, I wish I knew. He likes the horses. Yesterday he told me about the horses for about twenty-five minutes. His favorite is named Herb. He got to go into the stable and give Herb his oats." We smile at Herb. Jake smiles at me. He thinks we are coming out of things when in fact we are just getting started. Another day. I will let him go another day. He pecks me on the cheek and leaves with a number of slams: the kitchen door, the garage door, the car door. He is a noisy man.

Rhonda dances every day. Lately I have been going with her. This is not aerobics, it is serious modern dance. The other students are mostly in their teens and early twenties. The teacher is a black man who dances in a local company. I don't know why he lets me come, except that he is a friend of Rhonda's, and she is my sister. Rhonda, although she is thirty-two and has two children, turns out to have considerable talent for the dance. The first day I came, she warmed up, without shame, by stretching and then doing three slow cartwheels and a couple of handstands. I was amazed. I keep up well with the slower third of the twenty-year-olds, and mostly Henry doesn't pay any attention to us. We pay attention to him, though. Pas de cheval: Henry says, "You know how a puppy licks your arm? So that every pore and hair gets wet? Well, make the sole of your foot lick the floor." Deep second position: "You are in water! Your head is floating upward! Your knees are floating outward! Lift! Lift!" He tells us not to mimic him, but to feel ourselves, our muscles and tendons sliding and rolling, our balls and sockets rotating.

Today we have hamstrings and adductors for half an hour, then chaîné turns for half an hour. My days here, as everywhere, are numbered, and so when we lie on our backs and rotate our hips outward and find the place on each side where the tendons split, I am careful to note what it feels like. When we then curl up to standing, I think only of my spine, catlike, and my long, furry tail anchoring me to the floor. When we step and pivot across the floor, I push my toes through the wet mud Henry evokes, and leave long swathes filling with water behind me. After four times across the floor, we lie down and slither through that same mud, chests first, trying not to get our chins wet.

The first to go are Nancy and Ezra, who are active and well taken care of. Then I stop thinking about Rhonda, even though she is just ahead of me in line. Jake vanishes next, with his expectations that are soon to be betrayed. Now Dory, who never knew me as a dancer, who has no associations with this room or these people (they know my first name only, if that). After that, I forget I am pregnant, and at last, sometime in the triple prances ("Sli-i-ide snap! snap!" says Henry), even Jonathan lets go. Henry becomes Henry the dancer rather than Henry the man. We are panting. Henry tells the accompanist to speed up the tempo, and we are running. Henry goes first, down-up-up, arms and chin swooping then lifting. Someone in red and black does it after him, a flute passage on the heels of a bassoon passage, and then it is me, and the only thing I feel is the slick floor under my feet and the rush of my fingers through the air, up-up!

The one in red and black, of course, is Rhonda, who is damp with sweat from ponytail to heel, and when class is over, she says, "God, let's shower and eat at my place. I've got spaghetti left over from last night."

It is words that bring them all back with a suffocating rush. "God." "My place." "Last night." We are fixed in place and time after all. Henry passes us on the way out. "Lovely," he says. He is a big man, happy, Rhonda says, because he gets a lot of oxygen to the brain.

I should tell her in the locker room, naked in the shower, but I make excuses. Now that she is right here, it seems like Jonathan should be the first to know, then Jake, then her. Then our parents, then the children. That's the obvious order, just as Rhonda-Jake-Jonathan was last night, when Jake and Jonathan were standing with their hands in their pockets under the hackberry tree, considering ways to save it from whatever is infesting it.

There is this space, of course, this carefully made space in the day when I will see Jonathan. After the meatlocker, after lunch, before Nancy and Ezra get home from day camp. I enter the downstairs door quickly, and run up. The door opens at the first brush of my first knock. Jonathan is grinning. "Hi," he says, "Hi, hi, hi." He locks the door behind me. He looks me up and down. I catch sight of a pot of tea steaming behind him on the coffee table and I burst into tears. It isn't the first time, nor does it come from the press of present circumstances. All of this sadness has been there from the beginning. I think, in fact, that this affair was begun as a tribute to sadness, gathered force through sadness, and will result in more sadness for everyone than we can possibly stand.

I feel utterly comfortable weeping here.

Perhaps more importantly, Jonathan feels utterly comfortable with my weeping. I sit on the couch and he pours the tea and then he sits beside me and folds me into his chest, and soon I am weeping and kissing him, and he is wiping my face with a paper napkin and kissing me, and that is how it has gone for months, salty kisses, passion, and grief. I am, as they say, shameless. Often we don't make love, but today we do. Today when he kisses me with his lips, I give him my tongue, only my tongue, and then I feel his, meeting mine, and instantly my nipples, tender with pregnancy, stand up, burning. As much as they hurt, I long to have him lick and suck them, and when I think of that, they tingle suddenly, as if milk were about to come down. They haven't done that since Dory was nursing, and it is the most intense feeling of physical longing, the longing to give suck. I almost tell the news, but I don't.

Jonathan kisses my neck and shoulders, and his erection presses against my leg, presses into my imagination, the thick, smooth shape, the reddish color—I am as familiar with it as I am with my own hand, more familiar, since I have looked at it, tasted it, touched and held it, smelled it. A weighty, living object. Sometimes at night, after Jake goes to sleep and I am lying awake in fear and guilt, I just open my mouth and put my tongue out, wishing, thinking how I would lick the little crease and then run my tongue under the cap, marveling always at the warm shape of it. He sucks my breasts and I push both hands into his pants, unsnapping them, forcing the zipper down. He hops a little on the couch, then pulls my T-shirt up. It tangles in my arms and hair. I am still weeping. I am happy to be trapped inside this shirt with my nipples burning, my cunt throbbing. I open my mouth and put my tongue out.

"Sarah!" he moans. "Oh, Sarah oh oh." And then he strips off my shorts and shoes and sucks my toes and after that he licks my cunt, and licks and licks, parting the lips and putting his fingers in, licking, finding, at last, the spot that burns so that I push him away, his head, his shoulders. He pushes back, licking, his tongue fastened to that spot. My legs turn to water, and my back arches, and for a moment he is gone, and then he eases into me, slow and slick, and his tongue is in my open mouth and his fingers are in my ears and his chest, smooth and firm, in its way, as a penis, is sliding along my chest, and then he does something I always like, which is to lift my legs to my shoulders so that he can get in and in, and he gets in, so far that he relaxes a little, and closes his eyes. I push him off, out. He is shocked, his flesh is shocked at the suddenness of it, but before he realizes, I have it, his penis in my mouth, as I have wanted, and I am licking and stroking. I like to feel this, that he cannot stop himself. He does not. I swallow. He falls back on the couch, pulling me with him, holding me tight, panting. This is the way it has gone for months. I cling to him in desperate fear, but I am no longer weeping.

Sometimes I dream that I am just a torso, and blind, born that way, skin, a mouth, breasts, a cunt more open than any cunt ever, and Jonathan is engulfing me as well as penetrating every orifice. I dream that all I can do in life is fuck and suck and kiss and be embraced, and that I orgasm over and over and never get enough. Sometimes I daydream it.

The tension flows back into his flesh. I feel it along my chest, in his shoulder where my ear and cheek rest. His arm tightens over my back, and his other arm moves. When I lift my head to look at him, I see that he has covered his eyes with his elbow. I lower my head gently and wait, as still as possible. His heart has not relaxed, and is pounding steadily faster. As I open my mouth to speak, he says, "Sarah, talk to me."

I lift my head. "You want me to open the conversation."

"It's hopeless."

"What is hopeless." I can't make it a question, must make it a denial.

"Sarah—"

"Don't say anything, just don't say anything. Do you love me?"

He answers without hesitation but not without pain, "I tell you I do over and over. I do."

"Then don't say anything."

"Do you love me?"

"I think of you without ceasing, day and night."

"Do you love me?"

"You possess me."

"Sarah, do you love me?"

After minutes go by and I don't answer, he sits up and puts me away from him and pours the tea. I reach for my T-shirt and pull it on, but I don't stop shivering. I watch him drink his tea, catching tea leaves on the tip of his tongue and picking them off with his finger. He knows I am looking at him and from time to time turns his gaze to mine. This is another thing that we feel comfortable with, staring and being stared at. He is a big man, broad and muscular, utterly defeated, as an ox goeth to the slaughter. When we met, I was attracted to his self-reliance, his detached outlook. Both of those are gone now. I wonder how much he wants them back. He says, "I am terrified."

"Are you terrified that it will go on or are you terrified that it will stop?"

"Both."

"Are you frightened of me or for me?"

"Both."

"Will love find a way? If we stick together, can we make it?"

"Sometimes I think so. Weaker moments. Oh, Sarah." He covers his eyes again. A moment later I see tears on his cheeks. I look away. He goes on. "It's too painful. Sometimes I feel like our clothes are lined with nails and the tighter we embrace, the more blood we draw from each other."

I say, "It was fun at the beginning. That's important. A book I read says that you draw on the strengths of the relationship when you remember the beginning. I used to be known for my sense of humor, actually. Jonathan, suspend choice, all right? No action, no decision, just endurance." But he is slippery. As soon as he admitted fear, I felt it myself, telegraphed from him to me. I felt the size of the betrayal that would be possible just to escape that fear. Which arm, which leg, which sense would I have given just to escape that fear the moment I saw my daughter at the bottom of the stairs?

"A day," I say. "Only another day. Don't make up your mind or even think anything for another day. Go canoeing. Go to the movies. Eat something soothing, with lots of B vitamins. If I leave now, I might beat Nancy home by a minute." I run out the door, down the steps, out the lower door. I know he is watching me from the window. He fell in love with me when Dory died. That is why my chest closes up when I try to say that I love him. I don't want to

be loved for my belongings, even if that belonging is only an en-
largement that springs from tragedy.

I make a lot of mistakes. This time it is the potato salad, which I forgot, though Jake asked for it specifically. I forgot about it all the way
until he looked in the refrigerator and said, "Didn't you make the
potato salad?" and so there was no evasive action possible. I say,
"I'll do that thing."

"What thing?"

"That thing where I go to the deli and get some of theirs, then
redress it. You like that."

"You were going to put the potatoes on as soon as I left."

"I forgot."

"How could you forget? You were standing right here in the
kitchen. All you had to do was turn around and take the potatoes
out of the cupboard."

"I forgot."

"I'm not mad. I just don't understand you."

"You forgot your reports."

"I was working on them last night. I put them aside."

"I don't want to argue about fine points."

"It means something," he says. "The way people act means
something. You know that."

"I forgot."

He shakes his head and goes outside to start the fire. Before he
addressed me on the topic of potato salad, I was standing over the
dishwater, as always, washing up the cookie things and pondering
the recollection of Jonathan sucking my breasts, thinking that I
would like him to kiss all of my skin at the same time. Jonathan
knows in his heart that what I crave from him are impossibilities.
That is why he is afraid of me.

Out the kitchen window, Jake comes into view, carrying the
charcoal and the lighter fluid. Most people, including Jonathan, feel
lots of sympathy for him. Soon they'll feel more. They think he
must grieve a great deal for Dory. I don't know. I wish I had seen
the first look on his face when he got to her, but I started from back
in the closet in our bedroom upstairs, and by the time I reached

them at the bottom of the stairs, he was already practical, had already covered her with the afghan and was calling the ambulance, wouldn't let her be moved. He has never cried in my presence. Nor have I cried in his presence. But we do not pretend that everything is normal. We strive with all our might to make a routine, a little thread that will guide Ezra and Nancy, and maybe ourselves, out of the labyrinth.

That our sex life ended did not surprise me. Jake does not seek comfort in the flesh of others. He has to feel good to reach out. When he does not feel good, he avoids people. All of his brothers are the same way. When their father died three years ago, they gathered in Tallahassee for four days, five men. They built a bathroom out of the downstairs porch of their mother's house, taking maybe four hours out for the funeral and the burial. I asked Jake if they talked about their father in there, while they were grouting and caulking. He said, "Ralph did, a little." He didn't touch me for four months. I didn't mind. I think about Jonathan putting his face between my thighs and licking, sticking his tongue in; Jake comes up behind me and says, "Are you going to get the potato salad now or not?" and I start violently. He turns me around, his hands on my shoulders, and looks into my eyes. His face is very close to mine, and he is serious. He says, "Sarah, can't you pay attention? That's not an accusation. I want to know. Is that the problem, that you can't pay attention?"

"I'm trying. Don't watch me."

"I wish I could help myself."

I pull away. "I'll get the potato salad now, okay? Nancy is over at Allison's house, and Ezra is watching television."

"Don't get distracted. Half an hour, okay? Be back in half an hour."

"I will."

"I mean it."

"I will." It is for my own good, so I won't wander, so I'll keep my mind on the business at hand.

That is the beginning. The second incident takes place when I am coming out of Nancy's room after putting her to bed. Jake is in the hallway, looking at the bookshelves. I turn to say one last thing to Nancy, and Jake's arm goes around my waist. Distracted, I stiffen. Then I relax, but the stiffening doesn't go unnoticed. His arm drops. We stand there for an awkward second, then he chooses a book, and I turn and go down the stairs.

In the end, we argue about religion rather than sex. It is dark when I come into our bedroom, and I think Jake is asleep, but he speaks in a firm, clear voice, surprising in the dark. "Can I tell you something?" I push the top drawer of the dresser in, and he takes this for assent. I stand quietly, looking at the parallelogram of moonlight on the top of the dresser. "There was this time, when my mother's younger sister died of complications of childbirth. I guess I was about fourteen. Anyway, we had just moved to that house in Tallahassee, and I came in from doing something outside. Maybe we were helping Dad move that shed. That was one of the first things we had to do. It was almost dark, and Mom was sitting in the dark, snapping beans for dinner, and everyone else was outside, and when I went to turn on the light, she said, 'Jake, leave it dark,' so I left it dark, and she said, 'The Lord helps a man be good, Jake. If you let Him come inside you, He is a tide that carries you to goodness. But you've got to open the door yourself.' That was all she said, and then Richie came in and turned on the light and pretty soon we had dinner. Sarah, I know it's hard to find the door. It took me ten years to find the door, but I found it."

"It's not a door I want to find, Jake. Your mother was a religious woman, and she raised you, and so she was preaching to the converted. Before we got married, she said you'd come back to it, and you did. Big surprise."

"I tried the other way."

"You always thought of it as the other way. I don't believe, Jake. It's not in me. My brain doesn't have that bump. It's not in my horoscope. I went to Sunday school and read the Bible and it didn't take. If you didn't bring it up, I wouldn't think about it."

"But maybe me bringing it up is the Lord's way of trying to get your attention. I can't stop doing it. I *am moved* to do it. Don't you understand what that means?"

By now I have gotten, without realizing it, into the dark corner between the dresser and the wall. I open my mouth, but I know perfectly well how Jake's life looks to him: in retrospect, a series of perfectly timed nudges toward the right path that his mother would have, and often had, called miracles—a moment of despair, and then she looks up to see the minister on the porch, about to ring the bell. That happened more than once. I didn't necessarily discount her interpretation. It does seem to me that the world and the inner life mesh in mysterious ways more often than not.

I run my finger around the edge of the moonlight. More than anything, I want him to stop badgering me. I say, "I understand that you are driving me nuts with this God shit. I got some tracts in the mail again yesterday. Did you send them?"

He is out of bed in an instant, moved to rage by everything unbearable that we have to bear. I find that I am in a tight spot, between the wall and the dresser, and as I am trying to get out, he takes me by the shoulders and bumps my head on the wall. I press against him. His grip tightens, and I can feel the panic roll up from my toes all at once. I know he won't hurt me, but I feel that he will kill me. The walls behind me and to my left are unyielding, cold, terrifying. I bend down. His hands press harder on my shoulders, weights that I cannot evade. I do the only thing that I can possibly do, which is to push hard against the wall with my hip, and hard against the dresser with my hands. It falls over with a crash, and the stained glass box Jake keeps pennies in flies toward the window. I see this out of the corner of my eye. Jake does it again, bumps my head against the wall, this time hard, and simultaneously with the sound of breaking glass. Then I get out from under him, clamber over the dresser, and flee the room. For the rest of the night, which I spend on the sofa, every time I fall into a doze, I seem to feel my head being slammed into glass, and I wake up expecting to reach up and find blood pouring down my face.

When I loved Jake, when our relationship wasn't too complicated to have a label like that, it was this absolute quality that I loved, this straightness, this desire for goodness, and mostly the struggle he put up with himself, the manly difficulty of that. I didn't know anyone like him. I don't know that this appreciation is reciprocated—when he talks about me to his pastor and other men he likes who are religious, they will have a long tradition of misogyny to consult. He will not be guided to see things from my point of view. Well, deep in the night, curled up on the couch with the pillow over my head, somewhere in the realm of sleep, I do feel what he felt and see what he saw and hear what he heard: the flippant and dismissive tone of my voice, the indifference of my face in the half light, the inviting and unusual way I was wedged into that space, easy prey, and deserving of punishment too. I feel again the corner enclosing my flesh, the panic surging out of me in a flood, and I wake up with a start. Containing both points of view at once makes me short of breath. I sit up and gaze around the living room. For the first time in weeks, I don't want Jonathan. I try to make myself think of him, but my mind won't fix.

Jonathan used to run a millworks, producing hardwood moldings for lumberyards. He made some money and sold the business, and now he goes to school in horticulture and landscape architecture. He taught an extension course in tree fruits, which is where I met him, and which is why he has his days free and why he can talk to Jake, whose only ambition in life is to run a market garden with his brother Richie. Richie would grow only corn, Jake would do the other vegetables and press cider in the fall. I would do fresh-cut flowers in season and apples in the fall. Right now Jake and Richie have other jobs: Richie manages a big A & P in the next town and Jake works for the county government as an accountant. Jake and Richie and I own 57 acres, free and clear. Next summer, the five brothers are going to begin building a house on the land. Every weekend, all spring, Jake and Richie have gone out to the property and walked its every inch, looking for the best site for the house and the garden and the garden buildings. That gave Jonathan and me four or five extra hours every week that we wouldn't have had, and it was on one of those weekends, when I forgot my diaphragm, that I got pregnant. In the ten years of marriage, I have forgotten it off and on, without consequences, and each of the other pregnancies took a number of months, and so I was careless. Careless and lazy: I realized I had forgotten it before I was to the end of our street, but I couldn't bear to turn back and thought I would trust to luck, as I had in the past. Careless and lazy and possessed. There have been times in the last seven months

when putting off seeing Jonathan for even ten minutes was the
cruelest torture.

We bought the property two years ago, with savings and with
Jake's and Richie's portions of their father's estate. I like Richie. All
that summer he would come over about dinnertime and sit on
the porch swing, talking to Jake about what sort of house they
would build and watching Dory. Dory was sixteen months when
we bought the land. When Richie was here, we would prop open
all the doors and she would charge through all the rooms and in
and out of the house. He would help her down the front steps, and
she would tear around the yard, which was fenced. She was utterly
safe and utterly free, and maybe for that reason, much happier than
Nancy and Ezra were at that age. Rhonda and Walker came over a
lot too. We have all known each other for a long time. Lots of times,
Rhonda would go into the kitchen and open the cabinets and start
making dinner, and though I had disagreements with Jake that
everyone knew about, there was a largeness and comfort to family
life that soothed me. It spread in every direction, over the landscape, from the past into the future. It was enough to buy land and
plan, to care for the children, to dig and plant. Richie and Walker
distracted Jake, engaged him in conversation, made him feel at
ease. Whatever was missing between us got to seem like just a certain coloring, a certain way the landscape might be lit but wasn't,
nothing particular, considering everything else that was there.
Richie, after all, wasn't even married, had never, as far as we knew,
had a steady girlfriend.

Usually, these days, it seems like nothing, what we had at all
those dinnertimes, but just now, when I am cold and tired and
frightened of sleep, it seems like a thing of substance and weight,
safe as a vault, with the child rolling through it like a golden ball.

I don't know anyone who has had an abortion, but it can be
done. Rhonda would know all about it. And if this were the moment when it was to be done, I would do it, because no one else is
here, not Jonathan or Nancy or Ezra or Jake or Richie or Rhonda
or my mother. Only I am here, and for the moment Jake has
pounded sentiment out of me. Nothing in this room, which we
bought and filled with our purchases, means a thing to me, not

even the pictures. Nothing I have ever felt or thought or given voice to remotely interests me just now, no principle or affection or intention. I sit against the arm of the couch, waiting to make up my mind to have an abortion.

Instead it must be that I fall asleep, because Ezra wakes me, and it is daylight, though just barely. Ezra always comes down early and expects to have the house to himself for an hour. He says, "Mommy, can I turn on the TV?" and the day is begun. I look at him for a long moment, until he smiles in self-defense, and then I say, "Do you have riding again today?" and he grins. He says, "Alan, you know, the head of riding, he said I could ride Herbie every time, if I asked." He goes and turns on the TV, then glances back at me. "He's a real good horse, Mom. And he's a horse, not a pony."

"Hmm."

"Do you know the difference?"

"I do, actually."

"Well, he's a horse."

"Good, sweetie." I pull myself up the stairs and into the bathroom.

At breakfast I act as if nothing has happened, and Jake can think he is getting away with something if he wants. I put his eggs in front of him and meet his gaze, and I am nearly as tender with him as I am with the children, brushing their shoulders or hair with my hand. And then they are gone, and I pick up the phone and I call Jonathan and make a date with him for lunch. His voice is distant, distracted. After that I make sure that Rhonda is going to her dance class and that I can come along. Then I do the dishes and sweep the kitchen. In fact, I get down on my hands and knees with the butler's brush and sweep like I've never swept before, getting the dust and sand of seven years out of the corners, off the top edge of the moldings, out from under the stove and refrigerator. When I am finished, I am dusty and sweaty. I go around and open the windows, catching what breeze there is. After that I take another shower.

The fact is that this is the last hour of the old life. Things that are soft are about to harden and take the simple shapes that may last them the rest of my life. For example, I don't hate Jake and I don't love Jonathan. Whatever I feel for each of them is like one of those dye baths that you dip the endpapers of books in—a riot of colors swirled together, compounded of everything each has confided in me and everything I have confided in each of them. At this moment, I have the feeling that each time I have looked at each one of them is distinct and significant, that I know some discrete grain of truth about each of them as a result of every glance. The large thing that I know about them is that they are not each other, but that large thing is compounded of the numberless small ways in which they are not each other. I don't blame them for not being each other, but as soon as I speak, they will move into position. Jake, betrayed, will become my enemy. Jonathan, responsible, will become my partner. I would be deluding myself if I didn't know that Jake will consider my pregnancy a moral outrage in addition to an injury to himself. If he doesn't tell his brothers, and probably my children, that I am a whore, then he won't be the Jake I have known for ten years. And so the children will move into position too: confused at first, judgmental later, damaged forever. And Jonathan. Well, Jonathan. Just because I know that he will do the right thing, does that mean I planned for him to? At lunch I'll tell him I'm pregnant before he tells me we have to end our affair, and for a lot of reasons, he will swallow his doubts, and I will swallow mine, and sometime soon I will tell him that I love him, because I will love him. I will move into position too. Maybe.

A week after the funeral, when the children were back in school, I walked to the library and then to Jonathan's house. It was the day before Valentine's Day, warm and sunny, with snow melt trickling down every gutter. I had thrown away the valentine I intended to give him—it was one of those cynical and sexy ones, and when I found it in my purse the day after the funeral, it seemed to be cursed, so I tore it up, tore it up again, took it down the street, and threw it into some dry cleaner's dumpster. I was chastened. Everything having to do with Jonathan Ricklefs frightened me. We hadn't slept together very often—our friendship was more teasing and drinking tea than anything else. He seemed invulnerable, possibly dating someone else, though I wasn't sure. Jake was at work, my mother had left, the children were back in school, and I was walking down the street, glad to be put back together a little bit, glad that the previous night was over and the night to come wasn't yet upon me. I climbed the step and rang the bell, and I remember turning and looking down the street, idly, thinking of nothing for a moment. And then the door opened, and Jonathan was there, and his hand closed around my elbow, and he pulled me into the hallway where he hugged me and looked at me and put his hand on my face and then hugged me again, and just at that moment when he looked at me, I knew two things at once, that Dory was dead and that Jonathan loved me as he had not loved me ten days before. I don't know that any relationship can survive that sort of birth for long. Or maybe the root is this, that when I was standing in the closet that morning, buttoning my shirt, it was Jonathan I was thinking of, Jonathan who had delayed me in the closet, taking off one shirt and putting on another. I was thinking about him sucking my breasts; I could feel my nipples rise against the cotton of the shirt as I thought, *What's that noise?*

In the first hour of the new life, I will speak and act and justify and choose. I will summarize and simplify, in order to make the new life. I will start forgetting what I know in the last hour of the old life. I don't think this is the least of the things that will be destroyed.

I am pulling up my tights in the locker room when Rhonda comes in. She is lovely, my sister. She has two dimples, still, one just under her left eye, the other just to the right of her smile. In the humidity, her hair springs out of her bun with curly abandon. "Sary!" she roars. Her voice is always gravelly and ironic, because in spite of everything she still smokes cigarettes. "Am I late? I had to buy these new tights! Look at this! Is that shine? Don't you love it?" She goes over and stubs out her cigarette in the sink, then wets the end and throws it in the trashcan. "Shit. We've got to hurry. Henry always notices if you're late. Last week he wouldn't let one of them dance, that one who always wears the silver leotard."

I run after her. She snaps the front of her leotard as we trot down the hall. At the door, I put my hand on hers, holding it closed. She looks at me. I say, "Rhonda. Wait a minute." And I tell her. Then I open the door and walk in. Henry has started pliés. I take my place in line. Two minutes later, I feel Rhonda behind me, everything about her, her sadness and her fear as well as her presence. She gives out a little moan. Henry casts her a glance.

He says, "There is a thread attached to that spot on the back of your head where the hair swirls around. You know that spot? Just a thread. If you let your spine stretch upward as your buttocks drop down, you won't break that thread." My chin drops, the vertebrae seem to release one another and float. This is it, isn't it, what Jake calls God and Jonathan calls passion. I lift my arms and drop and spread my shoulders, then turn. Rhonda is there, and her face is white and her expression dismayed. She would like a cigarette. This is it, isn't it, this movement, movement, only movement, only the feeling of life running through the tissues. After all, it makes me smile. A second later, my sister smiles back.

The Little Yellow Dog

WALTER MOSLEY

When I got to work that Monday morning I knew something was wrong. Mrs. Idabell Turner's car was parked in the external lot and there was a light on in her half of bungalow C.

It was six-thirty. The teachers at Sojourner Truth Junior High school never came in that early. Even the janitors who worked under me didn't show up until seven-fifteen. I was the supervising senior head custodian. It was up to me to see that everything worked right. That's why I was almost always the first one on the scene.

But not that morning.

It was November and the sky hadn't quite given up night yet. I approached the bungalow feeling a hint of dread. Images of bodies I'd stumbled upon in my street life came back to me. But I dismissed them. I was a workingman, versed in floor waxes and bleach—not blood. The only weapon I carried was a pocket knife, and it only pierced flesh when I cut the corns from my baby toe.

I knocked but nobody answered. I tried my key but the door was bolted from the inside. Then that damned dog started barking.

"Who is it?" a woman's voice called.

"It's Mr. Rawlins, Mrs. Turner. Is everything okay?"

Instead of answering she fumbled around with the bolt and then pulled the door open. The little yellow dog was yapping, standing on its spindly back legs as if he was going to attack me. But he wasn't going to do a thing. He was hiding behind her blue woolen skirt, making sure that I couldn't get at him.

"Oh, Mr. Rawlins," Mrs. Turner said in that breathy voice she had.

The adolescent boys of Sojourner Truth took her class just to hear that voice, and to see her figure—Mrs. Turner had curves that even a suit of armor couldn't hide. The male teachers at school, and the boys' vice principal, made it a point to pay their respects at her lunch table in the teachers' cafeteria each day. They didn't say much about her around me, though, because Mrs. Turner was one of the few Negro teachers at the primarily Negro school.

The white men had some dim awareness that it would have been insulting for me if I had to hear lewd comments about her.

I appreciated their reserve, but I understood what they weren't saying. Mrs. Idabell Turner was a knockout for any man—from Cro-Magnon to Jim Crow.

"That your dog?" I asked.

"Pharaoh," she said to the dog. "Quiet now. This is Mr. Rawlins. He's a friend."

When he heard my name the dog snarled and bared his teeth.

"You know dogs aren't allowed on the property, Mrs. Turner," I said. "I'm supposed—"

"Stop that, Pharaoh," Idabell Turner whined at the dog. She bent down and let him jump into her arms. "Shhh, quiet now."

She stood up, caressing her little protector. He was the size, but not the pedigree, of a Chihuahua. He settled his behind down onto the breast of her caramel-colored cashmere sweater and growled out curses in dog.

"Quiet," Mrs. Turner said. "I'm sorry, Mr. Rawlins. I wouldn't have brought him here, but I didn't have any choice. I didn't."

I could tell by the red rims of her eyelids that she'd been crying.

"Well, maybe you could leave him out in the car," I suggested.

Pharaoh growled again.

He was a smart dog.

"Oh no, I couldn't do that. I'd be worried about him suffocating out there."

"You could crack the window."

"He's so small I'd be afraid that he'd wiggle out. You know he spends all day at home trying to find me. He loves me, Mr. Rawlins."

"I don't know what to say, Mrs.—"

"Call me Idabell," she said.

Call me fool.

Mrs. Turner had big brown eyes with fabulously long lashes. Her skin was like rich milk chocolate—dark, satiny, and smooth.

That snarling mutt started looking cute to me. I thought that it wasn't such a problem to have your dog with you. It wasn't really any kind of health threat. I reached out to make friends with him.

He tested my scent—and then bit my hand.

"Ow!"

"That's it!" Idabell shouted as if she were talking to a wayward child. "Come on!"

She took the dwarf mongrel and shoved him into the storage room that connected C2 to C1. As soon as she closed the door, Pharaoh was scratching to get back in.

"I'm sorry," she said.

"Me too. But you know that dog has got to go." I held out my hand to her. The skin was broken but it wasn't bad. "Has he had his rabies shot?"

"Oh yes, yes. Please, Mr. Rawlins." She took me by my injured hand. "Let me help."

We went to the desk at the front of the class. I sat down on the edge of her blotter while she opened the top drawer and came out with a standard teacher's first-aid box.

"You know, dog bites are comparatively pretty clean," she said. She had a bottle of iodine, a cotton ball, and a flesh-colored bandage—flesh-colored, that is, if you had pink flesh. When she dabbed the iodine on my cut I winced, but it wasn't because of the sting. That woman smelled good; clean and fresh, and sweet like the deep forest is sweet.

"It's not bad, Mr. Rawlins. And Pharaoh didn't mean it. He's just upset. He knows that Holland wants to kill him."

"Kill him? Somebody wants to kill your dog?"

"My husband." She nodded and was mostly successful in holding back the tears. "I've been, been away for a few days. When I got back home last night, Holly went out, but when he came back he was going to . . . kill Pharaoh."

Mrs. Turner gripped my baby finger.

It's amazing how a man can feel sex anywhere on his body.

"He wants to kill your dog?" I asked in a lame attempt to use my mind, to avoid what my body was thinking.

"I waited till he was gone and then I drove here." Mrs. Turner wept quietly.

My hand decided, all by itself, to comfort her shoulder.

"Why's he so mad?" I shouldn't have asked, but my blood was moving faster than my mind.

"I don't know," she said sadly. "He made me do something, and I did it, but afterwards he was still mad." She put her shoulder against mine while I brought my other hand to rest on her side.

The thirty desks in her classroom all faced us attentively.

"Pharaoh's a smart dog," she whispered in my ear. "He knew what Holly said. He was scared."

Pharaoh whimpered out a sad note from his storage room.

Idabell leaned back against my arm and looked up. We might have been slow dancing—if there had been music and a band.

"I don't know what to do," she said. "I can't ever go back there. I can't. He's going to be in trouble and I'll be in it with him. But Pharaoh's innocent. He hasn't done anything wrong."

As she talked she leaned closer. With me sitting on the desk we were near to the same height. Our faces were almost touching.

I didn't know what she was talking about and I didn't want to know.

I'd been on good behavior for more than two years. I was out of the streets and had my job with the Los Angeles Board of Education. I took care of my kids, cashed my paychecks, stayed away from liquor.

I steered clear of the wrong women too.

Maybe I'd been a little too good. I felt an urge in that class-room, but I wasn't going to make the move.

That's when Idabell Turner kissed me.

Two years of up early and off to work dissolved like a sugar cube under the tap.

"Oh," she whispered as my lips pressed her neck. "Yes."

The tears were all gone. She looked me in the eye and worked her tongue slowly around with mine.

A deep grunt went off in my chest like an underwater explo-sion. It just came out of me. Her eyes opened wide as she realized how much I was moved. I stood and lifted her up on the desk. She spread her legs and pushed her chest out at me.

She said, "They'll be coming soon," and then gave me three fast kisses that said this was just the beginning.

My pants were down before I could stop myself. As I leaned forward she let out a single syllable that said, "Here I am, I've been waitin' for you, Ezekiel Porterhouse Rawlins. Take my arms, my legs, my breasts. Take everything," and I answered in the same lan-guage.

"They'll be coming soon," she said as her tongue pressed my left nipple through thin cotton. "Oh, go slow."

The clock on the wall behind her said that it was seven-oh-two. I'd come to the door at six forty-nine. Less than a quarter of an hour and I was deeply in the throes of passion.

I wanted to thank God—or his least favorite angel.

"They'll be coming soon," she said, the phonograph of her mind on a skip. "Oh, go slow."

The desks all sat at attention. Pharaoh whimpered from his cell.

"Too much," she hissed. I didn't know what she meant.

When the desk started rocking I didn't care who might walk into the room. I would have gladly given up my two years of accrued pension and my two weeks a year vacation for the few moments of ecstasy that teased and tickled about five inches below my navel.

"Mr. Rawlins!" she cried. I lifted her from the desk, not to perform some silly acrobatics but because I needed to hold her tight to my heart. I needed to let her know that this was what I'd wanted and needed for two years without knowing it.

It all came out in a groan that was so loud and long that later on, when I was alone, I got embarrassed remembering it.

I stood there holding her aloft with my eyes closed. The cool air of the room played against the back of my thighs and I felt like laughing.

I felt like sobbing too. What was wrong with me? Standing there half naked in a classroom on a weekday morning. Idabell had her arms around my neck. I didn't even feel her weight. If we were at my house I would have carried her to the bed and started over again.

"Put me down," she whispered.

I squeezed her.

"Please," she said, echoing the word in my own mind.

I put her back on the desk. We looked at each other for what seemed like a long time—slight tremors going through our bodies now and then. I couldn't bear to pull away. She had a kind of stunned look on her face.

When I leaned over to kiss her forehead I experienced a feeling that I'd known many times in my life. It was that feeling of elation before I embarked on some kind of risky venture. In the old days it was about the police and criminals and the streets of Watts and South Central L.A.

But not this time. Not again. I swallowed hard and gritted my teeth with enough force to crack stone. I'd slipped but I would not fall.

Mrs. Turner was shoving her panties into a white patent-leather purse while I zipped my pants. She smiled and went to open the door for Pharaoh.

The dog skulked in with his tail between his legs and his be-hind dragging on the floor. I felt somehow triumphant over that little rat dog, like I had taken his woman and made him watch it. It was an ugly feeling but, I told myself, he was just a dog.

Mrs. Turner picked Pharaoh up and held him while looking into my eyes.

I didn't want to get involved in her problems, but I could do something for her. "Maybe I can keep the dog in the hopper room in my office," I said.

"Oh," came the breathy voice. "That would be so kind. It's only until this evening. I'm going to my girlfriend's tonight. He won't be any bother. I promise."

She handed Pharaoh to me. He was trembling. At first I thought he was scared from the new environment and a strange pair of hands. But when I looked in his eyes I saw definite canine hatred. He was shaking with rage.

Mrs. Turner scratched the dog's ear and said, "Go on now, honey. Mr. Rawlins'll take care of you."

I took a step away from her and she smiled.

"I don't even know your first name," she said.

"Easy," I said. "Call me Easy."

The Source

SHARON OLDS

It became the deep spring of my life,
I didn't know if it was a sickness or a gift.
To reach around both sides of a man,
one palm to one buttock,
the other palm to the other, the way we are split,
to grasp that band of muscle on the male

haunch and help guide the massed
heavy nerve down my throat until it
stoppers the hole behind the breastbone
    that is always hungry,
then I feel complete. To be lifted
onto a man—the male breast
so hard, there seem no chambers in it, it is
lifting-muscle—and set tight as a lock-slot down
onto a bolt, we are looking into
each other's eyes as if the matter of the iris were
a membrane deep in the body dissolving now,
it is what I had dreamed, to meet men
fully as a woman twin, unborn,
half-gelled, clasped, nothing between us
but our bodies, naked, and when those dissolve,
nothing between us—or perhaps I vanish
and the man is still there, as if I have been trying
to disappear, into them,
to be myself the glass of sourmash
my father lifted to his mouth. Ah, I am in him,
I slide all the way down to the beginning, the
curved chamber of the halls. My brothers
and sisters are there, swimming by the cinereous
millions, I say to them, Stay here—
for the children of this father it may be the better life;
but they cannot hear: Blind, deaf,
armless, brainless, they plunge forward,
driven, desperate to enter the other, to
die in her, and wake. For a moment,
after we wake, we are without desire—
five, ten, twenty seconds of
pure calm, as if each one of us is whole.

Full Summer

SHARON OLDS

I paused, and paused, over your body,
to feel the current of desire pull
and pull through me. Our hair was still wet,
mine like knotted wrack, it fell
across you as I paused, a soaked coil
around your glans. When one of our hairs
dried, it lifted like a bare nerve.
On the beach, above us, a cloud had appeared
in the clear air, a clockwise loop
coming in out of nothing, now the skin of your scrotum
moved like a live being, an animal,
I began to lick you, the foreskin lightly
stuck in one spot, like a petal, I love
to free it—just so—in joy,
and to sip from the little crying lips
at the tip. Then there was no more pausing,
nor was this the taker,
some new one came
and sucked, and up from where I had been hiding I as
drawn in a heavy spiral out of matter
over into another world
I had thought I would have to die to reach.

The Summer Dress

TOM ABSHER

It might have been a floral print—
for all I know it was the plan of
the Hanging Gardens of Babylon, or zodiacal,
revealing the arcana of all twelve houses
of heaven, or maybe it was patterned
after the emblems of the Tarot and
the Tree of Life.

Walking down the street behind you,
watching the lift and billowy flutter
of this flag, the way it sundered itself
in two, unfurling fore and aft above
your knees and thighs like a wing
splaying itself for flight, I felt
every gust of wind decompose another
layer of civilization from me
like steam: now the Age of Reason
is cast off, there goes medieval
scholasticism, Bye bye Byzantium,
blow a kiss to the Greeks.

Within two blocks I was back in time
with a pack of guys from the Paleolithic,
dudes who paint their bodies with mud
and red ochre and wear animal skins
over their heads: thank god you turned,
stepped into a building, another
hundred yards and I'd been down on
all fours, breathing, gasping
through my gills.

The War, at Home

GLORIA DYC

Operation Desert Storm breaks out the day my period is due. I feel blood rushing to my uterus, a heaviness and cramps but there's no blood. There's not much blood in the coverage of the war, either; like most Americans, I am spellbound by the television. The U.S. missiles light up the skies of Baghdad, spectacular explosions of red and green and white. The newscasters are tense and spontaneous. They duck as a reflex to the explosions in the distant city behind them, put a hand over one ear, trying to block out the thunder. The stoic generals and ex-generals are now in their glory. With pointers and maps, they precisely describe the targets, and talk about the casualties using the antiseptic language of war: *collateral damage*. In response to questions, they kept repeating, "I can't comment on that." How pleased our Defenders must be tonight, to see how our weapons actually perform.

I sit with my dinner in front of me, but I can't eat. I am out in the desert and cities beyond the lens of the press corps, and the steak on my plate might as well be a scorched corpse.

I haven't felt the world on such a brink since the escalation of the war in Viet Nam. There were days when I thought: *This is the end.* I remember my first boyfriend and I planning to move to the Wilderness before the entire world was engulfed in war, the cities destroyed. The Wilderness was somewhere out West. We sat on the pavement of a city street and planned. My boyfriend said we would need a good compass, knife, and plastic. What about Tampax? Birth control pills? He said the Indians had to have used something for absorbing blood flow, and as for birth control, we'd just have them. He flushed a little, and I remember thinking: how easy.

I have to smile now. I've backpacked into what is left of the wilderness lugging thirty percent of my weight in supplies; I've been humbled by snowstorms in August. I've lived with the Indians in South Dakota long enough to know about the loss of their survival skills: they have to attend workshops at schools to learn about butchering a buffalo and preparing the hides. And the idea that I may be a host to a cluster of inexorably dividing human cells is not at all easy to accept.

I see headlights outside the window; JB has arrived in his old Chevy, battered from travel all over the West, rodeo to rodeo. On this benign desert night, with snowcapped Mt. Taylor visible in the moonlight, it is hard to imagine war on the other side of the planet.

JB seems unaffected; he has brought a bottle of our favorite New Mexican wine.

I tell him a Scud missile has hit Israel. I tell him that a Jewish friend at work, a fan of Nostradamus, believes that this is the beginning of the End.

"Oh, I don't know. I don't think it's as bad as all that. I guess I believe everything will work out in the end. Besides, the world can't end until I make it to the finals," JB winks at me and begins to pour a glass of wine for me, but my stomach lurches when the glass is half full.

"My stomach. I'm queasy."

"Nervous about all this?"

"I don't know. My period is late. I skipped a few pills this past cycle, and then I took two each day to catch up . . ." I'm embarrassed and nervous.

"I knew you were going to say that." He looks at me, at the image of buildings bombed and reduced to rubble on the television, then back to me. He looks more frightened than when he settles himself on a bronc in a chute, the moment before the gate is opened. He is smiling though, to mask the emotion. "Well, I did my job," he says with mock heroism, then he becomes tense and distant.

I rub his lean, muscular thigh, encased in Wranglers. There is something incredibly sexy about a cowboy on a bronc, arm overhead, stomach and thighs taxed to the limit. If I could seduce him now, we might both feel better, but he jumps up to scan the other channels, declaring that he is sick of the war, until he finds a public television repeat on the ecology of the West.

A balding ecologist with expensive tennis shoes is talking about the ranchers on public land grants, who still graze their cattle the old-fashioned way. But the West is over-grazed, the land erod-ing, the Sonoran desert enlarging, spreading North. There is a map on the screen to show the spread of the desert and my mouth be-comes parched looking at it: where will the water come from in the future to support the population?

The days of the cowboy are gone, an anachronism.

"Shiiit, they don't know what the hell they're talking about," JB rails. He switches the channel and we are back to the explosion of missiles in the night skies of Iraq. JB is getting maudlin now, his mood intensified by the wine.

"This is it. I know. My kids won't be able to live like this. There probably won't even be rodeo in a generation or two. I'll have to steer them in another direction."

JB's father lost a ranch in the early eighties, when the price of cattle fluctuated dramatically. Since then he has worked in a mini-mum wage job at a trading post.

"Rodeo's a bad deal anyway," JB admits, "I either have money and spend it foolishly, or I'm a broke prick. But I'll tell you, there's nothing like working on a ranch. My grandparents get up every day before dawn. When we go out there to work, I'm the last son of a bitch to get out of bed, but I get used to it eventually. There's noth-ing like it. That's all I want to do really. Work on someone's ranch. In the middle of nowhere."

JB is remote, a solitary figure walking across the desert into his future.

He stretches out on the couch.

He isn't talking.

He doesn't want to make love.

"If I'm pregnant, it would be a fluke," I tell him, choking on the word *pregnant*.

"Mmmhuh," he responds skeptically. JB has always been con-vinced that women do these things on purpose, to trap men.

Now I am imagining my body is some inexorable transforma-tion. My abdomen stretches to accommodate a baby, a brown streak divides and discolors the swell. Then the abdomen deflates, leav-ing deep folds of skin, like a rotten pumpkin. My breasts, after nursing, have deep rivers and tributaries etched in my skin; they deflate and fall flat against my chest, like those of tribal women who have ten children.

And where is JB? He is in a bar after a rodeo, checking out the young things in their tight jeans.

This is irrational, I know. I am selfish and vain; the relationship too new, too insecure to accommodate such a change.

The bombs rain down, the oil fields burn, garbage floats out to sea. The generals look at their targets on computerized screens, in climate-controlled rooms, well-fed and clean. Are there spirits out there, like pollen in the dark desert wind, searching for hospitable wombs, desperate for the world to go on?

JB is sleeping. I shake him gently and he sleepwalks to the bedroom.

I call my friend Nicole. Her husband of just a few weeks is in the reserves and could get shipped out if more troops are needed.

"My soldier boy is getting shitfaced here," she reports in a low voice. "He's on leave from El Paso. I think he's worried about getting shipped over. But I think deep inside he wants to go and kick some butt."

"Kick some Third World butt, huh?"

"Yeah. Exactly. Kick some Iraqi butt."

"You know those pregnancy tests you buy at the supermarket? The ones that cost ten bucks? Do they really work?"

There is a lull, then Nicole laughs. "You think?"

"I'm worried sick. This cowboy is acting like a fox in a trap. I think he's going to bite his damn leg off."

Wes is sitting in his camouflage fatigues, which he hasn't taken off since he became active again, and he's on his third bottle of wine. I am watching his cigarette burn, unsteady between his fingers. I am prepared to jump up if he drops it. If he stands it up on the filter and puts it on the coffee table, I know I'll go into a rage.

I can't drink, since I have a night shift at the hospital. My purse and my car keys I keep close to the door, in case I have to make a quick exit. He's twice my weight but I'm sober and faster.

"So you think Bush is a warmonger? I mean, we gotta do it. We gotta get in there and kick ass." Wes's voice is slurred. I can tell he wants to trap me into a confrontation.

"You know what I think," I respond calmly. "You know how I feel about war. All war, not just this one."

Wes has been angry with me since I refused to quit my job and move to the base in El Paso. Who knows how long the war will go on, what with the damage the Americans are doing each day? Wes thought it might expand into some world war scenario. I told him, if it comes to that, I'll pack my bags and head back to the reservation. The Lakota can survive anything. Wes wanted to know if I'd leave him to perish, and I joked that I would take him along as my squaw man.

Besides, El Paso is a hellhole: ugly, industrialized. Everyone speaks Spanish, even in the Holiday Inn.

The cigarette burns Wes's fingers and startled, he flicks it into the ashtray, saving us a major scuffle over that one.

"But this guy's nuts," Wes continues. "Like Hitler. They have plutonium, research facilities, weapons factories. Hell, they'd nuke us back into the Stone Age if we gave them the chance."

"Oh, I'm sure *we*'ll nuke *them* into the Stone Age before they get a chance." I laugh and this provokes him.

"Oh. I forgot. You're Indian. You don't see any reason for war. The peace-loving Sioux. Now how much of that peace-loving Sioux blood do you have in you? Half? A quarter?"

"Only a *white* man would come up with the idea of measuring race by blood-quantum." Wes has me going, and he knows it. "I'm *all* Indian. My body rejected the white genes."

Wes smirks and drains the wine bottle, and I can tell he is disappointed in his half-full tumbler.

We keep circling back to this: white vs. Indian. Before Wes was called for the reserve, we battled it out over his work. Wes is training to be an archeologist, and he travels around digging up bones. I went to visit him on a site, once. They were exhuming Anasazi remains and reburying them so a road could be built. Wes seemed comfortable handling the bones, but all I felt was dread and anxiety. I could feel the presence of spirits, but not in a good way, like at a healing ceremony. When he got home I didn't want him to touch me.

Wes has reached the maudlin point in his drunk.

"I don't know. The bottom line is . . . I'm a soldier. That's what I am, Nicole. Do you understand? I don't want to go over there, but I'll do what I have to do. In a way, I'd like to go over there. Beats sitting around the barracks in El Paso with a bunch of illiterates."

The people over there don't stand a chance, I think. Like the Indians.

"We need more wine," Wes announces and begins to look for the keys to the vehicle.

"You don't need more wine."

"I don't *need* more wine I *want* more wine. Give me the keys."

The same old struggle. I would volunteer to drive, but I really don't want him to have more wine. He spots the keys and grabs them. I jump up and he sort of lunges at me. Of course I startle and he laughs to see my fear.

I give up. He doesn't have insurance or a license. We can't pay off the last car he totaled.

If it weren't for the war, we wouldn't be married. Last year we had plans, then Wes spent the rent on coke and all hell broke loose. That time the neighbors called the police, and they told me to cool it, because I had scratched him on the face in self-defense.

But when Wes was called up for duty, everything changed. We decided it was best. I think I was temporarily insane. There were so many details: buying a gown, flowers, booze, cold cuts, a hotel suite.

But when my gown split in back during the ceremony, the truth arrived like a narc. The gown was tight, but I hadn't had much to eat in three days. I'm sure everyone noticed, in the small front room of the suite, and I could feel the air conditioning on my back. I thought about the woman who sold me the dress: bitch. Not a good thought to have when you are supposed to be making a life-long commitment. But I do believe in signs.

Two days later I take the gown back to the store. I am in a rage. "I want my money back," I demand. "The wedding was ruined."

"But you've worn the dress," the saleslady said in a patronizing way. "I can't give you a full refund. That wouldn't be fair."

"I was totally embarrassed. This dress is a piece of crap. Perhaps I should have my attorney contact you." My face is shaking, I am so angry, and she has this tight smile on her face. Of course, I don't have an attorney.

When Wes returns from the store, he gets on the phone and talks to someone in a confidential tone. I'm wondering if he's talking to Roberto, the hot little coke dealer who drives the motorcycle.

He announces that a friend is going to pick him up and they are going to drive back to El Paso in the morning.

"But you don't have to be back until Monday," I protest.

"I want to go back. I want to be around people who understand."

I go into the bedroom, and sure enough, there's his duffel bag on the bed, packed.

I carry it out to the living room and sling it against the front door with all my strength.

"Go then," I hiss.

"Did you fill it with rattlers?" Wes asks. It's our private joke, but there's a real edge to his voice.

When I first met Wes, he took me to a VFW meeting in South Dakota. He's a vet of Grenada and very proud of it.

So we went to this dinner meeting in Sioux Falls, all white, and this asshole starts talking about Indians, guess he didn't know I was Lakota, or maybe he didn't care. And he said, "Oh, these Indians will do anything . . . they like to fill up suitcases with rattlesnakes and leave 'em beside the road for a white man to find." Wes looked at me, then at him, and he said, "Nicole, do any of your relatives do that? Do they fill up suitcases with rattlers and leave them at the side of the road?" I said, "Noooo, not that I know of. But it's a damn good idea!"

So that's what I say to Wes now. "That's a damn good idea!"

After I finish my last class at the college, I head for the pool, one of the few amenities the town has to offer. My students, I fear, sense that I am preoccupied. I tell them it's hard to carry on business as usual in the shadow of the war.

I spend a full hour going in and out of the steam room. I stay in the hot cloud until my heart is pounding, my lungs scalded, then I sit on one of the chairs outside and watch the swimmers do their relentless laps.

There are two Hispanic men steaming out, and like everyone they are discussing the war.

"These Scuds aren't worth a shit, you know, compared to the American weapons."

"Yeah, but they can't mess with Israel. Those people are serious. Can't blame them, no?"

JB has changed his pattern. Nights go by and he doesn't phone; I am immobilized by anxiety. When he does call, he is perfunctory, distant.

I broke down last night and called him, bolstering myself with a glass of wine. "What is going on with you, I don't understand."

"I don't know." JB sounded bewildered. "I don't know what to make of all this. I'm sorry. I wish I could talk to you. I'm not very good at this sort of thing."

The Hispanic men are talking about the cities that would be targets, if the Iraqis broke through our defense system.

"Hey, we're not so safe here, think about it. Los Alamos would be a prime target. Then all those weapons under the Monzanos. Eiiiii," one says.

His companion sits there for a beat, and then he throws up his arms and makes the sound of a bomb, just as the steam jet comes on and engulfs us all in a fresh cloud of heat and steam.

I startle; the steam could be smoke.

"I tell you, this world we live in, it's crazy, you know. Like you wonder what we're leaving to our kids, like this big debt."

"It don't make sense," the other one responds.

In the heat, the cramps I've been having intensify. I would be happy to bleed here. I imagine bright red blood running down my thighs, pooling beneath me on the white tiles, trickling down to my feet.

I try to imagine what else I could do to tempt the blood . . . sleep on a white satin sheet, try on white clothing at an expensive store.

"My period has arrived," I could announce to JB. Redeemed from this uncertainty, we could make love again, which I miss. JB is avoiding me, as if he might fertilize what is already growing inside.

JB's sister, a student at the college, arranged for our first date, thinking it would be good for her brother to meet someone outside the domain of rodeo. An unlikely match, perhaps, but I was intrigued by his occupation. My attraction to him was immediate: he was lean and muscular, cocky and yet a bit awkward, careful to stay within the corral of all that he considered male.

I found out that his skin was soft, his chest hairless. "I wear it off," he joked. He buckled under my touch, and made short and breathless confessions when he was out of control.

That first night, we watched Monday night football on a large-screen TV in a neighborhood bar; there aren't many choices in this town. I feigned polite interest in the game; he was distracted by my smile and my legs. He ran his finger up my calf, tried to read my facial expression, to see if he could move this fast.

"Well, I don't know how to ask you this," he said tentatively, "but sooner or later you're going to visit me at my place. What do you say we go over there now and watch one of the talk shows?"

"I don't know. They say you're not supposed to make love on the first date."

"We don't have to do that," he responded with some embarrassment.

"I don't know about you," I countered, "but I'd have a hard time keeping my hands off you."

His walls were decorated with rodeo memorabilia: photos of himself airborne on broncs, paper numbers the entrants pin to the backs of their shirts.

He turned on the television and paced awkwardly; I sat on the couch and watched him, smiling. He looked as if he was going to the next room, but he pivoted, and in a few short steps he was wriggling my skirt up over my hips.

Those first few times there was a scrim between us; he seemed detached, his eyes closed, focused on his sensation. He was a performer, processing the technicalities of the ride.

There was a furtive quality to his behavior; I wondered about his other lovers. Were they repressed or coy? Did they insist on darkness? One-night stands after rodeos? Tight jeans maneuvered down over hips, orgasms dulled by beer?

I want the lights on. "Look at me," I say finally.

He does, feels "weakened" by the emotion, and closes them again. "I love it when you come."

He rubs himself hard against me in the morning. I'm still very wet. He comes in from behind, reaches forward for my breast. He lifts my leg up, so he can go in deeper; he's very hard.

I am on my back, and he stretches my legs over my head. Kneeling he has a way of moving, a way of dancing there, and I watch how he sucks in his pelvis in the effort. He kisses the instep of my foot—no one has ever done this—and when he comes, he cries out freely, all of his muscles convulsing, unlike the first night when he put his face in the pillow. This choreography is original.

The steamroom is not working: there are cramps but no blood, thunder and clouds but no rain.

On my way home, I pick up a pregnancy test and a bottle of wine from the supermarket.

The phone is mute. I pick it up to see if there is a dial tone. Usually JB tells me his rodeo schedule, when he'll leave town and return. I know that his silence is a warning to me. When I call, I only hear his stilted message on his answering machine.

I try the pregnancy test, putting the little plastic stick in the cup of urine with trepidation. Then I go into the living room and watch the oil fires in Iraq on television. The air is black with smoke, the land a barren inferno. The desert is littered with debris from weapons.

If I am pregnant, I decide, I will go it alone. Child care, of course, might be a problem. I don't know what it costs, how to calculate it into a budget. I have no relatives in the area; would my mother fly out and stay? I imagine JB at some rodeo, preparing to ride by squatting and stretching, and I am overcome for a moment by anger.

I have waited twice as long as I need: I go to face my fate. There are two small windows on the stick; I am looking for the purple dot on the bottom window when I realize I have not followed directions by taking the cap off.

I laugh at my own ineptitude and try again. But this time I splash a bit of urine on the test stick, again violating the instructions.

Later, when I check the stick, there appears to be a very, very faint purple dot, and I strain my eyes as if looking for a newly discovered planet. I'll have to buy a new kit.

That night I have a dream: I have a child, but it is only a faint image, a shadow on the pavement, like those at ground zero after Hiroshima. I am leading the shadow down the pavement on a sort of leash, and I keep looking to see if it still exists, or if the child has evaporated, like liquid on hot cement.

There's a "Forget the War" party and opening at Alex's gallery, and I can feel myself get into one of my naughty moods. What the hell. Already I'm the disgruntled wife, wondering when Wes will call from El Paso.

When he finally calls, he asks, "Who's there?"

"Nobody's here."

"Be straight with me for once in your life. Who're you fucking? Roberto?"

"You babe, if you get your ass back to town."

Roberto is hot. He's part Hispanic; he teaches karate, deals coke, and rides a motorcycle. But I'm not fucking him.

Wes brings him to the house, and we sit around all night sipping wine and snorting coke. At four in the morning, Wes tells me I've been coming on to Roberto all night. That makes me laugh.

"You wanted him to stay." My laughter infuriates him. "You wanted him to stay so he'd keep the lines on the table."

For the party, I put on the bustier I bought at Victoria's Secret, a short jeans skirt and leather jacket. Wes was with me when I bought the bustier, and after we left the store, he wanted to know who I had bought it for.

Wes has been changing in bed, and I don't like it. He used to talk dirty once in a while, and I didn't mind. But now it's constant. Tell me about the biggest cock you've fucked. I'll make up a story, but then he's convinced that it's the truth. And he tells me these stories about other women . . . and I don't know if he's lying or telling the truth. He bought these dildoes and they're always in bed with us. I feel like a star in a bad porno movie.

When I walk into the gallery, I sense a high energy level. Everyone is ready to cut loose, as I am. We're sick of the war, and there's nothing we can do about it, anyway. I look around for my friend, Beth, who has been going through a pregnancy scare. We first connected here, at Alex's gallery, and recognized one another from the rez in South Dakota, where Beth had taught at the tribal college. Alex's studio is the place where people go when they haven't been raised in this god-forsaken town. We aren't part of the Hispanic enclave on the North side, or the Anglo business people who "live on the hill," or from the Navajo reservation. The people who come here are nurses or doctors from the Indian hospital, or lawyers or teachers, or artists, such as Alex, who came to the United States from Budapest in the 1960s and found his way West, to red rock country.

I am looking at Alex's photos; he has titled his exhibit "Broken." Beth is beside me, suddenly, handing me a glass of white wine, and raising her eyebrows in response to the images.

"These are a real downer. Shows you where Alex is at," I comment.

"Alex must still be working through his famous relationship," Beth sighs.

Alex is famous for dating woman after woman in this town, always breaking it off after six months. The women complain that he is still hung up on his former lover, a beautiful Japanese woman who left him to pursue her painting career on the West Coast.

The photos are of broken dolls in various settings: a doll with one eye and a few remaining tufts of hair, a doll with legs and arms twisted, a torso of a doll, superimposed with photos of breasts from a pin-up, then slashed with an "x" of red paint.

"I started my period," Beth whispers.

"Congratulations. I think." I'm not sure quite how to respond. This cowboy that Beth has been seeing isn't around much; not something I'd want to put up with. But he's handsome and good in the sack, Beth tells me.

"Oh, it's for the best. When I told JB, he threw up his arms and said, 'Thank you, God.' Now I know one thing. JB is emotionally unavailable. I told him that, and he kept playing with the sound of the words *emotionally unavailable* as if he was learning a new language."

"I'm sure it is new. Believe me, I've known cowboys from South Dakota. Now the Lakota men up there, they give you their hearts. They claim you. 'You're mine now.' Trouble is, you can't get rid of them."

I feel light. We circulate around the studio, looking at the photos, checking out the crowd. I realize how much fun it is to party without Wes around.

"You know," I admit to Beth as we fill up our glasses with the cheap wine, and check out the food on the table, "I wouldn't have gotten married if it weren't for this fucking war. I mean, Wes wanted to do it last year, remember? But we got into that big fight when he spent the rent money on coke. I've been waiting for him to call, but I'm sure he's partying on the base."

"I blame the war for this pregnancy scare. I must be really tense. I'm never late with my period."

There is a hand under my elbow. Roberto is standing next to me, and we are both wearing leather jackets.

"You know," he said in his soft and sexy voice, "I was so surprised when I found out you're from Rosebud. I have some Indian blood, but I don't like to talk about it, because I don't know the culture or anything, being a city boy."

"So why are you surprised about me?" I'm getting wet, just from his hand underneath my elbow.

"You're so . . . sophisticated."

"Oh, I lived in a trailer one year without running water. I did the Sun Dance. But I still know my wines and how to get around in a department store." Some men think I'm a real bitch, but I think Roberto can handle me.

"Some skins—I don't know—they get this superior attitude or just shy away when they find out I'm part Apache."

Alex comes into the room with a large, fresh bottle of wine and begins to fill glasses. "The ground war has broken out," he announces in his heavy, Hungarian accent. "Drink up, everyone." Everyone in the room groans. The lesbian lawyer yells, "They've got brown skin. Let's nuke 'em."

For a moment I worry that they have shipped Wes off. No, he's probably having a great time in El Paso, just hoping to get shipped off.

Now it feels like New Year's Eve. Roberto takes me in his arms and we both feel this electric animal energy. He squeezes one of my ass cheeks and whispers, "Let's go do a line."

Roberto takes my hand and pulls me down a long hall to Alex's bathroom. There is an oil painting on the wall from his ex; she was a decent artist. Roberto takes out a small vial of coke and looks around the small space we are in. He pulls the jacket off my shoulders, a little roughly, but I am giggling with excitement. Then he dribbles a spoonful of coke on the exposed top of each of my breasts. I hold my breath, then I feel his breath, his nose and chin against me, his tongue licking me clean. He pulls down the satin cup with one finger, exposes my nipple, erect as it can get, and takes it into his mouth, making a delicious noise; then he does the same with the other.

The muscles in my legs and ass are tight. Roberto tugs my skirt up and sticks two fingers up me, whistles softly at the heat and wetness, then I'm moving against him, going for an orgasm. There's a knock on the door, and someone outside is yelling something about Saddam Hussein. Roberto yells for them to go away, and we collapse against one another, weak and breathless.

"I know your old man can't be in town, because he hasn't called me. So let's go for a ride and continue at your house." I go back to the party to let Beth know, and she looks a little surprised and disappointed. I'm dressed for the occasion in my black leather jacket; Roberto insists I wear his helmet.

When we get to the house, my heart starts pounding and I can't breathe. I'm afraid that Wes has come back to town; that he's hiding in the house, or lurking outside. I look at the answering machine to see if the red light is on, but no one has called.

Roberto massages my back and keeps telling me that it's ok. I pour cranberry juice and vodka for us—a drink that goes down easy. Roberto puts out more lines, and lights a joint up to take the edge off. "That's an incredibly thick joint," I say, and he thanks me and then puts my hand on his erection.

I imagine Wes pounding on the door, the glass of the front window shattering. Roberto senses the spasms of anxiety, and tries to reassure me. He is so gentle, so softspoken, I have to keep asking him, "What?"

He takes off his clothes slowly, letting me appreciate his body, lean and hard. I have moments of ravenous desire, then I find that I've lost it, I've gone into some oblivion, and he tries to revive me with a line or a sip.

We are on the carpet, the arm of the chair, the bed. At one point I actually have the presence of mind to say, "No marks."

The next time I attempt to talk, I realize it is garbled, and then I realize I can't remember his name; then I start giggling and he says, "Tell me, tell me." I lose consciousness.

A vivid dream wakes me in the late morning: I am back on the reservation at the Sun Dance, sitting under the arbor. I am wearing my cotton flowered dress, my beaded belt, sage around my ankles and my head. There are other women dancers around me; we are on a break between rounds and one of the medicine men is talking. He is saying that the white man is always at war: with himself, with nature, with other people. "And we brown-skinned people always lose, and the four-legged ones, the winged ones, *maka*, our mother, we all lose." There is a commotion on the outside of the Sun Dance circle, and I join the others, to see what is going on. There is Wes; he has a shovel and he is hitting a copperhead snake: it is gruesome and violent. One of the women turns to me and points: "That's her man." A motorcycle pulls up. It is Roberto. He has tried to dress as a Sun Dancer, but it is all wrong, and the men laugh at him. He hands Wes a suitcase: "This belongs to Nicole," he says, and throws it on the ground. The suitcase opens under the force. Inside there are vibrators and dildoes of various sizes, and some resemble nuclear weapons. An old man and woman start to laugh. I feel deeply shamed.

I awake alone; Roberto has left, and I can't find any evidence of our night together. He has emptied the ashtrays, put the glasses in soapy water.

My head aches from the coke and the alcohol; my mouth is unspeakably foul.

I drink cold water and imagine packing my bags and moving back to Rosebud; Wes wouldn't have the nerve to drive up there and start asking around about me.

I wonder if the marriage can be annulled, given the war and the general level of hysteria.

I wonder if there is a restaurant that serves Bloody Marys, one without a television, one without much light, where I could sit and recuperate.

Then I wish that this were an ordinary Sunday, with Wes cooking his usual omelet, with green peppers, sausage, and potatoes.

Nicole is circulating, slinking about like a cougar, but I feel remote, and find myself watching people. Alex's studio is where the people who aren't from this town go. We aren't from the Hispanic North side, or the "hill," or the reservations. We are probably from the East, however that is defined, or maybe California.

Alex keeps filling my glass with cheap, white wine; he puts his hand under my elbow in an endearing way. Some women are drawn to him because he is an artist, but I've known too many artists; Alex has no aura for me.

My work is here, but I don't know if I can make a life here; others in this place, I'm sure, feel the same.

"The ground war has begun . . ." Alex announces. I hear someone say, "Son of a bitch." The woman who opened the New Age bookstore in town hurries to the back room where a group is crowded around a TV; the man who wrote a book about Santa Fe style seems more interested in his conversation.

Nicole is hooking up with Roberto, as good-looking and dangerous as men get.

I can't blame her, with the quantity of drugs and alcohol Wes has been putting away. But just weeks ago I stood up at Nicole's wedding and feel the guilt of one who has squelched all doubts in the name of romance.

The wedding was so rushed, there was no time to shop. I did buy a white push-up bra and bikini to wear under my red silk suit, to make the occasion somewhat special. On a later night, I wore the underwear for JB, who was appreciative, asking me to turn around and walk. He whistled and said, "Oh, what you're doing to me."

Of course he was too tied up with his rodeo schedule to go with me, and he's wedding phobic to begin with. He took me to the wedding of his boss's son and I remember he said, "Now don't get any ideas when they throw out that bouquet. Stay back here." In his mind, all women are hungry for that white lace, and he must remain agile to elude them. Later, after several more drinks, he became sentimental. "If I could find a woman who could put starch in my jeans the way the dry cleaners do, no telling what I'd do," he announced. "I thought I *did* put starch in your jeans," I said dryly.

To be in Nicole's situation would be the last thing I'd want: legally tied to a druggie who has locked her out of her own house. She slips over to quietly tell me she's leaving with Roberto, and I wonder if her latest choice is any better. But I know the pull of those sexy but dangerous men.

There is a void after Nicole leaves; I would have liked to talk with her and laugh, late into the night.

There is nothing new on the war front; they begin to recycle the same information about the ground war, the same images. I can see that people are getting bored. Someone flips from one channel to another, hoping for a new angle of coverage. Everyone has been drinking too much, as Alex has been refilling glasses regularly. People are drifting off.

Alex is sitting on the couch in his living quarters, looking at photographs of the old country. I sit next to Alex, trying to connect with the group.

"Do you have a picture of your wife?" the New Age bookstore owner asks.

"Yes. Show us pictures of all of your wives," the lesbian lawyer suggests.

Clearly Alex is in a nostalgic mood. He retrieves another box of photos from a storage closet. I am curious: I'd like to know what the women were like, how they compared in terms of coloring and build. What their personalities were like. The cause of the breakup. I am hungry for such domestic intrigue.

In the photograph of the first wife, we see a Hungarian Sandra Dee. The eyes of his first wife are heavily made up, her hair is stiff and dyed blonde. Alex looks young and uncertain in a suit and tie.

"Are you still friends?" the lawyer asks.

"I'm friends with all my ex-lovers, in spite of all the lies or crap that went down."

Others have drifted off, and I realize that only four of us are left now.

"The second wife is my favorite," Alex tells us. His second wife has been photographed looking into a mirror; her breasts are large and tilt upward.

"She's very proud of them. She'll show them to you, she carries herself so," Alex notes and thrusts out his chest.

"Did you lie to her?" the bookstore owner asks, with a tinge of judgment in her voice.

"Yes. I lied. I don't know why. It was necessary to survive." Alex shrugs and smirks. "I told her I was out all night in my studio, developing photographs. But you have to work at it to be good. I used to practice, looking in the mirror. Now, I'm not so good: you can see through me."

I think of all the artists I have known, and wonder if any of them were capable of any degree of fidelity to a woman. I know it is easy for Alex to get women, especially younger ones, because he is, by comparison with other local men, exotic. But I have known a number of male artists, so I am jaded; Alex is predictable. The third wife is the one who left Alex for a career as an artist on the West Coast, and her photo shows that she is a beauty. She also looks interesting, someone I'd like to get to know. Alex's discomfort is palpable, and a current of understanding passes between the women in the room: he is still in love with her. Alex returns to the pictures of the old country, and the lawyer and bookstore owner make their excuses and leave quite abruptly. Suddenly I am alone with Alex, sitting close to him on the couch. He is showing me a picture of a home in the countryside of Hungary.

"This was our country house. It brings back such good memories."

I nod; the pine trees around the house are tall, old. I feel awkward.

"Are you going to stay?" Alex asks, matter-of-factly.

I nod, not knowing if he means "stay for a while" or "stay the night." I am angry with my own capitulation, but also curious. I have often wondered what kind of lover Alex would make.

"Well, I'll go lock the door then," Alex resolves, and he pads down the stairs to lock the door to his studio, which opens to a busy street.

Alex sits next to me again, shyly and tentatively. He puts his arm around me, and I rest my head on it. He leans over and softly kisses my neck, then cups one of my breasts in his hand, as if it is a small bird. I laugh softly, and I sense a sardonic quality in my voice.

Alex gets up and puts on some New Age music tape. He sits next to me again. His large purebred dog is sitting and staring at us. We stare at the dog. The dog becomes anxious.

"Would you like to go into the other room?" Alex asks. I nod, and sense he is buying time.

In the next room there is a couch that folds out into a bed. The possibilities for intimacy are here, but intimacy seems remote.

"I can't do this," Alex confesses suddenly.

"Why?" I ask, confused.

"I've never known anyone quite like you. I usually go for the crazy artist types, you know?"

I shake my head, bewildered but amused. I wonder if he has had too much wine, if he is worried about getting an erection.

"I'm afraid," he continued. "I think this would be dangerous. I think you would have the power to hurt me."

Inside I am relieved, but I try not to show it. What I really want is to go home and sleep by myself, but it is reassuring to know that I am desirable.

"It's ok. This is too complicated. Maybe some other time or place." I'm afraid I sound too cheerful or flippant.

I get up to go, and I want to console him, as crestfallen as he looks, so I give him a quick hug. I fly lightly down the stairs.

I fantasize on the long drive home. I am thinking of my last birthday, and the lovemaking with JB. He sent flowers, and we sat across from each other in a dimly lit restaurant, desiring one another. "You've been getting to me," JB suddenly admitted, "but I've been resisting you. See, I have one shot in life with this rodeo, and it's the only thing I have, to tell you the truth. I figure I have three years left to make the finals, then it's over." I was wearing a low-cut lycra top and a push-up bra, and I kept lowering the material. In the car on the way back to his place, he reached over and pulled the top down, and kept squeezing my breasts. "You're so hot, I'm going to buy some ice," he said. Later at his place, he pulled the white silk of my pants aside and licked me, then put a small piece of ice up me. I was squirming, the water was dripping down my legs, and he lost himself in the moment and said, "I'm going crazy."

The fantasies help me sleep. In the morning, a dream is fresh in my memory: I am in a bookstore, wearing a push-up bra. My nipples stick out shamelessly, and I realize how inappropriate my dress is for a bookstore. I leave the store and walk down the street. I feel exposed. The streets are cobblestone, old and European. All of the doors are placed very high above the street level. I try to enter a building, but the door is so high, I can't stretch my leg that far, and my skirt is very short. Alex is waiting for me in a hotel. He tells me he wants to perform oral sex on me; it is a dry, clinical proposition. He gives me an egg to put up my vagina. I take it as if it is a cervical cap that I must insert. I go into another room and try to stuff the egg up me, but it is too large. The blood begins to drip down my legs; it pools at my feet. The blood seeps into my shoes. I begin to panic and think: I need a smaller egg.

I try to look into the far corners of the dream to see if I can retrieve more details. The dream is fading, like a rainbow. I think about how few years I have left. I will have to have a child soon, or not at all.

To Distraction

RONALD BAATZ

why must you lie in bed like that, with just blouse
and panties on, on your stomach, propped up on elbows,
reading that vegetarian cookbook you picked up in
the health food store. why don't you put some
clothes on and go sit on the back porch, where there
is a wonderful breeze this fine afternoon in late june.
and where did you dig those skimpy panties up from.
i swear i've never seen them before. i have all of your
underclothes memorized; they must be new ones. or
    maybe
i just never noticed them before because there isn't much
to them, although i hardly believe that this could be
the case. and why in heavens is your skin so incredibly
white. it's just a simple question; i am not nagging
you. when was the last time you ventured out into the
sunlight. but don't get me wrong, you know, since often
it is the sheer untouched whiteness of your skin that
drives me to distraction. look at me now, helplessly
standing here in the doorway, unable to go down the
stairs. i am riveted to this spot. and i am
absolutely mesmerized by the unbelievable roundness
of your ass. my eyes want to roll over this
roundness of your ass like i used to roll my small toy
trucks and cars over my mother's body in bed mornings,
when i would find her sleeping there after my father
would go off to work. i want to inhale the roundness
of your ass as i would inhale the beautifully ripe
pumpkin split open in autumn. i want to spit wet
watermelon pits on the roundness of your ass and
watch them stick there, so that i can pick them off
with my wet, excited lips to swallow whole. my god,

how the hell am i supposed to go out and water the
young flowers when you are occupying the bed as you
are. if we were at the beach you'd be asking me to
spray your long legs with water. other men would be
staring at me with envy in their eyes. it's true,
i've seen this happen i don't know how many times.
often i question myself: how is it that such
a beautiful woman has fallen in love with me.
but, there is no answer. all i can ascribe it
to is dumb luck. and if it is simply
an expression of life being kind to me,
well, i can only hope death is half so
kind.

Trust Muscle

LEASA BURTON

He has his fingers in her mouth
and she is not sucking.
She is letting him feel
how large a petal her tongue
can be, how velvet, how furred,
how thick as his two fingers
separate, slide down the sides
of it so that she notices
the salt on him, the bitter
and sweet, like blood, like leaf
and she thinks each taste
feels different—a darkness,
a moan, a shiver, a breath—
makes her want him
differently, every time, right

here, right now, her muscle
working hard to be still;
her teeth keeping their promise.

Two or Three Things i Know for Sure

DOROTHY ALLISON

I had this girlfriend once scared all my other girlfriends off. Big, blond, shy, and butch, just out of the army, drove a two-door Chevy with a reinforced trunk and wouldn't say why.

"What you carry in that thing, girl? You moving contraband state to state?" I was joking, teasing, putting my hand on her butt, grinning at her scowl, touching her in places she couldn't quite admit she liked.

"I an't moving nothing," she told me.

"Uh-huh. Right. So how come I feel so moved?"

She blushed. I love it when women blush, especially those big butch girls who know you want them. And I wanted her. I did. I wanted her. But she was a difficult woman, wouldn't let me give her a backrub, read her palm, or sew up the tear in her jeans—all those ritual techniques Southern femmes have employed in the se-duction of innocent butch girls. A basic error, this one was not from the South. Born in Chicago, she was a Yankee runaway raised in Barbados by a daddy who worked as a Mafia bagman and was never really sure if he was bringing up a boy or a girl. He'd bought her her first three-piece suit, then cursed at how good it looked on her and signed the permission form that let her join the army at seventeen.

"My daddy loves me, he just don't understand me. Don't know how to talk to me when I go back." She told me that after I'd helped her move furniture for two hours and we were relaxing over a shared can of beer and stories of how she'd gotten to Tallahassee. I just nodded, pretty sure her daddy understood her as much as he could stand.

I seduced her in the shower. It was all that furniture-moving, I told her, and insisted I couldn't go out in the condition I was in. Simple courtesy. I sent her in the shower first, came in after, and then soaped her back in businesslike fashion so she'd relax a little more. I kept chatting—about the women's center, books I'd read, music, and oh! how long and thick her toenails were. I got down on my knees to examine her toenails.

"Woman," I said, "you have the most beautiful feet."

I let the water pour down over both of us. It was a silly thing, to talk that way in that situation, but sex is like that. There I was, kneeling for her, naked, my hands on her legs, my mouth just where I wanted it to be. I smiled before I leaned forward. She clenched her fists in my hair, moaned when my tongue touched her. The muscles in her thighs began to jump. We nearly drowned in that shower.

"Don't laugh at me," she said later when we were lying limp on wet sheets, and I promised. No.

"Whiskey and cigarettes," she mumbled. "I move whiskey and cigarettes without tax stamps, for the money, that's what I move."

I smiled and raked my teeth across her throat. "Uh-huh."

"And . . ." She paused. I put one leg between her thighs and slid myself up and down until we fit tight, the bone of my hip resting against the arch of her pubic mound, the tangle of her blond curls wiry on my belly. I pushed up off her throat and waited. She looked up at me. Her cheeks were bright red, her eyes almost closed, pearly tears showing at the corners.

"Shaklee! Shaklee products. Oh God! I sell cleaning supplies door to door."

I bit her shoulder, didn't laugh. I rocked her on my leg until she relaxed and laughed herself. I rocked her until she could forgive me for asking. Then she took hold of me and rolled me over and showed me that she wanted me as much as I had wanted her.

"You're quite a story," I whispered to her after.
"Don't tell," she begged.
"Who would I tell?"
Who needs to know?

Under the Olive Tree

JS THOMAS

There's a whistle in your breath
as I approach you trembling, just
straining to tongue-twirl the buttons
of your chest, pitted, sour to the bone.

Soon enough, the grove will warm
as morning breakfasts on the moon
above us, her halo swearing eternal
hope, the two of us talking scandal.

Fresh christened by the breeze, will
you keep me clean, Love? Shall I
take you in my mouth again, roll you
over my teeth like that bitter fruit?

Oily and wet down to the seam
of your toes, you shimmer, graze
my thigh with the fair pulp I am
bursting to devour, skin and all,

so help me lord. And if tonight I die,
already I'm half gone, supine, chilled,
ready to be taken once, for all, the olive
branch heaving between my breasts.

Unto Her

TIM JOHNSTON

You find yourself in Tokyo on New Year's Eve, stuffed on seafood ravioli in a miraculous white sauce, lubricated from the toes up on the best Chianti the city can muster, staring her in the eyes. She is visiting at your suggestion, to see the country and to see if the two of you might, on the brink of your thirties, figure out a way to live with or without each other. She's been here ten days and leaves to-morrow—a fact you are certain, just now, you can live with despite the wine and the look in her eyes and the cut of the black brocade gown she's brought all the way here just for tonight, just for you.

You finish a final carafe and catch a cab back to Billy's apart-ment where you've been staying while you teach your English lessons and try to learn something about another culture. About a thousand years ago, it seems, you and Billy took drafting courses together in college. Billy went on to design buildings, you to build them, a nail bender when you can find the work.

In the cab, while a stone-shouldered Japanese driver speeds you through New Year's Eve traffic, she places a hand high on your thigh, higher still, then asks, garlic and wine on her breath, "Do you mind if I do this here?"

A scent rushing in the open window reminds you of leaves burning in the Midwest in October, the smell of first days on cam-pus, of first nights in her bed and the first, cautious negotiations of contact. "You mean this with your hand, here?" you say. "Or this in the cab, here?"

"Yes," she says, and black nylons sing as she shifts on the seat, dips to your lap, the applish scent of shampoo in your nostrils as she roots you out into cool air and then into warm mouth, brings you to spinning bliss behind the driver's unmoving head, crisp reddish oak leaves burning somewhere in Tokyo.

On the slow elevator up to Billy's apartment, the bust of the gown comes down, along with lace panties, which you stuff in your pocket and will not find again for several days, a slug to your heart. She is hot down there, she's running some kind of fever, and when the elevator dings and the door whisks open you are only half-relieved that nobody is waiting to see the topless redhead Westerner with one bare leg hiked up around her date, telling him, "I want you inside me."

She consents to waiting until you're in Billy's bedroom before whisking the gown to the floor and tugging at your belt.

In seconds you are on the bed, on your back, arms pinned by hers, testicles squashed and aching with the weight of hips, noticing for the first time that a Japanese ceiling looks exactly like one from home, like oatmeal flung thickly and painted white.

"What's the matter?" she asks. "Don't you want to fuck me?"

You manage a smile. In her use of profanity she is like, you decided long ago, many well-raised, God-fearing Midwestern girls: forbidden words turn her on. You understand even if you don't always sympathize. Lately, you understand a lot without sympathy. Your mind and heart have never seemed so much like separate beings, like two bickersome, estranged parents. You have no idea which to trust.

"I'd love to," you say at last.

"To what?"

"Fuck you."

The bones of her neck seem to soften with the word, and red hair splashes your face. Strong freckled thighs spread further. "Then fuck me," she suggests.

You tell her you can't—you're wasted, emptied, sucked inside out—until she laughs and rolls from you like a giddy child and you laugh too, big loose laughter like you haven't felt, you realize, since she dropped The Big One, a bomb any moron could have seen coming from a thousand miles away but which caught you standing straight as a plumb line. She had not, she confessed on the second day of her trip, been completely honest.

She'd met someone in your absence, a thirty-six-year-old pianist divorcée with a kid. She wanted you to know this, she explained, for the sake of fair play, so that you'd know she was prepared, if necessary, to get on with her life. She wanted to be honest. She didn't want to hurt you.

Which, you decided, was a lie. She may have really cared for The Pianist—you'll give her that—but telling you about him was an act of purest cruelty, though neither of you would have guessed at the results. That first night was the hardest, the night you'll never forget but mercifully never fully recollect: the dizziness, the knotting of viscera, the unceasing pain of your physical heart. All of that will fade and you will only remember crawling on your hands and knees to the other bedroom, locking the door behind you, wanting to be knocked somehow into another world and time. What flaw in the construction of your life, you wondered, had left you so unprepared for such a blast?

The next morning, as she slept, you dressed and took the elevator down, crossed the alley and took another elevator up to Heidi and Ron's apartment. Like Billy, they'd left for the holidays, and you'd promised to water plants. You got as far as the philodendrons before calling Billy's travel agent. It would take three days and nearly 150,000 yen to get her out of Japan.

You hung up and stepped outside and saw, standing on the balcony across the way, a woman, rolled up in a bedsheet like sushi, staring west. It was the same woman you'd known for five years, lived with for two, nearly married before the call from Billy: *Come see the Orient, man. The time of your life.* It was the same woman you'd thought about as you hiked Mount Fuji, gathered rose petals from the floor of the Taj Mahal, watched beautiful young Thai couples copulate for your amusement in the bars of Bangkok.

You called, "Why did you come here?"

She turned, pulling hair from her face. "To see another world. To be dazzled."

"Hey," you answered, "that's why I'm here."

She squinted in the sun. "I came to see you, too, okay? But you wanted me to. You got me here. What are you going to do, send me back?"

Your mind raced: *Find her a hotel? Find yourself one? Jump the hell off this balcony?* A forgotten cluster of words from childhood, from before your parents gave up on vows and catechism, assail you like bees: "If a man put away his wife, and she go from him, and become another man's, shall he return unto her again?"

Could you have actually been listening, you wonder, through all your daydreaming? Could the nuns of St. Joe's be skulking, still, in the aisles of your soul? What did it matter if the girl you left behind opened her heart, and her thighs, to another man? What right did you have to feel betrayed?

When you said nothing she returned her attention to the west, her hair a small blaze, bedsheet rippling.

In the remaining days of her visit you slowly returned to her. You bought her snapdragons from a hunchbacked Japanese woman on a street corner, paid four thousand yen apiece so you could dance like teenagers at a Rappongi "disco," taxied her to Tokyo Tower for a bird's-eye view of the city, all the while wanting nothing so much as to have some part of you inside her. No place was too public for your fingers: the subway, the movie theater, the disco, the crowded tower elevator going up and up. You fondled and probed and called her a whore when the mood struck, which it did often—as it does now, lying naked and impotent on Billy's bed on New Year's Eve, laughing with her. You are struck by a vision of The Pianist, holding his remarkable joint with concerto fingers, aiming it squarely at her mouth, until you suddenly want nothing more than to smother her laughter with one of Billy's pillows.

You jump from bed as one jumps up from an embarrassing fall. "Maybe I'll take a shower," you say.

She rolls to her stomach and spanks you playfully. "Good idea. Get it good and steamy in there."

You stand over her a moment, looking down coldly while she looks up with inebriate affection, crossing and uncrossing skinny ankles in the air above her buttocks.

You leave for the bathroom and she gives you a few minutes, no doubt sensing the most recent uprising of The Pianist; she is smart, you think—and goddess-assed. You take yourself in hand and discover hardness. Hardness pleases you, just now, like no laughter ever could. After all, you think, you'd left her for the seduction of travel, abandoned her to the other men of the world and yet, here she was, an ocean crossed despite a desperate aversion to flight, just to be with you. It is this cock she wants, you console yourself, this cock that had her nearly raping you in the elevator, this cock she comes for now as she steps into steam.

A smaller hand replaces yours. Her voice is sibilant, like water. "I see you've rallied the troops."

"Yes," you answer. "We're ready for the siege."

With spray and steam buffeting from all directions, you press her against the tiles of the wall, kissing hard, jamming a finger deep inside her. The water runs into and out of your mouth and you raise her legs around you and she guides you in with a sigh.

You push into her, against the tiles, push again.

"Wait," she says. "That kind of hurts."

"Sorry."

She seeks your eyes through steam. "I bet you are."

"Too rough?" you ask.

"You want rough?" She's on her own feet now, fingernails deep in your arms, turning you around. "You want to fuck me rough?" she asks.

Yes, you concede, you do, and with a smile she turns her back to you, plants her feet well apart, bends, and grips the rim of the tub. Over her shoulder, wet ropes of hair clinging to the tub, she says, "Okay. Let's go."

It's all too absurd, you think, trashy and staged, yet you are lightheaded with the invitation, that white freckled backside lifted, buttocks spread so that every detail of her anatomy looks you in the eye and dares you to look back.

You step over to her, grab hold of hips and watch yourself enter, slowly. Back out again just as slowly, fascinated by the interaction of flesh, the tug and pull, as if you've never seen anything like it.

"Faster," she says. "Please."

Fascination fades. You spread your own feet and bear down hard.

"Yes," she says. "Fuck me."

The word hits you, just then, like a bad swing, like a 20 oz. hammer missing the nail and smashing your heart. A blush invades your vision, turns the world red.

"Did he fuck you like this?" you ask.

"Please," she says, her head sagging slightly. "Don't talk."

"Did he?"

"Did he what?" Her voice has all the energy of water slipping down the drain.

"Did he fuck you like this," you repeat. "From behind."

She shakes her head.

"Say it." You despise your monstrosity. You despise her for suffering it.

"No, God damn it," she says at last. "He didn't fuck me like this. He didn't fuck me from behind."

Outrageous curses burn your throat. You want to set them loose, feel you have to, are about to—when something shifts behind your ribs, like organs trading places, and it's all you can do not to fall, to drop to the tiles and curl up in the tightest knot possible.

"Jesus," you say after a moment. "Christ." You slip out and rest against her, hands on her shoulder blades, your resolve all soft and mashed into the sleeve of her buttocks.

She sighs and seems to soften as well, the sturdy posts of arms and legs giving way slightly, listing beneath your weight, and it's here you experience a moment of clarity, a kind of glimpse into a future state of mind, it seems, when all of these days, since that first brutal night until now, will all seem like something you dreamed. All the sexual intensity and emotional chaos of the last ten days, you are suddenly certain, all your groping attempts to diminish and accuse and repossess, will amount, finally, to nothing more than some kind of bout, a lapse, a horrible but temporary madness. As early as tomorrow, you think, after she has boarded the plane and left the country, you will be able to return to your quiet, displaced life among the Japanese. You do not yet realize, and would not believe—with her bent like so before you, your sorry cock pinned in the seam of her ass—the immensity of feelings to come.

But there you are, flaccid and tired, wishing only to get her on that plane, when she reaches across the tub.

She hands a bottle back to you. "Do you mind? All this water . . ."

The bottle contains baby oil. Raised on the tundra of Minnesota she has used the stuff since childhood, and you recall, in another burst of clarity, the applications you'd devised in college, the slick massages, buttery grips, those hilarious sucking sounds.

You take the bottle. You direct a thin stream onto her back, working it into her skin with your free hand. She lowers her head and dips slightly, knees briefly buckling. You blink away steam, wait for a warm tremor to spend itself in your gut, then spill more oil, watch it river down her spine, flow quickly between buttocks. You reach down there with a palmful and splash her, spank her wetly, spread the oil thoroughly.

"Yes," she says in a breath.

All at once, obvious as if she's told you, you understand what she's asking. You drop the bottle and slowly, carefully, slip the tip of your index finger into her anus. You cannot believe the heat and tightness of this place, as you cannot believe she wants your finger there. You begin to withdraw it, but she moves toward you.

"Stay," she says. "If you want to."

You don't answer but stay put. It occurs to you that this is the first time you've ever had your finger inside an anus—any anus, including your own—and you are genuinely surprised by your lack of revulsion. You find yourself floating in a mist of candor and tenderness like you've never felt before, as if the last ten days have been layers of sheetrock, broken through one by one to expose, finally, this room where you've never been and where you feel yourself capable of kindnesses unimaginable before.

Certain she shares this feeling, you slip in another finger.

"Too much?" you ask.

"I don't know. It's the first time."

"A virgin, then," you say, hoping for a nod.

"Yes," she says, shuddering slightly.

You stand like this for some time, your fingers inside her, until desire becomes stronger than tenderness, and you pull your fingers out and aim yourself at the tiny puckering.

She stops you with your name, softly spoken, a one-word question.

"Yes?" you answer.

"Slowly?"

"Slowly," you promise.

When you enter she catches her breath, and it seems for a moment as if she's trying to pull away, but it's really just her knees giving out again, her strength collapsing and you collapsing with her, the both of you easing as one to the tiled floor, to hands and knees, you holding her firmly and forcing yourself in incrementally, one heartbeat at a time. You keep your promise until slowness itself, the steady tight grip of it, becomes unbearable and you push the rest of the way in, deep as you can, raising a low wailing from both your throats, a stretched cry echoing as you fall like wreckage all the way to the floor, a wet tangle of mutual limbs, mouths open and forming each other's names, breathless and repeatedly and urgently until pain and bliss spike through you like ampage, like crossed wires, and you seem to actually lift from the tiles, to hang weightless for an extended, trembling moment before returning, gradually, to the floor.

Flesh slowly settles, muscles twitch. Names trail off to small giggles and whimperings, then sighs and soft whisperings, then nothing: deep breaths and water, a calm so necessary you can't imagine its end.

Vespers

TIMOTHY LIU

So many want to be blessed.
I only want to kneel in a quiet room.
To love what we have or not exist
at all. Nothing to help me sleep.
Only a scrap of paper slipped
into my hand: *your body an ocean,*

a song without end. Votive candles
flickering in the dark that made us
larger than life: hip-thrust,
back-arch, mouth-grip, you on top
till we collapsed in the coiled
springs that came to rest. A chair
where you once sat. A bowl of fruit
neither one of us would touch.

The Storm

TIMOTHY LIU

Black ants crawl in the sugar bowl,
me no longer checking the mail.

How stars in the window shift as I
begin to forget. Cricket song

instead of your voice. That fire
we started nothing more than ribs

of ash on an iron grate. A time
when we spoke. Come to me in a dream

where I don't appear. Closer still—
as if love were more than a fever

of moths crowding a lighted square
moments before the power goes out.

What it Sounds Like

DORIANNE LAUX

You called it screwing, what we did nights
on the rug in front of the mirror, draped over
the edge of a hotel bed, on the balconies
overlooking the dark hearts of fir trees or a city
of flickering lights. You'd whisper that word
into my ear as if it were something real: a sliver
of apple, a swirl of chocolate, thick and black
on the tongue. I was used to the rough
exuberant consonants of fucking, and this
soft s and hard c had a new feeling—sad, slow,
like the moments of leaving between thrusts.
I don't know what to make of it
now that you're gone. I think of metal
eating wood, the delicate filaments quivering
inside a bulb of thin glass, harsh light, corks
easing up through the wet necks of wine bottles,
a silver lid turned tight on a jar of skinned plums.
I see two blue dragonflies hovering, end to end,
above the pond, as if they are twisting
the iridescence deep into each others' bodies,
long segmented abdomens writhing, spiraling
into the beaten air, and your voice
comes back to me through the trees,
this word for what we couldn't help doing
to each other, a high, thin cry unwinding.

What She Wrote Him

KATHRYN STEADMAN

If you want to excite me not just for this moment but so that I'll carry you inside of me, and at a word entering grow hot for you. Then pull your hand back away from my body. Talk to me.

Speak in front of a mirror to see how your mouth moves as you say certain words. I'll be watching. Talk into a tape recorder to practice making the perfect sound. A sound clear and fluid so it enters me secretly. Roll your r's so I see them spiraling off of your tongue. Have the right amount of shush in your sh's to quiet my heart pounding. Onomatopoeia, what a beautiful word. Learn what it means and use it daily to express yourself. Press your mouth to my skin, so I feel the vibration of letters. Sharpen your tongue, enunciate. Speak without hesitation and I can't help but do whatever it is you demand. Practice, practice, practice. Talk to the purple iris in the garden, talk to the child, the whore.

And then the words. Choose carefully, be sure you know their exact meaning. Don't say penis when you mean cock. Don't say cock when you mean the bold stamen of a calla lily. My name is a good one. You'll want to say it often, as though it comes from deep inside your belly, as if you named me.

Use poetry, it is the root of all language. Think of line breaks rather than sentences. Pause in all the right places. Be aware of timing. I don't like periods, I don't believe in endings of any kind, you must go on and on the way the sky does. Don't overpunctuate, most of it's designed to stop sensation. Talk in metaphors. Tell me I'm sand under your nails, tell me I'm the rope that'll hang you.

I'll begin to moan.

And when you're not with me I'll remember the tone of your voice and what was said. I'll find a corner half hidden in shadow, half in light that angles in from a nearby window. The window is cracked to let a warm breeze in. Lying on the hard wooden floor, I'll hear your voice speaking from inside of me the way it has in the past. Saying my name. I'll pull my red skirt up, gather it up around my waist, slip my hand inside purple lace panties. All the time your voice talking to me, "come for me" you say.

In the background I hear the song of children from the school next door, the crack of my neighbor's hoe hitting a stone in his garden. Closer is the hum of the fluorescent light left on in the study where I was writing, and the whirl of the washer as it spins cum, sweat, and hairs from the blue sheets.

Then you enter. And you tell me what you said in secret to the purple iris, the child, and the whore.

So that when my back begins to rise off of the floor, and my legs bend back and away from my body, and it feels as if I'm breathing through a mouth filled with thistles, I'm speaking in tongues or making the kind of noises I imagine people who speak in tongues make, though I've never heard them, but I know this is surely one God speaking through me. I'm calling your name, I'm holding the gold sex of bees, I'm praying to the Patron Saint of Fornication, I'm tasting red honey, I'm pleading with Our Lady of the Brilliant Fuck. Iris delivers me to you, into the bed of purple flowers in our garden where there are no voices. Where we have no name.

You Are The Girl i Love

GABRIELLE GLANCY

That was an April. Sixteen
Sycamores harbored South Portland
And the Slope rose Westward
In a breeze that blew Brooklyn
Clear from the sea to the bridge.
Now the wind chases us wildly,
The light chases the wind and even
Long days won't slow us down.

(What is the name of those
Fierce yellow flowers that smell
Like the sweet part of lemon?) How
The view here is broader and more
Sudden. How you are the girl I come
Home to: You are the girl I love.

Too near

GABRIELLE GLANCY

everywhere such breathing as will unclose me
first petal-by-petal (deeper still) descending
a meaning that compels your slightest look away
I perceive in equal parts the closeness of this

careful world carefully opening me and closing
the first touch of me too near to everywhere,
suddenly, in peculiar agreement with this heart
the trees lie in waiting each breathing to each

about you something discloses itself to me

Contributors

TOM ABSHER has taught literature and writing at Goddard College and Vermont College since 1968. He received his M.F.A. from Goddard in 1978, and has two books of poems in print, *Forms of Praise* (1981, Ohio State University Press), and *The Calling* (1987), as well as a book of essays, *Men and the Goddess* (1991, Park Street). A YMHA/Nation Discovery winner in 1978, Absher has won two N.E.A. poetry fellowships over the years, and he received a Vermont Council on the Arts grant in the early eighties.

DOROTHY ALLISON is the author of the novel *Bastard Out of Carolina*; the essay collection *Skin: Talking About Sex, Class and Literature*; *Trash*, a collection of short stories; and *The Women Who Hate Me*, a volume of poetry. She has won numerous awards for her work. She lives in northern California.

RONALD BAATZ lives in an old farmhouse in upstate New York.

CAROLYN BANKS most recently authored a five-book comic mystery series set in the equestrian world. The latest of these paperback originals is *A Horse to Die For*, the final entry. She has had four hardcover suspense novels published as well as a collection of her short stories, *Tart Tales*. In addition, Banks has served as book editor for several national publications and regularly reviews books for the *Washington Post Book World*. Harking back to her earlier work, she's presently writing an erotic thriller entitled *His*.

DAVID BIESPIEL was born in 1964 in Oklahoma and grew up in Texas. He is the author of *Shattering Air* (BOA Editions). The recipient of many awards, he has taught at several universities, most recently at Stanford University. He is a contributor to *The New York Times*, *American Poetry Review*, and other literary quarterlies.

TARA BRAY teaches elementary school in Georgia. Her work has appeared or will soon appear in *Poem*, *Atlanta Review*, *Georgia Journal*, and *New York Quarterly*.

LEASA BURTON is an editor at Cleis Press and teaches writing in the Pittsburgh community. Her poems have appeared in *Central Park*, *Quarterly West*, *Sojourner: The Women's Forum*, *The Louisville Review*, among others, and in the anthology *A Gathering of Poets* from Kent State University Press. She received an M.F.A. from the University of Pittsburgh in 1992, and has been awarded an Associated Writing Programs Intro Journal Award and an Academy of American Poets Prize.

J. DUNNE is currently pursuing his interests in both writing and the fine arts. He has been working with the concept of the book as an artifact, making one-of-a-kind handbound artist books as well as taking book pages out of their bindings and arranging them in odd fashions as three-dimensional drawings. Also, he is taking steps to publish his first novel.

GLORIA DYC is a poet and fiction writer who lives in Continental Divide, New Mexico. One of her short stories will appear in *Southwestern Women: New Voices* (Javelina Press). An associate professor at The University of New Mexico-Gallup, Gloria Dyc is working on a novel.

EDWARD FALCO is the author of the novel *Winter in Florida* (Soho, 1990), the hypertext novel, *A Dream with Demons* (Eastgate Systems, forthcoming), and a recently completed novel, *High Falls*. He has published two collections of stories: *Acid* (Notre Dame, 1996) and *Plato at Scratch Daniel's & Other Stories* (University of Arkansas Press, 1990). A story of his from *The Atlantic Monthly* was chosen for *The Best American Short Stories 1995*; other stories have appeared in *TriQuarterly*, *Ploughshares*, and many other places. Edward has won numerous fellowships and awards, and he lives in Blacksburg, Virginia, where he teaches writing and literature at Virginia Tech.

ALISON FELL is a Scottish poet and novelist who lives in London. Her previous novels include *Every Move You Make*, and *Mer de Glace*, which won the 1991 Boardman Tasker Award for Mountain Literature. Her poetry is widely anthologized, and appears in the individual collections *Kisses for Mayakovsky* and *The Crystal Owl*. She edited and contributed to the three women's collections *The Seven*

Deadly Sins, *The Seven Cardinal Virtues*, and *Serious Hysterics*. This book's story is from her novel *The Pillow Boy of the Lady Onogoro*.

THAISA FRANK is the author of fiction collections *Enchanted Men*, *A Brief History of Camouflage*, and others, and *Finding Your Writer's Voice*, a guide to creative fiction. A two-time PEN award winner, she teaches writing at U.C. Berkeley and the graduate program at San Francisco State University.

CARLOS FUENTES is author of numerous novels, including *The Old Gringo*, *The Death of Artemio Cruz*, and most recently *The Campaign*. In 1987, he received the Cervantes Award, the highest award bestowed on a Spanish-language writer. Mr. Fuentes divides his time between Mexico City and London. This anthology's story is an excerpt from a story in his recent collection, *The Orange Tree*.

JESÚS GARDEA is a prolific writer, born and bred in northern Mexico. His initial field was dentistry, which he practiced and eventually taught. Years of reading in the library, however, led him to become a writer, altogether self-taught. He published his first novel while in his forties and a year later, in 1980, received the prestigious Xavier Villarrutia Prize for his collection of stories *Septiembre y los otros días*. An anthology of his short stories entitled *Stripping Away the Sorrows from This World*, edited and translated by Mark Schafer, will be published by Editorial Aldus in 1997. It will include "Forty Springs."

GABRIELLE GLANCY'S poems have appeared in such publications as *The New Yorker*, *The Paris Review*, and *The American Poetry Review*. Her work has been anthologized in *Sister and Brother Lesbians and Gay Men Write About Their Lives Together* and many other anthologies. She was recipient of a New York Foundation for the Arts grant in 1990 and a Writers at Work Prize in 1991. Born and raised in New York City, she now lives in San Francisco and is at work on a novel that chronicles the exploits of a girl-casanova in search of her Russian lover, who has mysteriously disappeared.

JOHN GOLDFINE. June 7, 1995. Borscht two nights back from beets I put up a year ago and pesto last night with the very last of last summer's basil. This year's garden is all planted, except for the potatoes, which go in so late in June (to stymie Colorado potato beetles) that one can hardly believe they will throw a crop, but they will. It's raining as I write—fresh weeds to chop tomorrow and chores everlasting.

KARL HARSHBARGER lives and writes in Germany, where he also teaches English as a foreign language. Stories of his have appeared in such magazines as *The Atlantic Monthly* and *The High Plains Literary Review*. "The Escort," which appeared in *Oasis*, was nominated for the 1995 Pushcart Prize.

LINDA VANESSA HEWITT, who grew up in a working-class neighborhood of Boston, served as Assistant Director of the Isabella Stewart Gardner Museum for twelve years. She writes fiction and poetry for herself and nonfiction for social service agencies and cultural organizations. Her poetry has been accepted for publication in the *California State Poetry Society Quarterly*, *The Cream City Review*, and *Anthology of New England Writers* (1996), and her short story, "Desert," appeared in the Winter 1996 issue of *Excursus*. She lives near the south coast of Massachusetts and now and then teaches creative writing workshops.

JANE HIRSHFIELD is the author of *Alaya* (1982), *Of Gravity and Angels* (1988), *The October Palace* (1994), and *The Lives of the Heart* (1997); she is also co-translator and editor of *The Ink Dark Moon* and *Women in Praise of the Sacred*. She has received a Guggenheim Fellowship, the Poetry Center Book Award, the Bay Area Book Reviewers Award, and the Commonwealth Club Poetry Medal, and her work appears in *The New Yorker*, *The Atlantic*, *The New Republic*, *The Nation*, *The American Poetry Review*, *The Paris Review*, and elsewhere.

DAVE HOWELL lives with his wife and daughter in the Palouse region of Washington. He received an M.F.A. at The University of Alaska, Fairbanks, and a Ph.D. in Interdisciplinary Studies at Washington State University. He presently works as a writing consultant.

TIM JOHNSTON is living in Los Angeles, working on a novel. His stories have appeared in the *New England Review*, *Missouri Review*, and elsewhere. As in most cases, "Unto Her" is a mix of facts and lies forced into the same small room. After a while, looking in on them, you forget which is which.

GINU KAMANI is the author of *Junglee Girl* (Aunt Lute Books, 1995), a collection of short stories exploring the sensual recklessness of Indian women. Her writings have appeared in *On a Bed of Rice: An Asian American Erotic Feast*, *Dick for a Day*, *Herotica 5*, *au Juice: the journal of eatin drinkin & screwin 'round*, and *Traveler's Tales: Food*. She lives in northern California and is finishing a novel.

GALWAY KINNELL'S poetic career spans thirty-five years and includes such poetry collections as *Imperfect Thirst*, *Three Books* (*Body Rags; Mortal Acts, Mortal Words*; and *The Past*), *What a Kingdom It Was*, *The Book of Nightmares*, and *When One Has Lived a Long Time Alone*. He lives in Vermont, where he has been State Poet of Vermont, and New York City, where he is Erich Remarque Professor of Creative Writing at New York University. He is a former MacArthur Fellow, and in 1982, his *Selected Poems* won the Pulitzer Prize and the American Book Award.

EDWARD KLEINSCHMIDT'S poems in this book are included in a book of love poems, *Bodysongs*, due out from The Heyeck Press this year (1997). His second book of poems, *First Language*, won the Juniper Prize, and his first book, *Magnetism*, received the 1988 Poetry Award from the San Francisco Bay Area Book Reviewers Association. His poems have appeared in *American Poetry Review*, *The New Yorker*, *Poetry*, *The Best American Poetry*, and many other places. He teaches at Santa Clara University.

PETER KUNZ lives near Point Reyes Station, California. His work has appeared in *Yellow Silk* as well as *Barnabe Mountain Review*, *convolvulus*, *Lullwater Review*, *Poetry at the 33*, and *Steelhead Special*.

DORIANNE LAUX is the author of two collections of poetry from BOA Editions, *Awake* (1990) and *What We Carry* (1994), which was a finalist for the National Book Critics Circle Award. She is also co-author, with Kim Addonizio, of *The Poet's Companion: A Handbook and Guide for Writers* (Norton, 1997). Among her awards are a Pushcart Prize for poetry and a fellowship from The National Endowment for the Arts. In 1994 she joined the faculty at the University of Oregon's Program in Creative Writing.

LISA LEITZ works as a reporter for *The Royal Review* and for the Northwest Association of Mothers of Twins. She has an M.F.A. from Eastern Washington University, her work has been published in *Willamette Week* and *The Red Rock Review*, and she has edited a historical novel. She has three delightful, persistent young sons, and a gracious sister and husband who make her writing possible.

TIMOTHY LIU's books of poems are *Vox Angelica* (Alice James Books) and *Burnt Offerings* (Copper Canyon Press). A new book, *Say Goodnight*, is forthcoming in 1998. He lives in Iowa.

JOAN LOGGHE has lived in rural northern New Mexico since 1973 and teaches writing workshops locally and nationally. Her most recent book, *Twenty Years in Bed with the Same Man* (La Alameda Press, 1995), was a finalist in the Western States Book Award. She was poetry editor for *Mothering Magazine* for seven years and received an N.E.A. in poetry. She is project director for Write Action, a writing workshop for Santa Fe's AIDS community, an educational outreach program from which she edited *Catch Our Breath: Writing from the Heart of AIDS* (Mariposa, 1996).

MARY MACKEY is the author of eight novels, including, during the last five years, a trilogy including *The Year the Horses Came*, *The Horses at the Gate*, and *The Fires of Spring* (all published by HarperSanFrancisco). Based on the research of archaeologist Marija Gimbutas, the trilogy explores how an eros-based culture, as it may have existed in 4000 B.C.E. Europe, can defend itself against a culture based on violent conquest, without giving up its most basic values. Mackey also reviews for the *San Francisco Chronicle*. Her most recent collection of poetry is *The Dear Dance of Eros* (Fjord Press).

STEFANIE MARLIS'S book *Slow Joy* won the Brittingham Prize from the University of Wisconsin in 1989 and the Great Lakes Colleges New Writers Award in 1990. In 1994, she received an N.E.A. fellowship. Floating Island Press published her small chapbook: *Sheet of Glass*, and she has been published in numerous journals including *Arshile*, *APR*, *Poetry*, *Manoa*, and *Gettysburg Review*. Marlis has received three California prizes: two Marin Arts Council Awards and the Joseph Henry Jackson Award, and Sarabande Books will be publishing her manuscript, tentatively called *The Other Wakes*, in early 1998. She makes a living as a freelance copywriter.

CAROLE MASO is the author of *Ghost Dance*, *The Art Lover*, and *The American Woman in the Chinese Hat*. She teaches at Brown University.

JILL MCDONOUGH is really a very nice girl. To prove it, she worked briefly as a librarian after graduating from an expensive university. She teaches English in rural Japan and watches X-Files in Japanese while preparing spinach for her dinner. She was the 1995 National English Language Poetry Slam Champion of Japan, which isn't nearly as impressive as it sounds.

PHILIP MEMMER currently lives and writes in Pittsburgh. His poem is from a manuscript-in-progress entitled *One Luxury*. Other poems from the manuscript have recently appeared in *Puerto del Sol* and *Poetry*.

STEVE MILES teaches writing and literature courses at Colorado State University and has published book reviews, poems, and essays in various magazines including *The Southern Poetry Review*, *The Chattahoochee Review*, *Atlanta Review*, *The Sun*, *Poem*, *New Letters Review of Books*, *Hawaii Review*, *Sundog*, *The Southeast Review*, *Colorado Review*, *The William and Mary Review*, and the anthology *New Voices*. Steve has been a Poet in Residence for both the Colorado and Wyoming State Arts Councils, and received the 1995 Literature Recognition Award from the Colorado Council on the Arts.

WALTER MOSLEY is the author of four previous novels in the Easy Rawlins series, *A Red Death*, *White Butterfly*, *Black Betty*, and *Devil in a Blue Dress*, which was made into a motion picture with Denzel Washington. In 1995 he published his first nongenre novel, *RL's Dream*. The former president of Mystery Writers of America, he is on the board of PEN American Center, where he founded the Open Book Committee, and on the board of the National Book Awards.

D. NURKSE was appointed Poet Laureate of Brooklyn in 1996. He has recent work in *The New Yorker*, *Grand Street*, and *The Kenyon Review*. His fourth book, *Voices Over Water*, was reissued in 1996 by Four Way Books.

SHARON OLDS was born in 1942, in San Francisco, and was educated at Stanford University and Columbia University. Her books include The Wellspring; The Father, which was shortlisted for the T. S. Eliot Prize in England; The Dead and the Living, which won the National Book Critics Circle Award and was the Lamont Poetry Selection for 1983; and her first, Satan Says (1980), which received the inaugural San Francisco Poetry Center Award. She teaches poetry workshops in the Graduate Creative Writing Program at New York University, and helps run the N.Y.U. workshop program at Goldwater Hospital on Roosevelt Island in New York.

DONALD RAWLEY is the author of five books of poetry: Mecca (1991), Malibu Stories (1991), Steaming (1993), Duende (1994), and Sirens (1996). His first novel, Dark Hands, will be published by Avon Books in the spring of 1998, and a collection of short stories, Slow Dance on the Fault Line, is due out in July 1997 from HarperCollins-London. His short fiction, essays, and poetry have appeared in The New Yorker, Yellow Silk, BUZZ, Genre, Geo Germany, the Olympic Review, and many other places. He is a contributing editor at BUZZ and is working on his second novel. He lives in Sherman Oaks, California.

JAY ROGOFF'S book-length sequence of poems, The Cutoff (Word Works, 1995), won the 1994 Washington Prize for Poetry. He has recent or forthcoming poems in American Literary Review, Chelsea, Confrontation, DoubleTake, The Kenyon Review, Manoa, The Paris Review, Partisan Review, Press, Salmagundi, and The Sewanee Review, among others. His reviews of poetry and prose have also appeared in Kenyon, Sewanee, and Shenandoah. He is at work on Terpsichore Variations, an extended sequence of poems concerning dance. A resident of Saratoga Springs, New York, he teaches in Skidmore College's Liberal Studies program.

MARK SCHAFER is a literary translator and visual artist who lives in Boston and Tepoztlàn, Mexico. His translation of "Springtime" was supported by the Fund for Culture USA-Mexico and the National Endowment for the Arts. He has translated a wide range of Latin American authors, including novels by Virgilio Piñera and Alberta Ruy Sánchez, essays by José Lezama Lima and Julio Ortega, short stories by Jesús Gardea and Juan Bosch, and poetry by Alvaro Mutis, Gloria Gervitz, and David Huerta.

MARILYN SIDES teaches literature and creative writing at Wellesley College and is working on a novel to be published by Harmony. Her first story, and her first story in *Yellow Silk*, "The Island of the Mapmaker's Wife," was published in the 1990 *O. Henry Prize Stories*, and is included in a collection of short stories of the same name, from which this book's selection was taken. *The Kenyon Review* has honored her with an award for "Best Emerging Writer." She lives in Wellesley, Massachusetts.

EDWARD SMALLFIELD'S poems and stories have appeared in *Caliban*, *Ironwood*, *Manoa*, *Yellow Silk*, *Zyzzyva*, and other periodicals. He has taught creative writing at San Francisco State University and now teaches at the University of California at Berkeley Extension. With Toni Mirosevich and Charlotte Muse, he is the author of *Trio*. He lives in Albany, California, with his wife and daughter.

JANE SMILEY was born in Los Angeles and grew up in St. Louis. She studied at Vassar and the University of Iowa, where she received her Ph.D. She has published eight novels, including *Moo*, *The Age of Grief*, *The Greenlanders*, *Ordinary Love and Goodwill*, and *A Thousand Acres*, which received the Pulitzer Prize and the National Book Critics Circle Award. She teaches at Iowa State University and lives in Ames, Iowa.

KATHRYN STEADMAN is a poet and fiction writer. Her work has appeared in *Fireweed*, *The Other Paper*, and *Denali*. "What She Wrote Him" is a piece taken from her completed manuscript *Seeking the Pleasure God*, a novel of obsession between two sexually scarred adults.

E. BETH THOMAS lives in New York City.

JS THOMAS is a post-graduate fellow at the University of Texas in Austin, where she lives, loves, writes, practices Aikido, and on Tuesdays goes swing dancing. Her poetry has appeared in such journals as *The Quarterly High Plains Literary Review*, *Southwestern American Literature*, and *Midwest Poetry Review*. In her own words, "I wanted to make music or love, / and having the talent for neither, / I settled on both."

DEBRA VIOLYN has been the editor of an international erotic literary magazine for fifteen years. She gardens, unlocks mysteries in the songs of frogs, tapes mockingbirds, sleeps curled in the sun like a small cat.

THOM WARD is Editor/Development Director for BOA Editions, Ltd., and also teaches poetry workshops in elementary and secondary schools and through The Writers & Books Literary Center in Rochester, New York. His poems have been published in many journals, anthologies, and newspapers, including The Atlantic Monthly, The Christian Science Monitor, Tar River Poetry, Chelsea, Poetry Northwest, and Yankee. Six of his poems were nominated for the 1995 Pushcart Prize: Best of the Small Presses. He and his wife and three children live in Paltry, New York.

LEONORE WILSON teaches creative writing at Napa Valley College. Her work has been published in such magazines as Yellow Silk, Five Fingers Review, Laurel Review, Poet and Critic, and Berkeley Poetry Review.

TOBIAS WOLFF'S publications include The Night in Question, In Pharaoh's Army, In the Garden of North American Martyrs, and This Boy's Life, which was made into a motion picture. His stories have appeared in numerous periodicals, including The New Yorker, Antæus, Granta, Esquire, and others. Among his prizes are the Rea Award for excellence in the short story, the Los Angeles Times Book Award, and the PEN/Faulkner Award; his stories have regularly appeared in the Best American series. Wolff lives with his family in upstate New York, where he is writer-in-residence at Syracuse University.

ROBERT WRIGLEY'S books include Moon in Mason Jar, What My Father Believed, and In the Bank of Beautiful Sins. He is a 1996–97 Guggenheim Fellow and lives with his wife and family in Lenore, Idaho.

RICHARD ZIMLER has lived in Porto, Portugal, since 1990. His most recent novel is Unholy Ghosts (GMP Publishers, 1996), from which the story "Pushing Me Into the Past" is an excerpt. His first novel, The Last Kabbalist of Lisbon, was published by Quetzal Editores of Lisbon in April of 1996 (in Portuguese translation) and became an immediate bestseller. It is now in its third printing and will next be published in France. Richard's short fiction has been anthologized recently in The Book of Eros, Men on Men: 6, and His. In 1994, he won a National Endowment of the Arts fellowship in fiction.

This constitutes an extension of the copyright page. Grateful acknowledgment is made for permission to use the following:

TOM ABSHER "The Summer Dress," copyright © 1997 by Tom Absher.

DOROTHY ALLISON From *Two or Three Things I Know for Sure* by Dorothy Allison. Copyright © 1995 by Dorothy Allison. Used by permission of Dutton Signet, a division of Penguin Books USA Inc.

RONALD BAATZ "To Distraction," copyright © 1997 by Ronald Baatz.

CAROLYN BANKS "His," copyright © 1997 by Carolyn Banks.

DAVID BIESPIEL "Each Touch the Future" from *Shattering Air* by David Biespiel. Copyright © 1996 by David Biespiel. Reprinted by permission of BOA Editions, Ltd., New York.

TARA BRAY "Grayton Beach Cottage," copyright © 1997 by Tara Bray.

LEASA BURTON "Trust Muscle," copyright © 1997 by Leasa Burton.

J. DUNNE "Kathy Soffia, Kathy Soffia," copyright © 1997 by J. Dunne.

GLORIA DYC "The War, at Home," copyright © 1997 by Gloria Dyc.

EDWARD FALCO "Tell Me What It Is," copyright © 1997 by Edward Falco.

ALISON FELL "The Cold Fish" from *The Pillow Boy of the Lady Onogoro* by Alison Fell. Copyright © 1994 by Alison Fell. Reprinted by permission of Harcourt Brace & Co. and Serpent's Tail.

THAISA FRANK "Animal Skins," copyright © 1997 by Thaisa Frank.

CARLOS FUENTES "Apollo and the Seven Whores" from *The Orange Tree* by Carlos Fuentes. Translated by Alfred Mac Adam. Translation copyright © 1994 by Farrar, Straus and Giroux.

JESÚS GARDEA "Springtime" translated by Mark Schafer. Translation copyright © 1997 by Mark Schafer.

GABRIELLE GLANCY "You Are the Girl I Love" and "too near," copyright © 1997 by Gabrielle Glancy.

JOHN GOLDFINE "A Sun to Shine on Them," copyright © 1997 by John Goldfine.

KARL HARSHBARGER "Harry Pickering," copyright © 1997 by Karl Harshbarger.

LINDA VANESSA HEWITT "The Fourth Child," copyright © 1997 by Linda Vanessa Hewitt.

JANE HIRSHFIELD "If the Rise of the Fish," copyright © 1997 by Jane Hirshfield.

DAVE HOWELL "Making love, Embracing the gentleness," "Whenever the unbelievable," and "My wife sleeps," copyright © 1997 by Dave Howell.

TIM JOHNSTON "Unto Her," copyright © 1997 by Tim Johnston.

GINU KAMANI "The Goddess of Sleep" reprinted by permission of author. Copyright © 1997 by Ginu Kamani.

GALWAY KINNELL "Rapture" and "Telephoning in Mexican Sunlight" from *Imperfect Thirst*. Copyright © 1994 by Galway Kinnell. Reprinted by permission of Houghton Mifflin Company. All rights reserved. "Rapture" was originally published in *The New Yorker*.

EDWARD KLEINSCHMIDT "Holding Your Hands Up" and "Say So," copyright © 1997 by Edward Kleinschmidt.

PETER KUNZ "If I Could," copyright © 1997 by Peter Kunz.

DORIANNE LAUX "What It Sounds Like," copyright © 1997 by Dorianne Laux.

LISA LEITZ "Fall Courting Rituals" and "Only-Child Agriculture," copyright © 1997 by Lisa Leitz.

TIMOTHY LIU "Vespers" and "The Storm," copyright © 1997 by Timothy Liu.

JOAN LOGGHE "Post Coital," copyright © 1997 by Joan Logghe.

MARY MACKEY "Blue," copyright © 1997 by Mary Mackey.

STEFANIE MARLIS "Bells," copyright © 1997 by Stefanie Marlis.

CAROLE MASO "Make Me Dazzle" from *Aureole* by Carole Maso. Copyright © 1996 by Carole Maso. Reprinted by permission of The Ecco Press.

JILL MCDONOUGH "New York Public Library" and "The Story of Joe," copyright © 1997 by Jill McDonough.

PHILIP MEMMER "Love," copyright © 1997 by Philip Memmer.

STEVE MILES "Sailing," copyright © 1997 by Steve Miles.

WALTER MOSLEY From *A Little Yellow Dog: An Easy Rawlins Mystery* by Walter Mosley. Copyright © 1996 by Walter Mosley. Reprinted by permission of W.W. Norton & Company, Inc. and Serpent's Tail.

D. NURKSE "July Lover," copyright © 1997 by D. Nurkse.

SHARON OLDS "The Source" and "Full Summer" from *The Wellspring* by Sharon Olds. Copyright © 1996 by Sharon Olds. Reprinted by permission of Alfred A. Knopf Inc.

DONALD RAWLEY "Mother of Pearl," copyright © 1997 by Donald Rawley.

JAY ROGOFF "The Door" copyright © 1997 by Jay Rogoff.

MARILYN SIDES "Kites!" from *The Island of the Mapmaker's Wife and Other Tales* by Marilyn Sides. Copyright © 1996 by Marilyn Sides. Reprinted by permission of Harmony Books, a division of Crown Publishers, Inc. and Brandt & Brandt Literary Agents, Inc.

EDWARD SMALLFIELD "Geography," copyright © 1997 by Edward Smallfield.

JANE SMILEY "The Life of the Body" reprinted by permission of author. Copyright © 1996 by Jane Smiley.

KATHRYN STEADMAN "What She Wrote Him," copyright © 1997 by Kathryn Steadman.

E. BETH THOMAS "Coyote and the Shadow People," copyright © 1997 by E. Beth Thomas.

JS THOMAS "Under the Olive Tree," copyright © 1997 by JS Thomas.

DEBRA VIOLYN "My Shadow Has Blond Hair," copyright © 1997 by Debra Violyn.

THOM WARD "The Breeze at Dawn" and "Barbara," copyright © 1997 by Thom Ward.

LEONORE WILSON "The Implausible Lovely" and "Sex While Driving," copyright © 1997 by Leonore Wilson.

TOBIAS WOLFF "Bullet in the Brain" reprinted by permission of International Creative Management, Inc. Copyright © 1995.

ROBERT WRIGLEY "On the River Road," copyright © 1997 by Robert Wrigley.

RICHARD ZIMLER "Pushing Me into the Past" from *Unholy Ghosts* by Richard Zimler. Copyright © 1996 by Richard Zimler. Reprinted by permission of Gay Men's Press, London.

All original material used by permission of the authors.

For information about *Yellow Silk*, please write us at:
P.O. BOX 6374, Albany, CA 94706